NEW MERMAIDS

BEN JONSON

VOLPONE

edited by Robert N. Watson

Professor of English
University of California, Los Angeles

Methuen Drama • London

New Mermaids

Second Edition 2003

5 7 9 10 8 6 4

Methuen Drama
A&C Black Publishers Limited
36 Soho Square, London W1D 3QY
www.acblack.com

ISBN: 978 0 7136 5433 2

First New Mermaid edition 1968

A CIP catalogue record for this book is
available from the British Library

Printed in the UK by CPI Cox & Wyman, Reading, RG1 8EX

This book is produced using paper that is made from wood grown in
managed, sustainable forests. It is natural, renewable and recyclable.
The logging and manufacturing processes conform to the environmental
regulations of the country of origin.

NEW MERMAIDS

General editors
William C. Carroll: Boston University
Brian Gibbons: University of Münster
Tiffany Stern: University College, Oxford

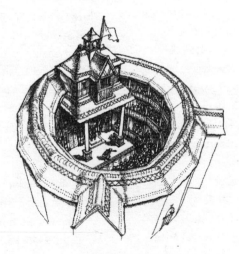

Reconstruction of an Elizabethan Theatre
by C. Walter Hodges

NEW MERMAIDS

CONTENTS

ACKNOWLEDGEMENTS

I am deeply indebted to the remarkable work of previous editors of *Volpone*, especially Alvin Kernan, Brian Parker, Philip Brockbank, and John W. Creaser, as well as to the great edition of Jonson's complete works by C. H. Herford, Percy Simpson and Evelyn Simpson. My debts to the cumulative work of other learned commentators on the play are so manifold that they cannot be specifically acknowledged without turning this general-interest edition into a stack of scholarly footnotes. My work has been further supported by conscientious research assistants from the Center for Medieval and Renaissance Studies and the Clark Center for Seventeenth and Eighteenth Century Studies at UCLA, the wisdom and learning of Brian Gibbons and my UCLA colleagues, and research funds from the Faculty Senate at UCLA.

INTRODUCTION

The Author

Ben Jonson was an astonishing character: a passionate man with no apparent interest in love, a working-class child who became the exemplar of high court culture, a decorous classicist given to extreme drunkenness and murderous violence, a self-proclaimed Stoic driven by violent appetites for praise and pleasure, a dedicated social climber who stubbornly sabotaged his own advancement, a moralistic writer who always seems to side with his rogues, a genius of comic drama who repeatedly withdrew bitterly from the theatre. Indeed, Jonson is a victim of his own success: having systematically used the mantles of classical literature and royal employment to conceal his common origins and wild tendencies, Jonson has convinced many potential modern readers that he is yet another formal snob in the literary establishment.

Jonson's father, a minister, died before his son was born in 1572; his stepfather was a bricklayer. Intelligence and diligence won the boy a scholarship to the prestigious Westminster School in London where he met his lifelong mentor, William Camden. After apprenticing unhappily to his stepfather's trade, Jonson volunteered for the wars in Flanders, where – evidently not deeming that slow campaign dangerous enough – he reportedly challenged an enemy soldier to single combat, and killed him.

In his early twenties, Jonson married and had several children; the deaths of his first daughter and first son are lamented movingly in his *Epigrams*, and there is no evidence that any of his legitimate offspring survived to adulthood. By 1597 he was acting and writing in the nascent theatre industry – and heading for jail. He had played the lead in Thomas Kyd's *Spanish Tragedy*, and was designated one of England's best tragic playwrights in Francis Meres's 1598 *Palladis Tamia* (though neither Jonson nor anyone else preserved any of the plays on which that judgement must have been based). But in August of 1597 he went to prison for his part in finishing a satiric play called *The Isle of Dogs* (also now lost). The next year, within a few days of the opening performance of his *Every Man In His Humour*, with William Shakespeare in the cast, Jonson killed another fellow-actor (Gabriel Spencer, who had been in prison with him) in a duel; he escaped execution – any man able to read Latin could claim exemption as a clergyman – but had his thumb branded and his belongings confiscated. To make things worse, he announced his conversion to Catholicism, which was then effectively illegal. After his release, his characteristic pugnacity (already evolving into its adult guise of scholarly arrogance) propelled him into a prolonged literary brawl – now hyperbolically known as the War of the Theatres – with Thomas Dekker and John Marston, a brawl that carries over into the Prologue to *Volpone*; he also boasted (in his revealing 'Conversations with Drummond') of battering Marston physically and taking his pistol. He dined with the conspirators only weeks before the Gunpowder Plot, and was secretly enlisted in the subsequent investigation.

Despite disgrace and debt – or perhaps because of them – Jonson used his literary skills and scholarly reputation to gain the patronage of powerful aristocrats, whom he followed to their country houses – leaving his family in London, at risk of bubonic plague, which killed his first son. He wrote intricate elegies of praise to anyone who supported him, and brutally nasty epigrams against anyone who crossed him. When verse satires were made illegal, he (along with Chapman and Marston) invented the 'comical satire' mode of drama. When the Scottish King James succeeded Queen Elizabeth in 1603, Jonson co-authored a play called *Eastward Ho!* that satirized Scots and landed him again in prison.

Jonson emerged to write a series of great and popular comedies, including *Volpone*, *Epicoene*, *The Alchemist*, and *Bartholomew Fair*, as well as the best of his surviving tragedies (*Sejanus*, based on ancient Roman history) and a number of his great lyric poems. During the same time period, having worked his way back into favour, he became James's leading author of masques: elaborately produced ceremonial allegories designed to instruct and flatter the high-ranking persons who watched and often performed them. But he feuded bitterly with the physical architect of these productions, Inigo Jones; and the new king, Charles I, turned to other authors. Jonson was even hired by Sir Walter Ralegh to tutor Ralegh's son in Paris – until the drunken Jonson (weighing close to three hundred pounds by this time) was carted mockingly through the streets by his pupil. Virtually every claim to glory brought with it a threat of disgrace: along with the instances already mentioned, the early *Poetaster*, the mid-career *Sejanus* and *Epicoene*, and the late *Devil is an Ass* each somehow landed him in trouble with the authorities.

Jonson's lifelong struggle to construct and project a dignified self through his literary art culminated in the 1616 Folio of his *Works*. Despite some mockery of the idea of presenting mere 'plays' under the grand traditional title of 'Works', Jonson had become a revered figure, a kind of poet laureate, winning honorary degrees, state employment, and a pension (including an annual barrel of wine). The 'Tribe of Ben', a loose association of leading Cavalier poets, worshipped him as their 'father' at many bibulous occasions. Still, disasters befell him, including a fire that destroyed his books and papers in 1623, and a stroke in 1628 that rendered him paraplegic – and a far less successful comic playwright – until his death in 1637.

The Play, and the Plays Within It: Jonson and Genre

The sharpest, funniest comedy about money and morals in the seventeenth century is still the sharpest and funniest about those things in the twenty-first. The satire is devastating: Jonson's *Volpone* depicts unprincipled selfishness thinly covered by sanctimonious speeches, lust and possessiveness poorly disguised as love and marriage, cynical legalism passing itself off as pure justice, boastful name-dropping that pretends to be cultural sophistication, snobbery congratulating itself that it is decorum, and greed deluding itself that it is really prudence, responsibility, even religion. Volpone likes to be flattered that he is not like the misers despised in medieval literature, but this evasion only casts him as a more modern version of the figure – the mega-billionaire unaccountably determined to acquire further billions, whatever the ethical and social costs, if only to assert his superiority to his fellow-billionaires. This modern self is defined by its performances and its acquisitions, with no stable or satisfactory person at the centre of it; it sits surrounded by a sterile caricature of family, and protected by the illusion that wealth can claim priority even over death. It is a game for the man who has everything except a life or a heart, and Volpone plays it well.

The legacy hunters have prominent sources in classical literature (Horace, Petronius, Lucian, Juvenal), but they emerge here as venture-capitalists, investing more and more of their considerable wealth in flattering Volpone, in hopes of inheriting even greater wealth when he dies. As this new capitalist economic system came to predominate in the Renaissance, the old, feudal rules of social order collapsed; money became regarded as a goal in itself, and as the primary measure of status. Yet the limited imagination of those who succeed financially, then and now, generally leaves them with little idea of what to do with their fortunes other than try to make them into larger fortunes, and to try to put on the style and seek the power of a feudal aristocracy – to become (at best) high-brow patrons or (more often) petty barons. In this sense, Jonson's *Volpone* conveys the same warning as Marlowe's *Doctor Faustus*: that the modern world –though it may lack the explicitly diabolical tempters of the old morality-plays – offers to buy our souls in exchange for some superficial power and glory that never really transcends the banal and the mundane. Gold replaces God, as it does for Volpone in the opening lines, though it can buy nothing except more gold. Opulent possessions become the new form of demonic possession.

This most praised and most performed of Jonson's brilliant comedies is, paradoxically, a moral story in which every character is wrong; and, despite the extremely wide moral spectrum they seem to represent, they are all wrong in some deeply similar ways. The play's primary satiric target is greed, but it also recognizes that greed is merely one facet of the insatiable human desire to continue desiring (even, perhaps especially, where there is no pressing need), and of the fundamental human tendency (which Jonson exposes throughout his comedies) to live in grandiose egoistical fantasies rather than in the real world.

Rivalries in trade and religion encouraged English authors to depict Venice as a scene of Italianate corruption, but this city-state is also apt (as in Shakespeare's *Merchant of Venice*) as a place where there is only mediated value; in the absence of land and other natural resources, Venice built its economy and even identity entirely around exchange. So it provides a perfect setting for greed, and for a sophisticated understanding of greed as desire that has broken loose from real objects and real needs. As among the wealthy in many major twenty-first century cities, money in *Volpone* becomes (like Celia for the men who seek to control her) more a symbolic marker than a substantial instrument, in a costly competition for personal pride rather than mere survival. Nobody in this story is obliged to any manual labour, at least until Mosca is finally sentenced to the galleys. Neither Volpone nor the three men pursuing his inheritance lack anything that more money could buy. In an emerging capitalist world, however, they still crave wealth as an index of power and status, one that can be multiplied without limit, like the sexuality Volpone vainly offers to Celia.

That sexual offer also involves costumes and roles: all of Jonson's Venice is a stage, a world of plays superseding reality, as well as of play superseding work. In a volume called *Coryats Crudities*, for which Jonson wrote a commendatory poem, Venetian mounte-banks match Volpone's showmanship in the role of Scoto, and Venetian courtesans match Lady Would-Be's equally ill-fated attempt to seduce Volpone with heavy make-up and elegant rhetoric; Jonson's actors would have been performers imitating per-formers imitating performers. As in the 'humours' plays Jonson had been writing during the preceding years, various characters in *Volpone* are led astray largely by over-confidence in the flattering scripts they have adopted or adapted for themselves. What is new here is the degree to which the satiric manipulators delude and injure themselves in the process of deluding and injuring their vic-tims. Jonson's audience, meanwhile, is rebuffed for confidently awaiting either the victory of virtue which concludes most popular comedies, or else the victory of satiric wit that concludes so many other Jonsonian comedies. Behind his ostensible purpose in punish-ing the rogues, which (his Epistle asserts) is to disarm the moral crit-ics of the theatre, Jonson may also intend to unsettle any spectator who complacently believes he or she has caught onto Jonson's comic formula. Much of the play's remarkable tautness and energy comes from Jonson simultaneously spurring on and reining in his own roguish impulses.

One unrecognized basis for Jonson's plot is the tradition of moot cases at the Inns of Court. These were mixtures of festivity and pedagogy, testing legal scholars with scenarios designed to generate hilariously complex disputes about the rights to inherited property. The playlet staged by Volpone's servants about the Pythagorean reincarnations of a soul provides a perfect overture to this topic. Jonson then replicates many favourite conundrums of the moot cases by giving Volpone so many potential heirs, each with different claims and different disqualifications – including the rumour that his servants are his children and the implication that those children are sterile, Voltore's status as his lawyer, Sir Politic's status as a foreigner and possible traitor, the exchange of wills with Corbaccio, the questions about women's eligibility to inherit property, proposed forfeitures to the state or to charity, and Volpone's own temporary death.

Volpone also leans heavily on the tradition of Aesopian beast-fables, especially the legends of Reynard the Fox, many of whose adventures – extremely popular in Renaissance European folklore – suggest parallels to Volpone. As Parker's edition observes, Reynard too is tried by a corrupt court, first for attempted rape, then for feigning death in an attempt to capture the crow's wife. He pretends to be a doctor, and is often depicted preaching from a platform like the one Volpone uses to play Scoto of Mantua. Like Volpone (and like some real foxes), Reynard often plays dead in order to trap the predatory birds who gather to feed on his corpse. The vulture (here, the lawyer Voltore) is a notorious carrion-seeker. The raven was a long-lived bird whose croaking voice was associated with death, and who was thought sometimes to abandon its offspring (as old Corbaccio disowns Bonario). The crow (the jealous merchant Corvino) is another scavenger, and ironically a bird traditionally associated with marital fidelity. Flies also feed on the dead, and were associated (as Mosca is here) with demonic possession. Sir Pol displays the parrot's devotion to loud, mindless mimicry, and is hunted down by the sharper hawk Peregrine. The fable thus conjoins with the overall ethical thrust of the play: as traditional social and religious principles yield to the avaricious appetite, human beings inevitably sink to the level of beasts.

Jonson combines this bestiary tradition with the popular tradition of Italian improvisational theatre known as the *commedia dell'arte*, in which stock roles (such as the cuckold Pantalone with whom Corvino explicitly associates himself, and the nattering Punchinello with whom Jonson associates Sir Pol) were reflected by exaggerated masks and plumes that, as Parker has suggested, could easily have doubled as bird costumes. Suitors in the *commedia* often try (as Volpone does) to woo a sequestered woman by playing a mountebank or apothecary under her window, assisted by zanies, until the master of the house chases them away; Volpone's speeches here add another meta-theatrical level by suggesting an ironic commentary on Jonson's own turbulent career as a playwright (see the note to II.ii.33).

Eventually Volpone becomes truly as sick and immobile as he had pretended to be, Mosca is sentenced to the total servility he had feigned, the legacy-hunters reveal themselves as essentially the animals after which they are named, and Sir Pol becomes a victim of his own grandiose paranoid politics. So acting controls reality in this play, but (as in fairy-tales) not in the way the wishers had hoped. The characters each have ingenious plans, all of which backfire. The joke is finally on everyone, including the audience.

But, while the narcissistic aspect of theatre is mortified, the pleasure of theatre is thereby reborn. Here – as usual in his comedies, which work deliciously on stage – Jonson offers the thrill of watching swift, death-defying manoeuvres in a tight space, of watching the protagonists improvise and integrate an ever-increasing number of subplots, each reflecting some deluded character's egoistic fantasy. Mosca must keep all these incompatible story lines running on the same stage, without collisions; it is a bold juggling act that earns gasps of admiration as it endures through mounting complications and several near falls, and provides a satisfying series of crashes when Jonson brings it all tumbling to earth at the end.

Mosca and Volpone

Discussions of *Volpone* often begin at the beginning, with Volpone's famous panegyric to gold (I.i.1–27). Critics and editors sift through the variety of literary echoes the speech offers, seeking evidence that the play is essentially another condemnation of greed, that it is a subversive celebration of appetite, or that Volpone suffers from a perversion of his religious or sexual instincts. Perhaps, instead, the flood of conventional motifs suggests a man searching for a satisfactory role in which to cast himself. The fate of miserly characters in literature is so unappealing that Volpone tries (with temporary success) to translate it into the more exalting roles of worshipful saint and devoted romantic lover, with gold as his deity and paramour. He also leans on a wide range of classical allusions to give his avarice the dignity it so conspicuously lacks in English literature (see H&S, IX, 689).

Mosca amplifies Volpone's interest in Celia with the most hackneyed sort of romantic imagery (I.v.107–22), as if he knew that Volpone could not resist writing himself wholeheartedly into this sort of bodice-ripping love-story. Volpone consciously assumes the role of Scoto of Mantua in order to make contact with Celia, but his subsequent seductive song to her in his bedroom betrays a care-

Act II, Scene ii; Mosca (Guy Henry), top, playing zany to
Volpone's performance as the mountebank Scoto of Mantua,
leads Castrone, Androgyno, and Nano in song; RSC Swan,
Stratford, 1999, dir. Lindsay Posner (photo © Colin Willoughby/
Arena PAL).

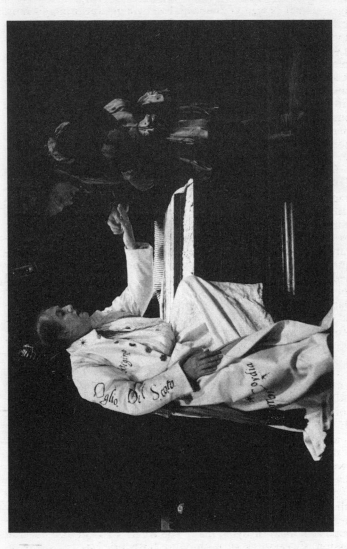

Volpone (Michael Gambon), in a robe advertising 'Oglio Del Scoto', communes with Mosca (Simon Russell Beale); Royal National Theatre, London, 1995, dir. Matthew Warchus (photo © Ben Christopher/Arena PAL).

lessness about the interplay of literature and life: the song is lovely in its way, but dangerously second-hand. The literary precedent from Catullus foreshadows the ill-fatedness of Volpone's corrupt schemes, sexual as well as financial. Even when expressing his most powerful private desires, Volpone thus remains a puppet to conventions. Furthermore, he has miscast his play: he assumes that Celia will prove to be like Lucrezia in Machiavelli's *La Mandragola*, a typical wife in the world of Italian satire, quite willing to be seduced away from her worthless husband. Like the manipulators in Jonson's earlier comedies, Volpone promises Celia a set of participatory literary allusions which they will consciously control to maximize their own pleasure (III.vii.157–238). Unluckily for him, the play drifts out of the gravitational field of satiric comedy, and temporarily into that of sentimental melodrama. When, as a result, he lies uncomfortably trapped in the courtroom, Volpone momentarily fears that his role as an invalid will become real and permanent (V.i.1–10), a fear that soon proves prophetic (V.xii.121–24). He had mistakenly assumed that he inhabited a genre that favours cynical exploitation, rather than an equally familiar (but less Jonsonian) genre that enforces poetic justice.

Just as Volpone imagines himself the triumphant fox of several ancient beast-fables, so Mosca envisions himself as the all-conquering wily servant of the ancient mode still known as New Comedy, and of the satiric city-comedies based on that classical model. As his plot progresses, Mosca asks his master to 'applaud my art', even while hoping to avoid the kind of 'epilogue' that punished Volpone's strategic role-playing as Scoto of Mantua (II.iv.32–8). Preparing to turn against his long-time master and ally, Mosca declares, 'this is called the fox-trap' (V.v.18), which may remind us of the dramatic 'mouse-trap' trick Hamlet uses to expose King Claudius. But by pursuing a plan merely because it seems to fit a dramatic precedent, Mosca virtually assures his doom in the context of Jonson's iconoclastic comedy; Jonson would never let a Shakespearean plot triumph within his own.

What makes Mosca's fate particularly bitter is that the pattern he relies on is essentially Jonson's own, in which the sharpest predatory wit – often a wily servant – ends up triumphant. Like Volpone, Mosca is finally defeated less through his own weakness than through betrayal by his creator, who is experimenting with a sternly moralistic ending. When Volpone calls an end to all the playing by throwing off his disguise as the sergeant, all the other roles – Volpone as a dead or dying man, Voltore as a victim of diabolical possession, Corvino as an upstanding husband, Mosca as a *magnifico* – collapse too. In Jonson's other plays, characters who try to end the play by casting off their own masks fail to crush the theatrical and picaresque spirit; when Surly in *The Alchemist* and

Justice Overdo in *Bartholomew Fair* throw off their disguises, they succeed neither in ending the play, nor in punishing the rogues. If Jonson does manage (as his Epistle promises) 'to put the snaffle in their mouths, that cry out, We never punish vice in our interludes', it is only by putting the irons on the legs of the characters who assumed that such critics were right, and that theirs would prove to be another amoral Jonsonian world.

Through most of the play, Volpone and Mosca control their gulls by the same principle that functions in the other comedies: they exploit the fact that people would rather misperceive reality than surrender their self-aggrandizing fantasies. Like Clement and Brainworm in *Every Man In His Humour* or Lovewit and Face in *The Alchemist*, they are exploiters of cognitive dissonance. Mosca comments that each of the legacy-hunters

> Is so possessed, and stuffed with his own hopes,
> That anything unto the contrary,
> Never so true, or never so apparent,
> Never so palpable, they will resist it –
>
> (V.ii.24–7)

While Voltore daydreams happily about the new role, costume, and name he supposes he is about to acquire, Volpone and Mosca delight themselves (as do the schemers and the audience alike in the earlier plays) by envisioning the moment when this inflated image will collide with the degrading reality of the situation (I.ii.97–113).

When Volpone's performance as Scoto enrages Corvino by threatening to cast him as the humiliated Pantalone of the *commedia* (II.iii.2–9) , Mosca distracts him by offering to cast him as (in effect) the understudy to the role of *magnifico* now played by the supposedly dying Volpone. The prostitution of his wife suddenly becomes, in Corvino's eyes, merely a piece of stage-business peripheral to this grand transformation. Volpone will get what he wants, not so much through his virtuosity as an actor in the role of mountebank, as through Mosca's virtuosity as a reviser of old plays: Corvino can only stumble from one script to another. Even when he finds out the truth, his impulse is to resort to a literary-conventional expression of his despair, 'with a rope, and a dagger, / To visit all the streets' (V.ii.93–4). But finally, in yet another facet of the play's pattern of poetic justice, Volpone and Mosca fall into the trap of literary formulas they had set for their victims.

Celia and Bonario

Celia and Bonario provoke the greatest confusion among the critics of *Volpone*, and generate what is probably the play's most remarkable instance of Jonson's manipulation of generic formulas. The extreme and apparently authentic virtue of these characters makes them anomalous in the world of satiric city-comedy. Are we to take them as the sole remaining locus of true goodness, or as yet another naive and pretentious target of ridicule? The question is impossible to resolve, as the protracted critical disagreements suggest, because these characters are one thing on their own terms, and another within the dramatic context Jonson imposes on them (just as they are transformed from heroes to villains by the little play of demonic possession in the Venetian courtroom). What critics have tried to resolve by analyzing personality traits can be understood only by analyzing literary conventions: these are exiles from the world of sentimental melodrama, which is the one place their sort of virtue has any real relevance or force.

The fate of these characters has disturbed readers of *Volpone* in revealing ways. William Butler Yeats found these innocents poignant in their isolation. Samuel Taylor Coleridge's oblique objection took the form of a suggestion that 'a most delightful comedy might be produced, by making Celia the ward or niece of Corvino, instead of his wife, and Bonario her lover'. Since then, scholars have repeatedly puzzled over the fact that Jonson neglects to propel Celia and Bonario into the romantic union that would conventionally have been their lot. It often seems as if the pair themselves expect their life-trials to be resolved as they would be in such a comedy. But those who call on the heavens for aid in *Volpone* (as even more grimly in Shakespeare's *King Lear*) will meet some rude surprises; and though they may survive, they will never be allowed to fulfil the roles that they proudly assign themselves. Jonson thus again turns our conventionalized expectations of romantic theatre against themselves, in favour of his own realism. If we try to perceive Celia and Bonario entirely as heroes, the play calls us fools; if we try to perceive them entirely as fools, the play calls us rogues. The discomfort felt by readers is natural under such circumstances, and we can escape the dilemma only by recognizing the novelty of Jonsonian comedy.

Celia is not inherently a simpleton; that would dull the edge of the parody. She is guilty, not (as critics have asserted) of stupidity exactly, but (like so many of Jonson's victims) merely of misunderstanding the nature of the play-world she inhabits. The eccentric perspective of her extreme and conventional virtue causes her repeatedly to misread the plot. Because she is constitutionally incapable of fathoming the greed and cynicism of the schemes enmeshing her, Celia misinterprets her husband's urgings (as Mistress Fitzdotterel in Jonson's *The Devil is an Ass* misinterprets the advances of Pug) as a conventional ploy to test her doubted fidelity. Corvino's actual plot is, of course, quite different – virtually the opposite (III.vii.24).

Act IV, Scene v; Voltore (Mark Bramhall) accuses Bonario and Celia (Richard Soto and Allison Sie); the Avocatori watch from above, while Mosca and the other legacy-hunters watch from below; A Noise Within, Glendale, CA, 1998, dir. Art Manke (photo © Craig Schwartz Photography).

As Volpone attempts to rape her, Celia's pleas for divine rescue sound very much like an actor repeating a cue waiting for a saving entrance – which is very much what they are. She keeps calling upon heaven to stand up for the right (Bonario joins in this practice at the trial), because that is what would happen in a traditional maudlin tale of threatened innocence. But here, as in *King Lear*, the lack of any divine response to these repeated calls is an exploitation of the audience's desires and expectations, used to remind us yet again that the real world does not work in the reassuring manner of the play-worlds we are used to witnessing.

Celia begs to be allowed to 'take down poison, / Eat burning coals, do anything', rather than submit to sexual dishonour. She tells Corvino that she is his 'martyr', and goes on spouting – with perfect sincerity – the classic clichés of female virtue (III.vii.94–107). Celia behaves, in other words, just as a conventional heroine should behave. But no one – not her seducer, her husband, her God, or her author – seems to be impressed. The world of satiric city-comedy is like the world of the Venetian court: a place 'Where multitude and clamour overcomes', and where calling as witnesses 'Our consciences' and 'heaven, that never fails the innocent' is equivalent to having 'no testimonies' at all (IV.vi.15–19). What would become of the archetypal tragic rape victim, Lucrece, in a cynical comic universe?

Bonario looks at Mosca's outrageously insincere show of sad humility, and tells himself, 'This cannot be a personated passion' (III.ii.35), probably because it is exactly the sort of behaviour that occurs sincerely in the sort of sentimental melodramas that populate Bonario's mind in place of the real world. The rhetoric of Bonario's dramatic entrance to prevent the rape can only be characterized as corny:

> Forbear, foul ravisher, libidinous swine!
> Free the forced lady, or thou diest, impostor.
> But that I am loath to snatch thy punishment
> Out of the hand of justice, thou shouldst yet
> Be made the timely sacrifice of vengeance,
> Before this altar, and this dross, thy idol.
> Lady, let's quit the place: it is the den
> Of villainy. Fear nought, you have a guard;
> And he, ere long, shall meet his just reward.

(III.vii.266–74)

This play is not an allegory, nor do its speeches begin in alliteration and end in rhyme; these anomalous signals of more exalted genres involving heroic Anglo-Saxon warriors or heroic couplets reinforce the impression that the virtuous couple and their sentiments are badly out of place, comic-bathetic in a comic-satiric universe. A morality-play tradition in which Good Conscience had to rescue Innocent Humanity from the clutches of the Vice rings deliberately hollow on Jonson's stage.

The Would-Be Plot

One other aspect of *Volpone* that has long troubled critics, editors, and directors is the questionable integration of the Sir Politic Would-Be subplot into the play as a whole. But the follies of this English couple often generate useful parallels, in both plot and theme, to the Venetian vices in the main plot; and, as their name suggests, the Would-Be family provides further occasions for Jonson to attack self-aggrandizing literary delusions. If at times their story seems irrelevant to the centre of the play, that may itself be Jonson's point. The Would-Be subplot is a would-be main plot.

Lady Politic acknowledges that she derives her behaviour from Castiglione's *The Courtier* (IV.ii.35), but she ends up seeming more like a courtesan, and her speech is an obsessive chain of literary allusions (III.iv.79–97). Characteristically, Jonson attacks this affectation indirectly, through the framing of the plot, as well as by direct ridicule. Lady Politic's ability to mistake the Englishman Peregrine for a Venetian courtesan, because she believes Mosca's hints that her life is becoming a standard story of Italianate sexual connivance, typifies her self-dramatizing tendencies. She is too enthralled with her role as the righteous detective to notice how little Peregrine resembles such a courtesan, and there is no way for her to recognize that Mosca's advice is merely a ploy in the main line of Jonson's story, to which her marital problems remain extremely peripheral.

Sir Politic, too, feeds his melodramatic fantasies on discarded scraps from the main plot. He is obsessed with clothing and scripted behaviour (IV.i.8), and his grandiose schemes resemble not only those generated by the 'projectors' of the other comedies, but also those triumphantly executed by figures such as Gresham in Thomas Heywood's wonderfully titled *If You Know Not Me You Know Nobody, Part Two* (1606), which appeared at the same time as *Volpone*. Sir Pol is absorbed in such outlandish schemes and tales that Peregrine is left wondering, 'Does he gull me, trow? or is gulled?' (II.i.24). The answer, of course, is both: Sir Pol is so enthralled with his imaginary intrigues that he starts believing his own lies. What his diary reveals is that he takes the painfully banal events of his daily life – such as replacing shoelaces and urinating – and writes them down in books ('quotes' them) as if they were indeed the makings of an international spy-thriller (IV.i.128–147). In letting us know that we would not be interested in reading Pol's closely-guarded diary, Jonson is partly letting us know why he has forestalled Pol's efforts to make the play into a political melodrama, and to cast himself as its Machiavellian protagonist. A genial and sociable idiot (the opposite of the cruel, isolated, and clever Volpone) who repeatedly flees from petty brawls is unlikely to star in that genre.

That does not, however, preclude Sir Pol from proving useful in another genre. Peregrine concludes that Pol 'would be a precious thing / To fit our English stage', were it not that everyone would dismiss him as an exaggeration (II.i.56–60). He finally decides to punish Pol by pretending that these dangerous plots are actually occurring, that Pol's spy-fantasies have been misread as real by real spies. Pol's reaction is to confess, too late, that he drew all his politic schemings 'out of play-books' (V.iv.41–2). His fate (analogous to that of Volpone) is to find the world all too willing to play along with his role, in a way that makes him confront its costs and limitations. He tries to cloak himself in a cleverness, as in the tortoise-shell which was a Renaissance symbol of Polity, but in both cases the put-on cover-story finally serves only to hurt and humiliate him. Peregrine wonders whether his 'counter-plot' (IV.iii.24) will end up causing Pol's 'Adventures' to be 'put i' th' *Book of Voyages*, / And his gulled story registered for truth?' (V.iv.4–6). Such punishment would ironically fit the crime. After Pol is humiliated, one witness describes the scene as 'a rare motion, to be seen in Fleet Street' (V.iv.77), and Pol moans that he 'shall be the fable of all feasts; / The freight of the *gazetti*; ship-boys' tale; / And, which is worst, even talk for ordinaries' (V.iv.82–4). He will become, as he had hoped, renowned, but not at all in the way he had hoped: this master of gossip about prodigies has himself become a prodigious subject of gossip. In Jonson's comedies, the effort to play an exalting literary role remains the surest path to humiliation.

Peregrine's uncertainty about whether Pol is a coney-catcher or a coney – a clever exploiter or a gullible victim – arises from the formulaic fervour of Pol's self-important fantasies. But Peregrine's fear that he is being tricked enmeshes him in this same pattern of error: he, too, ends up misreading Jonson's plot. Commentators often assume that Peregrine is the wise hero of the play, but his one decisive action is a misreading of a misreading, rather than a perfect moral insight: when Lady Would-Be mistakes him for her husband's supposed courtesan, Peregrine misinterprets her behaviour as evidence that she is a courtesan, and Pol her pander. So Peregrine's punishment of Pol for this supposed outrage is hardly the triumph of the all-knowing satirist exploiting folly, but instead the delusion of another victim (however witty) of Jonson's control of the plot. The gallant Peregrine, even more clearly than Mosca, is a plausible version of Jonson's usual triumphant satiric wit, and English audiences were clearly invited to identify with him; but these clever characters eventually become the prey of the very devices that had empowered them in earlier Jonsonian comedies,

Act V, Scene iv; Peregrine (Robertson Dean) and the merchants torment Sir Pol (Mitchell Edmonds) in his tortoise disguise; A Noise Within, Glendale, CA, 1998, dir. Art Manke (photo © Craig Schwartz Photography).

and earlier in this comedy. Peregrine is the least wrong, perhaps, of all the characters in *Volpone*, but also probably the least interesting.

The critics who commonly see Peregrine as a Jonsonian hero may thus be missing an important point. Even the role of punitive satirist – one Jonson has usually exalted, as a surrogate of the role he claims for himself – fails in Volpone. Peregrine is finally a marginal character, so much so that productions have often cut him, and his battle of errors with Sir Pol, completely.

The Ending

Several objections have commonly been raised to the harshly moralistic conclusion of this play. Except for the attempted rape of Celia (which is stylized toward farce), Volpone's and Mosca's crimes are really poetic justice against loathsome and over-privileged scavengers, and audiences generally find themselves quite ready to forgive both lead characters 'for the wit o' the offence' (as the scheming servant is forgiven at the end of Jonson's *Every Man In*, and similarly *The Alchemist*). Audiences are further discomfited by the way the severe sentences jumble the genre of the play, which Northrop Frye's *Anatomy of Criticism* cites as an anomaly in being 'a kind of comic imitation of a tragedy'; and it certainly seems like a satire as well. Why does Jonson insist on wedging a severe sentence against Volpone in the few lines between his delicious performance as the exploiter of vices and his applause-winning appearance speaking the epilogue?

Perhaps the strain we feel at the end of *Volpone* is Jonson pulling back on the bridle of his own satiric spirit; he projects into the audience his own dilemma as a comic moralist. The surprisingly blunt exposure and punishment in *Volpone* pits the indulgent conventions of satiric comedy, in which wit is the sole criterion for success, against the forces of conventional morality that were, through the Puritans, exerting renewed pressure against the popular theatre. What is imprisoned at the end of the play, but escapes into the epilogue, is an aspect of comedy that conspires with the cruel, selfish, cynical exuberance of the spectators. Volpone and Mosca betray each other, but in a deeper sense they are both betrayed by Jonson. The lead characters and the audience alike confidently await the vindication of the clever, exploitative plot, only to have it explode as badly as the more naive plots.

Audiences understandably wonder why Mosca refuses to accept half of Volpone's fortune, insisting instead on a total triumph that practically forces Volpone to seek out vengeful counter-measures; or why Volpone chooses a counter-measure that essentially assures him of a fate far worse (even for such a greed-driven personality) than poverty. Perhaps neither of them can conceive that their play could really end so bluntly and brutally, any more than the audience can, because they all share the same set of expectations about Jonsonian comedy. Volpone's announcement of his true identity at the end of the play may indeed be 'a flourish of defiance' like those of Webster's Duchess of Malfi or Shakespeare's Richard III (Leggatt), but the result is a long, dull, painful penance, not a glorious final conflagration. Editors and critics have long striven to identify the many literary sources of *Volpone* and to understand how Jonson translates them into Volpone's speeches and schemes. They have also struggled to explain why someone as clever and generally disillusioned as Volpone makes such grave errors in predicting the reactions of Celia and Mosca at crucial points in the plot. Combining the questions offers some plausible answers: Volpone, deluding himself by expecting his story to conform in full to its literary precedents, becomes yet another Jonsonian character defeated when his world stubbornly refuses to imitate conventional art.

Volpone apparently believes exactly what many commentators now believe: that his story is essentially a retelling of old beast-fables about the clever fox who outwits the birds of prey and finally entraps them by feigning death. These parables resemble the typical satiric city-comedy, with the cleverest creature feeding himself fat on gulls whose over-confidence has made them vulnerable. Volpone, disguised as a court-sergeant to taunt Corvino further, evidently understands himself as the moralizing spokesman at the end of such a fable:

> Methinks
> Yet you, that are so traded i' the world,
> A witty merchant, the fine bird, Corvino,
> That have such moral emblems on your name,
> Should not have sung your shame, and dropped your cheese,
> To let the fox laugh at your emptiness.
>
> (V.viii.9–14)

If only Volpone had the option of ringing down the final curtain right there, as he gloats about fulfilling a familiar little literary piece in which he plays the triumphant role. The mouldy tale in which Volpone has cast himself with too much confidence, vanity, and literary-mindedness becomes instead a different story, 'called mortifying of a fox' (V.xii.125), as Volpone himself ruefully acknowledges. It is as if Volpone – despite having robbed so many others by indulging their dreams of glory – starts to believe that he himself is the hero of the Reynard tales, who ends up escaping from such a similar series of accusations. Jonson out-foxes that belief by importing the variant on the story – best known in Chaucer's 'Nun's Priest's Tale' – in which Reynard squanders his victory by insisting on jeering at his victims.

If Peregrine had exposed Sir Pol's schemes as mere self-inflation, exposed the fraud of Volpone and his co-conspirators, punished them merely with shame and impoverishment, and bestowed the ill-gotten fortune on Celia and Bonario, the play would have been much more conventionally satisfying. The Jonsonian hero would achieve his usual moral and practical sovereignty, the two plots would be unified, the fate of the evil-doers would be just without marring the comic atmosphere, and the romantic couple would be vindicated. But Jonson chooses to challenge us, rather than merely satisfy us. Specifically, he challenges the preachy critics mentioned in the Epistle (here printed at the end of the play-text), telling them that a strictly ethical conclusion in Jonsonian comedy will not take the customary and comfortable form envisioned by Celia and Bonario, because the real world seldom works that way. If his critics demand a moral ending, they will receive it only in the harsh discordant form of the court's official sentences, where power and money crush playfulness, and those critics will have to decide whether they really prefer that to the comic spirit that survives in Volpone's epilogue, and in Jonson's other comedies.

The striking oddities of *Volpone* make sense as part of Jonson's struggle to keep his audience ethically and theatrically alert. Things that do not seem to fit are, for the most part, not intended to fit. The Would-Be subplot is, in this sense, not nearly so superfluous as it might have seemed. The characters of Celia and Bonario are indeed anomalous, but it is an anomaly that forces us to confront our assumptions about both comedy and morality. The ending may seem too sternly punitive as a response to the plotters who, for the most part, merely allowed the wickedness of the fortune-hunters to punish itself; the play, as a result, may give confusing signals about its genre. But that confusion allows Jonson, characteristically, to undermine the complacencies of his audience, including any assumption that the victory in Jonson's comedies must always go to the strongest predatory wit.

Several things thus present themselves simultaneously, even synergistically, in *Volpone*:

1) a critique, at once extremely bitter and extremely funny, of decadent human greed;
2) an extended parable that echoes ancient and popular fables about the crafty fox;
3) an indirect critique of the literary conventions accepted by Jonson's competitors; and
4) a series of satiric depictions of other follies epidemic in Jonson's society.

Together they make *Volpone* the most wickedly delightful piece of comedy produced by the English Renaissance – the greatest dramatic culture (with the possible exception of the Greeks of two thousand years earlier) in the history of the world.

Stage History

As the preceding analysis has suggested, *Volpone* incorporates a critical history of drama; but it also has a notable theatrical history of its own. It opened at the Globe in 1606, with the same cast that performed Shakespeare's masterpieces of that period (and had recently performed Shakespeare's *Othello*, with some notably similar views of Venetian society). For one hundred and eighty years following that successful debut (except when the theatres were closed from 1642–1660), it was frequently in performance – long after most other Jacobean plays had been forgotten. In 1733–4, there were twelve productions of *Volpone* by England's leading companies. After a mid-century lull, it regained prominence in the later eighteenth century, though it began to suffer decorous cuts to its lower-comic parts (such as Volpone's servants and the Politic Would-Be subplot). Performances became rare after the retirement of Garrick in 1776, and the play finally fell into disuse after a 1785 Drury Lane production, while more sentimental comedies and puritanical attitudes – the very things the play itself sought to subjugate – dominated the English theatre.

Since its revival at the Lyric Theatre Hammersmith in 1921 (which won a rave review from T. S. Eliot), however, *Volpone* has been produced more often than any other non-Shakespearean play of the period, and more often than several of Shakespeare's. It has also inspired adaptations such as a 1936 French film, scripted by Jules Romains, which begins with a back-story resembling Shakespeare's *Merchant of Venice*, then follows a 1926 socialist reworking of the play by Stefan Zweig that allows Mosca to share the hoarded wealth with the poor (Joan Littlewood's superb 1955 production, reflecting the leftist values of the Theatre Workshop, also gave Mosca the final triumph). Larry Gelbart's 1976 hit Broadway play 'The Sly Fox', set in San Francisco, also drew on Zweig, and starred George C. Scott as Foxwell J. Sly. The 1967 feature film 'The Honey Pot' starred Rex Harrison as a Mr. Fox testing three money-hungry mistresses. The 1960s also produced opera and musical-comedy versions of the play. If these adaptations have anything in common, it is the effort to make *Volpone* a more conventional comedy, softening the cruelty, allowing at least a glimmer of romance and the possibility of a happy ending.

Staging the play in its original form seems to require at least some kind of upper balcony (from which Celia can throw her handkerchief out of a window, and Bonario can later observe Volpone's attack on her), a large curtained bed (where Volpone can rest and conceal his treasure, and from which he can partly emerge to whisper to Mosca or the audience), and a court bench large and dignified enough for the four *Avocatori* in the trial scenes. Otherwise, directors have great leeway, and they have used it.

Act II, Scene ii; Celia (Allison Sie) throws her handkerchief down to Volpone/Scoto (Dan Kern); A Noise Within, Glendale, CA, 1998, dir. Art Manke (photo © Craig Schwartz Photography).

Act V, Scene iii; Mosca (Francois Giroday) taunts Corvino, Corbaccio, and Voltore over the will of the supposedly dead Volpone; A Noise Within, Glendale, CA, 1998, dir. Art Manke (photo © Craig Schwartz Photography).

A crucial question in staging the play, as in reading it, is how to balance the beast-fable allegory with realistic human psychology. Many productions have costumed Volpone in vulpine furs, and the legacy-hunters at least partly as the birds their names suggest, giving Voltore a long vulture-like beak, Corbaccio the stooped posture and croaking voice of a raven, and making a black-robed Corvino chase, crow-like, the disguised Volpone away from his nest. Sometimes (as in Donald Wolfit's landmark productions) the *Avocatori* become owls, though the text does not propose it (Wolfit stretched Jonson's fable further by making the diabolical Mosca snake-like and the pugnacious, sexually obsessed Corvino bullish). In the 1952 production in Stratford, England, Anthony Quayle's fabulously unctuous Mosca not only wore shiny black clothes and rubbed his hands together like a fly, but emitted a strange buzzing laugh, and (thanks to matching table legs) appeared to have six black legs as he took inventory of Volpone's treasures.

Though the tendency early in the twentieth century was to keep the play nimble (and affordable) with simple traditional costumes and minimal sets, subsequent major productions were designed to emphasize the beast-fable further. For the 1968 National Theatre version, Tyrone Guthrie sent his actors to study animals at the London zoo, and aptly extended the avian repertoire by costuming the mindless mimic Sir Pol and his garishly dressed Lady as parrots. In 1972 the Bristol Old Vic – which had successfully emphasized the animal aspects in voice and movement in a 1955 production – pursued the same idea with emphasis on the sets, allowing the bird-characters to swoop down from on high, and Volpone to emerge from a kind of burrow. A delightful 1998 version at the Noise Within in California featured a raucous chorus of crows. The lively 1990 English Shakespeare Company version – which cleverly suggested comparisons between Volpone's three servants and his three male legacy-hunters, and hinted at the depravity of late capitalism – kept some gestures from the beast fable, but mostly modernized the setting by giving Volpone an invalid's intravenous drip and having donations arrive in shopping carts.

Other sets have ranged from traditional simplicity, such as Wolfit's basic proscenium stage that used the front curtain to divide venues, to the opulence of the 1952 version, which featured functional gondolas and an elaborate background depiction of the ornate Piazza di San Marco, thus highlighting the Venetian materialism which the play so centrally criticizes. Like all major Renaissance plays, *Volpone* has also been modernized, as in the 1971 Stratford, Ontario production that (like Thomas Mann's 'Death in Venice') evoked the city's 1890s decadence, and turned the Politic Would-Be couple into ugly-American tourists from Texas.

The pre-eminent modern Volpone was Wolfit, who for over twenty years played Volpone as an almost Falstaffian force of playfulness and appetite, cutting Volpone's weaker moments to assure the audience's admiration (this Volpone was also Falstaffian in his ruthlessness toward his underlings and victims). To keep Volpone as the commanding force, Wolfit also cut lines suggesting Mosca's readiness to mock and betray Volpone long before Volpone's fatal decision to play dead; how early and eagerly Mosca considers such betrayal is crucial for that role. Wolfit trimmed the Sir Pol subplot, too, thereby keeping the focus more on greed and cruelty than on lighter social follies.

Others (such as Ralph Richardson, whose 1952 Volpone was condemned as meek, and William Hutt's nastier 1971 portrayal) depicted Volpone more coolly, as a decadent aristocrat merely battling his own boredom (with the servants usually reflecting that decadence grotesquely); several more recent productions have begun the play with Mosca rousting whores (female and sometimes male) from Volpone's bed, or starting Volpone's day with a cocktail. The implicit blasphemy in the subsequent worship of gold has been heavily emphasized, to the point that (in the 1968 National Theatre production) Volpone's 'take of my hand' became the offering of a golden coin, in place of a Communion wafer, to the kneeling Mosca; and (in the 1971 Ontario production) Volpone elicited mass responses from a procession of monks who then stripped for an orgy. Modern productions have occasionally underscored the play's distorted sexuality by having a man in drag play Lady Pol (as would necessarily have happened in the all-male Jacobean theatre).

Celia has sometimes been performed as a meek little victim, other times as a strident moralist, and even occasionally as a hypocritical temptress, more vixen than victim. A lot depends on how one stages her encounters with Volpone, from the mountebank scene – where her body-language can answer many questions that the text leaves open – to the attempted-rape scene.

The mixed tone of the ending of this play – a comedy that culminates with harsh sentences and no winners – has troubled directors as much as it has critics. The Bristol Old Vic production changed the ending several times during its run, unable to decide whether to suggest that Volpone (like Reynard) would finally escape; Guthrie, having played up the light comic pleasures of the story, tried adding a madrigal between the sentencing and the epilogue to overcome the closing bitterness; in later stagings Guthrie surrendered by eliminating the epilogue and letting the *Avocatori* lead sadistic laughter at the prisoners. A production in New York in 1985 ducked the problem by keeping the atmosphere morally sombre from the start, and the 1999 RSC Swan production, though funny, was effectively dark and menacing throughout. Many other productions (including the Wolfit and the Ontario versions) have sought to emphasize the separation between the defeated exit of Volpone and the potentially triumphant return, in the epilogue, of the actor who played him.

Collectively, the stage history seems to warn against trying – perhaps misled by Jonson's Prologue – to hide the tough, sinister side of the play behind cheerful laughter (as in Jose Ferrer's scorned 1948 slapstick version, the 1965 Nottingham Playhouse version, and Guthrie's 1962 Minneapolis and 1968 Old Vic versions), or trying to hide the essential theatricality of the play and of the plays within it. Evidently *Volpone* needs to be savage and stagey. Efforts to conceal what are assumed to be Jonson's incompatibilities with modern sensibilities do him more harm than good (this is true on the page as well as the stage, I will now argue). The man may often have been difficult for no good reason, but the difficulties of the works are usually for very good reasons indeed.

The Text

This edition is a modern-spelling text based on facsimiles of Jonson's 1607 Quarto *Volpone* and 1616 Folio *Works*, both of which I believe he supervised carefully, though not fanatically. F appears to be based on a copy of Q marked, presumably by Jonson, with minor revisions. Ordinarily this would lend greatest weight to F, which is how editors of *Volpone* (with the exception of Henry de Vocht's little-known 1936 version) have tended to proceed. But revisions are not always improvements, and Jonson was surely a sharper playwright around 1606, as he began his string of great comedies, than he was approaching 1616, with *Bartholomew Fair* his only recent play, and no theatrical successes in his remaining decades.

Some of F's corrections are indeed corrections, its punctuation is often more expressive, and some changes may have emerged from performance. But the fresh wisdom of the genius at the start of his remarkable comic period deserves more respect than Jonson himself or his editors have given it. Furthermore, some changes apparently arose from tightened censorship rather than artistic reconsideration.

And, in truth, the differences between Q and F (about a hundred substantive changes, not counting small corrections and shifts in punctuation) are quite minor, and do not suggest any coherent change in view, any basic differences in intention – except perhaps for re-punctuation in the rape scene that renders Celia commandingly rational in F, rather than breathlessly desperate as in Q (in performance, Siobhan McKenna's defiance of Ralph Richardson epitomized the implications of F, Rosalind Iden's panic over Donald Wolfit's attack epitomized the implications of Q). Not even the myopia of an editor, and the accompanying narcissism of small differences among editions, can justify an absolute preference between the Q and F texts of *Volpone*, which are here therefore conflated to provide the best possible communication of this biting and hilarious play, with all its verbal and moral complexities, to a general modern audience.

With that goal in mind, I have worked as Jonson evidently did, using corrected versions of Q as a basis susceptible to small revisions: mostly modernization of spelling and punctuation, along with selective endorsements of revisions Jonson himself offered in F, and a few emendations (especially where authorized by the 1640 Second Folio) of what appear to be minor errors that slipped through both editions. Unlike previous editors, I have favoured the Q text of Jonson's Dedicatory Epistle, since it presumably reflects his thoughts at the time the play was composed, and certainly reflects the date at the end of the letter, more accurately than the F revision. The showy and archaic complexity of Jonson's syntax (in either version), evidently designed to flatter his university audience, makes this Epistle so difficult that I have placed it at the end of the text, rather than the beginning, to avoid discouraging modern readers before they reach the delights of the play proper. Several commendatory Latin and English poems from fellow-authors such as John Donne and Francis Beaumont also preceded the text – Jonson clearly designed Q to exalt himself as a literary artist – but are omitted from this edition.

At the beginning of each scene, the original texts list all the characters who appear in that scene; I have replaced that group listing with individual entrances at the likeliest moment in the text. These and other added stage directions appear in square brackets, and readers and performers are encouraged to reconsider them. Aside from the group entrance listings, and parentheses around lines to be whispered aside from one character to another, Q provides no stage directions; all unbracketed stage directions here come from F, which was more intent on reflecting the theatrical experience than on presenting a literary credential.

I have sought to retain some impression of Jonson's characteristic verbal rhythms, which he conveyed by elisional apostrophes and heavy punctuation. Modern usage generally dictates exchanging Jonson's colons and semicolons, as when Mosca remarks, 'There, he is farre enough; he can hear nothing: / And, for his father, I can keepe him off' (F, III.vii.17–18); occasionally the original texts use a colon in place of a modern exclamation point. Otherwise, however, this edition retains (to an unusual degree) Jonson's elaborate punctuation, which provides a valuable guide at times to sense for the reader, at other times to performance for the actor. A comma often represents the space, the lightly emphatic pause (between a predicate and its objective or subjective clause), in which a modern speaker would insert 'that', as when Corbaccio offers a drug by claiming to 'know, it cannot but most gently worke' (Q, I.iv.16), or when Mosca describes Celia's 'soft lip, / Would tempt you to eternity of kissing!' (Q, I.v.111–12). At other times the comma provides a pause for dramatic effect: modern writers – indeed, most modern editors – would remove at least the second of the commas in Mosca's almost pornographic description of Celia as 'a beauty, ripe, as harvest' (Q, I.v.109); but Jonson's commas suggest the provocative pauses that give Mosca's description the quality of a cumulative, developing series of thoughts; 'ripe' works by itself, before becoming subsumed into the conventional comparison. The same effect explains the even more peculiar insistence of commas when Mosca evokes, for Voltore, the wealth supposedly awaiting him upon Volpone's death: 'When you do come to swim, in golden lard, / Up to the armes, in honey' (Q, I.iii.70–1); for an editor to decide, merely for the sake of eliminating commas, that the swimming should be associated only with the lard, and the immersion separately with the honey, is a waste of Mosca's mesmerizing artistry, and Jonson's behind it.

The mid-sentence question marks of Mosca's 'Am not I here? whom you have made? your creature?' (Q, I.v.78) demand preservation for similar reasons: the phrases are each separate expressive units, as well as finally blending into a single sentence that, normally punctuated, would be less than the sum of its parts. Ironically, editors have inadvertently made Jonson seem old-fashioned by over-eagerly modernizing the oddities of his syntax and punctuation which, in their original form, reveal exactly the process of a human subjectivity spontaneously and realistically developing from moment to moment that Jonson's drama is commonly accused of lacking.

ABBREVIATIONS

Brockbank   *Volpone*, ed. Philip Brockbank, New Mermaids (London: A&C Black, 1968)

F   Ben Jonson, *Works*, First Folio edition (London, 1616)

F2   Ben Jonson, *Works*, Second Folio edition (London, 1640)

H&S   C. H. Herford, Percy Simpson, and Evelyn Simpson, eds., *Ben Jonson* (Oxford: Clarendon Press, 1925–52)

Kernan   *Volpone*, ed. Alvin Kernan (New Haven: Yale Univ. Press, 1962)

OED   *Oxford English Dictionary*, J. A. Murray et al., eds. (Oxford: Oxford Univ. Press)

Parker   *Volpone*, ed. Brian Parker, revised edition, Revels Plays (Manchester: Manchester Univ. Press, 1999); a Revels student version, with some updating of text and notes by David Bevington, appeared simultaneously

Q   *Volpone*, first Quarto edition (London, 1607)

Tilley   M. P. Tilley, *A Dictionary of Proverbs in England in the Sixteenth and Seventeenth Centuries* (Ann Arbor: Univ. of Michigan Press, 1950); the proverbs can generally be traced under the same numbers in the indexes by R. W. Dent

Citations of Shakespeare are based on *The Riverside Shakespeare*, ed. G. B. Evans (Boston: Houghton Mifflin, 1974)

FURTHER READING

Anne Barton, *Ben Jonson, dramatist* (Cambridge: Cambridge Univ. Press, 1984); the most helpful and perceptive modern study of Jonson's plays

Harold Bloom, *Ben Jonson's Volpone, or the Fox: Modern Critical Interpretations* (New York: Chelsea House, 1988); a selection of essays by major critics

Ian Donaldson, 'Volpone: Quick and Dead', *Essays in Criticism* 21 (1971), 121–34

William Empson, *'Volpone', The Hudson Review* 21 (1968–69), 651–66

Brian Gibbons, *Jacobean City Comedy*, 2nd ed., (London: Methuen, 1980); the best overview of play's genre, which Jonson would bequeath to the wittiest playwrights of subsequent decades

Richard Harp and Stanley Stewart, eds., *The Cambridge Companion to Ben Jonson* (Cambridge: Cambridge Univ. Press, 2000); an excellent new introduction to the author and his contexts

Harriet Hawkins, 'Folly, Incurable Disease, and *Volpone*', *Studies in English Literature, 1500–1900*, 8 (1968), 335–48

C. H. Herford, Percy Simpson, and Evelyn Simpson, eds., *Ben Jonson* (Oxford: Clarendon Press, 1925–52); the great modern edition of the complete works, well annotated

Alexander Leggatt, 'The Suicide of Volpone', *University of Toronto Quarterly* 39 (1969–70), 19–32

Gail Kern Paster, *The Idea of the City in the Age of Shakespeare* (Athens, Ga.: Univ. of Georgia Press, 1985); includes a perceptive study of Jonson's Venice; see also the David McPherson's helpful studies of this topic

James D. Redwine, 'Volpone's "Sport" and the Structure of Jonson's *Volpone*', *Studies in English Literature, 1500–1900*, 34 (1994), 301–21.

David R. Riggs, *Ben Jonson: A Life* (Cambridge: Harvard Univ. Press, 1989); a brilliant biography, rich in historical detail and psychoanalytic insight

Robert N. Watson, *Ben Jonson's Parodic Strategy: Literary Imperialism in the Comedies* (Cambridge: Harvard Univ. Press, 1987); a more extended application, to this play and others, of the argument outlined in this Introduction

Robert N. Watson, ed., *Critical Essays on Ben Jonson* (New York: G. K. Hall, 1997); the most recent general collection of Jonson criticism, including commentary on *Volpone* from John Dennis in the seventeenth century to Stephen Greenblatt in the twentieth

BEN: IONSON

his

VOLPONE

Or

THE FOXE.

— Simul & iucunda, & idonea dicere vitæ.

Printed for *Thomas Thorppe.*
1607.

VOLPONE, *a Magnifico* Volpone meant 'an old fox' and hence 'an old craftie, slie, subtle companion, sneaking lurking wily deceiver' (according to a popular 1598 dictionary, *A Worlde of Wordes*, by John Florio, to whom Jonson sent a copy of Q thanking him for 'the aid of his Muses'). A *Magnifico* was a name for a Venetian magnate or plutocrat, and also an alternative name for the Pantalone character in the *commedia dell'arte*. Though Jonson's Epistle warns against such 'applications', and editors have generally dismissed this one, several commentators in Jonson's own time suspected that Volpone was based on Thomas Sutton, the wealthiest commoner in London, and a controversial figure whose lack of direct heirs apparently allowed him to profit by manipulating those who were scheming to gain his legacy, which eventually founded the Charterhouse hospital (as Volpone's wealth finally goes to 'the hospital of the *Incurabili*' at V.xii.120).

MOSCA, *his Parasite* Mosca meant a kind of fly, and became thereby a term for human parasites, those who live and feed on others (usually by servile flattery); as references to demonic possession accumulate later in the play, we may also suspect a reference to Beelzebub, 'Lord of the Flies'.

VOLTORE, *an Advocate* Voltore meant 'a ravenous bird called a vultur' (Florio), and – because vultures feed on dead animals – the name was applied to legacy-hunters. It was also applied to persuasive lawyers; an Advocate was the equivalent of an English barrister or American defence attorney.

CORBACCIO Italian for a raven, a bird believed (as in Psalm 147, Proverbs 30:17, and Luke 12:24) to neglect its offspring, who (like Bonario) therefore had to rely on heaven for protection; its croaking was thought to signal death.

CORVINO Italian for a small crow – an emblem of marital fidelity, and an enemy of the fox.

NANO Italian for dwarf; dwarves were popular as court jesters.

CASTRONE 'a gelded man' (Florio), one who has been castrated, often to preserve a high singing voice or to preclude sexual intercourse.

ANDROGYNO 'he that is both male and female' (Florio)

POLITIC WOULD-BE a would-be schemer in affairs of state, one who wishes (like many English Renaissance travellers) to be thought important, clever, prudent and worldly. Shortened to Pol, his name links him to the parrot, which suits his mindless efforts to mimic the fashionable phrases and sophisticated schemes of those around him.

PEREGRINE a traveller; also a kind of hawk, birds which Jonson's Epigram LXXXV says 'strike ignorance' and 'make fools their quarry'; an emblematic tradition made them the opposite of the tortoise.

CELIA literally, 'heavenly one', celestial; sometimes the name of the heroine in the *commedia dell'arte*

BONARIO 'debonaire, honest, good, uncorrupt' (Florio), though it can also thereby imply 'naïve'

FINE MADAM WOULD-BE cf. Jonson's satiric Epigram LXII 'To Fine Lady Would-Be'; she probably has a large red beak of a nose that emphasizes her kinship to Pol the parrot

AVOCATORI Venetian officials who served as prosecutors and sometimes (as in Jonson's version) as judges

COMMANDATORI lower officials who enforced subpoenas summoning witnesses and malefactors to court hearings

2

THE PERSONS OF THE COMEDY
[in order of appearance]

VOLPONE, *a Magnifico*
MOSCA, *his Parasite*
VOLTORE, *an Advocate*
CORBACCIO, *an old Gentleman*
CORVINO, *a Merchant*
NANO, *a Dwarf*
CASTRONE, *an Eunuch*
ANDROGYNO, *a Hermaphrodite*
POLITIC WOULD-BE, *a Knight [from England]*
PEREGRINE, *a Gentleman-traveller [from England]*
CROWD
CELIA, *the Merchant's wife*
SERVATOR[I], *Servant[s]*
BONARIO, *a young Gentleman,* [Corbaccio's son]
FINE MADAM WOULD-BE, *the Knight's wife*
WOMEN, [*Attendants waiting on* Lady Would-Be]
AVOCATORI, *four Magistrates*
NOTARIO, *the Court clerk*
COMMANDATORI, *Officers*
MERCATORI, *Merchants*

The Scene: Venice

3

THE ARGUMENT

V *olpone, childless, rich, feigns sick, despairs,*
O *ffers his state to hopes of several heirs,*
L *ies languishing; his parasite receives*
P *resents of all, assures, deludes; then weaves*
O *ther cross-plots, which ope' themselves, are told.*   5
N *ew tricks for safety are sought; they thrive; when, bold,*
E *ach tempts th'other again, and all are sold.*

As in the comedies of Plautus, the first letters form an acrostic of the play's title.
  2 *state* estate, property
  5 *ope'* open
    told exposed
  7 *sold* betrayed, ruined

PROLOGUE

Now, luck God send us, and a little wit
  Will serve, to make our play hit,
According to the palates of the season:
  Here is rhyme, not empty of reason.
This we were bid to credit, from our poet,   5
  Whose true scope, if you would know it,
In all his poems, still, hath been this measure:
  To mix profit, with your pleasure;
And not as some (whose throats their envy failing)
  Cry hoarsely, 'All he writes, is railing',   10
And, when his plays come forth, think they can flout them,
  With saying, 'He was a year about them'.
To these there needs no lie, but this his creature,
  Which was, two months since, no feature;
And, though he dares give them five lives to mend it,   15
  'Tis known, five weeks fully penned it,
From his own hand, without a co-adjutor,
  Novice, journeyman, or tutor.
Yet, thus much I can give you, as a token
  Of his play's worth: no eggs are broken;   20

Prologue This Prologue may be spoken by Nano, Androgyno, and/or Castrone, since it shares the clunky poetic meter of their show in I.ii, and Mosca and Volpone will be needed onstage in character as soon as the Prologue ends.
1 *God* This word was changed to a meaningless 'yet' in F, probably because of the 1606 Act against Blasphemy.
5 *credit* believe, understand
6 *scope* intention
8 *profit* didactic value, as in Horace's formula of *utile dolci*; but perhaps quipping also on the playwright's financial motive in writing for the public theatre.
10 *railing* a tirade of abuse, complaint, and criticism; theatrical rivals such as Dekker and Marston voiced this objection to Jonson.
12 *about them* in writing them; Jonson proudly contrasted his careful workmanship with the hasty play-writing of his competitors, including Shakespeare, but here he boasts that he can also outdo them in writing quickly.
13 *To these ... creature* To refute these critics requires no lie, only this play he has created; or, he does not need to call them liars – 'give the lie' – only show this play
17–18 *co-adjutor ... tutor* Various kinds of assistant, each common in the play-factory that was the Elizabethan public theatre, ranging from a full collaborator to an apprentice, a hack assistant and scene-doctor, or a mentor and corrector.

Nor quaking custards with fierce teeth affrighted,
  Wherewith your rout are so delighted;
Nor hales he in a gull, old ends reciting,
  To stop gaps in his loose writing,
With such a deal of monstrous, and forced action,   25
  As might make Bedlam a faction;
Nor made he his play for jests stol'n from each table,
  But makes jests, to fit his fable.
And so presents quick comedy, refined,
  As best critics have designed: 30
The laws of time, place, persons he observeth,
  From no needful rule he swerveth.
All gall, and copp'ras, from his ink he draineth,
  Only, a little salt remaineth;
Wherewith, he'll rub your cheeks, till, red with laughter,   35
  They shall look fresh, a week after.

21 *quaking custards* the stock cowards of comedy, with reference also to pie-in-the-face slapstick and the fool's leap into a giant custard at the Lord Mayor's banquet; here, as in *Poetaster*, V.iii.525, Jonson mocks the phrase 'Let custards quake' from his rival Marston's *Scourge of Villainy* (1599), an example of what was called 'biting satire'.

22 *your rout* the rabble, 'your basic mob'

23–4 *Nor hales ... writing* Nor will this playwright haul in a gullible fool reciting stock phrases or bits from other plays

26 *make Bedlam a faction* add a new group to the madhouse, or competitor to the show people went to see there, or possibly, gain the endorsement of madmen; Bedlam was the common name of the insane asylum of St Mary of Bethlehem in London.

27 *jests stol'n from each table* jokes stolen like random leftovers from a feast, or picked up as table-talk, or plagiarized from a jest-book

29 *quick* lively

31 *The laws of time, place, persons* Sixteenth-century Italian critics developed precepts from Aristotle's *Poetics* into an insistence on the Dramatic Unities, which lent verisimilitude and thus believability to a play by having it all occur in a single day and area, with suitable and consistent character-types (since *Volpone* has a distinct subplot, Jonson conveniently omits the law governing unity of action here); Jonson often used his adherence to these laws to attack his theatrical rivals, who generally did not observe them.

33 *gall, and copp'ras* substances used to make ink, but standing here for animosity (attributed to the gall-bladder) and bitterness (ferrous sulphate, known as copperas, tastes extremely harsh)

34 *salt* sediment; edible salt was a metaphor for pungent wit, and was also used in cleaning and food preservation, leading to 'fresh' in line 36.

VOLPONE
OR THE FOX

Act I, Scene i

[*Enter*] MOSCA, [*pulling back the curtains to discover*]
VOLPONE [*in bed*]

VOLPONE
Good morning to the day; and, next, my gold:
Open the shrine, that I may see my saint.

[MOSCA *uncovers the treasure*]

Hail the world's soul, and mine. More glad than is
The teeming earth, to see the longed-for sun
Peep through the horns of the celestial Ram, 5
Am I, to view thy splendour, darkening his;
That, lying here, amongst my other hoards,
Show'st like a flame by night; or like the day
Struck out of chaos, when all darkness fled
Unto the centre. O thou son of Sol, 10

0 s.d. Though his entrance could be delayed until just before he speaks, Mosca
probably enters here, perhaps opening the curtains around Volpone's bed, or
opening curtains to admit the morning sun.

2 *shrine ... saint* Volpone asks Mosca to open curtains concealing the gold, to
which Volpone then addresses a kind of matins prayer, which would normally
have been addressed to God in praise of the morning sun. His subsequent speeches
are permeated with religious language blasphemously redirected toward gold.

3 *world's soul* the Platonic *anima mundi*, but punning on *sol* – the French word
for the sun; Volpone sees gold (which alchemists called 'the son of Sol', as at line
10 below) as the soul of worldly desires; *sol* was also the name of a French coin
(as at IV.v.97 below).

4 *teeming* full of life, and ready to give birth

5 *horns ... Ram* Aries in the zodiac, the beginning of spring, when the increasing
sunlight nurtures renewed life

6 *thy splendour ... his* the gold's splendour making the sun seem dim by comparison

7 *hoards* secret treasures, presumably including jewels and silver plate

9–10 *Struck ... centre* Established amid the primal Chaos, driving all darkness to the
centre of the earth (described in the opening of Genesis)

10 *son of Sol* in alchemy, the sun was described as the father of gold

But brighter than thy father, let me kiss,
With adoration, thee, and every relic
Of sacred treasure in this blessèd room.
Well did wise poets, by thy glorious name,
Title that age which they would have the best,   15
Thou being the best of things, and far transcending
All style of joy, in children, parents, friends,
Or any other waking dream on earth.
Thy looks when they to Venus did ascribe,
They should have giv'n her twenty thousand Cupids;   20
Such are thy beauties, and our loves! Dear saint,
Riches, the dumb god that giv'st all men tongues;
That canst do nought, and yet mak'st men do all things;
The price of souls; even hell, with thee to boot,
Is made worth heaven! Thou art virtue, fame,   25
Honour, and all things else! Who can get thee,
He shall be noble, valiant, honest, wise –
MOSCA
And what he will, sir. Riches are in fortune
A greater good than wisdom is in nature.

14–15 *thy glorious name ... best* The great poets called the first and best period in
   human history 'the Golden Age' – the classical equivalent of the Christian
   Garden of Eden; e.g. Ovid's *Metamorphoses*, I.89–112 and XV.96 ff.
16–20 When Seneca translated the portion of Euripides's *Danae* on which this pass-
   age is based (*Epistles* CXV.14), he reported that Euripides had to placate the
   original audience by assuring them that this impious greedy speaker would be
   punished – very much the same promise Jonson makes in the Epistle accompanying *Volpone* (lines 121–4) (Parker).
19–20 *Venus ... Cupids* the goddess often called golden – *aurea Venus* – by Homer
   and classical Latin poets would need to have many supplementary beauties (typ-
   ified by the son she produced, the god of love) to be worthy of that adjective; but
   Volpone is also unwittingly confessing that he has perverted the love inspired (in
   the classical tradition) by Cupid into the greed defined (in the Christian tradition) as *cupiditas*.
22 *dumb* mute; Compare the proverbs 'when gold speaks every tongue is silent'
   (Tilley G295) and 'silence is golden'.
23 *That ... things* Recalling Aristotle's definition of divinity as the unmoved mover
   (Parker)
24 *with thee to boot* with gold as a compensation (playing perhaps also on 'booty',
   stolen treasure); where Christ's sacrifice had paid 'the price of souls', gold can
   buy them back for damnation.
28 *what he will* whatever he desires
28–9 *Riches ... nature* It is better to be wealthy than wise (playing on a conventional
   debate about the relative importance of nature and fortune).

VOLPONE
   True, my belovèd Mosca. Yet, I glory   30
   More in the cunning purchase of my wealth,
   Than in the glad possession, since I gain
   No common way: I use no trade, no venture;
   I wound no earth with ploughshares; fat no beasts
   To feed the shambles; have no mills for iron,   35
   Oil, corn, or men, to grind 'em into powder;
   I blow no subtle glass; expose no ships
   To threat'nings of the furrow-facèd sea;
   I turn no monies, in the public bank;
   Nor usure private.
MOSCA   No, sir, nor devour   40
   Soft prodigals. You shall ha' some will swallow
   A melting heir, as glibly as your Dutch
   Will pills of butter, and ne'er purge for't;
   Tear forth the fathers of poor families
   Out of their beds, and coffin them, alive,   45
   In some kind, clasping prison, where their bones
   May be forthcoming, when the flesh is rotten.
   But your sweet nature doth abhor these courses:
   You loathe, the widow's, or the orphan's tears
   Should wash your pavements; or their piteous cries   50
   Ring in your roofs, and beat the air for vengeance.
VOLPONE
   Right, Mosca, I do loathe it.
MOSCA   And besides, sir,
   You are not like a thresher, that doth stand
   With a huge flail, watching a heap of corn,
   And, hungry, dares not taste the smallest grain,   55

33 *venture* speculative business scheme
35 *shambles* slaughterhouse
37 *subtle glass* Venice was (and still is) famous for its artistic glass-blowers.
38 *furrow-facèd* covered with dangerous waves
39 *turn* exchange
40 *usure private* loan-sharking; as Shakespeare also shows, Venice was a hot-bed of
   usury in the Renaissance.
41 *Soft prodigals* Gullible spend-thrifts; foolish heirs are often cheated by clever
   urban operators in the plays of this period, especially Jonson's.
42 *melting* wasteful (continuing also the play on their 'soft' edibility, one of countless cannibalistic metaphors in the play)
42–3 *Dutch ... butter* The Dutch appetite for butter was notorious.
43 *purge* suffer diarrhoea or vomiting, or possibly, need a laxative
44–7 *Tear ... rotten* Hold men in debtors' prison, letting them out only when they
   have been reduced to mere bones

But feeds on mallows, and such bitter herbs;
Nor like the merchant, who hath filled his vaults
With *Romagnìa*, and rich Candian wines,
Yet drinks the lees of Lombard's vinegar;
You will not lie in straw, whilst moths, and worms   60
Feed on your sumptuous hangings and soft beds.
You know the use of riches, and dare give, now,
From that bright heap, to me, your poor observer,
Or to your dwarf, or your hermaphrodite,
Your eunuch, or what other household trifle   65
Your pleasure allows maint'nance.
VOLPONE   Hold thee, Mosca,
Take, of my hand: [*Gives him money*] thou strik'st on
    truth, in all;
And they are envious, term thee parasite.
Call forth my dwarf, my eunuch, and my fool,
And let 'em make me sport.

                                      [*Exit* MOSCA]

                          What should I do,   70
But cocker up my genius, and live free
To all delights my fortune calls me to?
I have no wife, no parent, child, ally,
To give my substance to; but whom I make,
Must be my heir; and this makes men observe me,   75
This draws new clients, daily, to my house,
Women, and men, of every sex, and age,
That bring me presents, send me plate, coin, jewels,

---

56 *mallows* a common plant family which Pliny (among others) believed to be med-
    icinal. Cf. Horace's *Satires* II.3.111–21: 'If beside a huge corn-heap a man were
    to lie outstretched, keeping ceaseless watch with a big cudgel, yet never dare,
    hungry though he be and owner of it all, to touch one grain thereof, but rather
    feed like a miser on bitter herbs' (Parker).
58 *Romagnìa . . . wines* sweet wines from Greece and Crete
59 *Lombard's vinegar* The wines of Lombardy were notoriously harsh.
63 *observer* lowly, worshipful follower
66 *Hold thee* Stop talking, and/or, You may hold this coin or jewel
68 *term* [who] call
71 *But cocker up my genius* Except indulge my natural talents and tendencies (with
    a suggestion of rousing his genital powers to pleasure)
74 *substance* wealth
    whom I make whomever I designate
75 *observe me* treat me reverently
76 *clients* persons depending on patronage, as in the decadent phase of ancient Rome
78 *plate* gold or silver dishes

With hope, that when I die, which they expect
Each greedy minute, it shall then return   80
Tenfold upon them; whilst some, covetous
Above the rest, seek to engross me, whole,
And counterwork, the one, unto the other,
Contend in gifts, as they would seem, in love;
All which I suffer, playing with their hopes,   85
And am content to coin 'em into profit,
And look upon their kindness, and take more,
And look on that; still, bearing them in hand,
Letting the cherry knock against their lips,
And draw it by their mouths, and back again.   90
How now!

Act I, Scene ii

[*Enter* MOSCA,] NANO, ANDROGYNO, CASTRONE

NANO
Now, room for fresh gamesters, who do will you to know,
   They do bring you neither play, nor university show;
And therefore do entreat you, that whatsoever they rehearse,
   May not fare a whit the worse, for the false pace of the verse.
If you wonder at this, you will wonder more, ere we pass,   5

82–4 *engross me ... love* take over my wealth wholesale, and undermine each other,
    competing in gifts that masquerade as true affection
85 *suffer* allow
88 *bearing them in hand* leading them on
89 *cherry knock against their lips* This refers to a tantalizing game called chop-
    cherry, much like bobbing for apples.
Act I, Scene ii Like many Renaissance play-texts, the printed *Volpone* seems too long
    to have been acted in two hours; this scene is often cut by modern directors who
    favour rapid plot-development over arcane set-pieces.
1 *room* make room
2 *neither play, nor university show* neither from the public theatre, nor from the
    academic pastimes or classical revivals performed by the Cambridge and Oxford
    students Jonson addresses in his Epistle. The cluster of learned references in this
    scene seem better suited to a university than a general audience.
4 *whit* the slightest bit (with a pun on 'wit', on which the academic plays especially
    depended)
    false pace Nano is speaking in an awkward old-fashioned type of verse, familiar
    from medieval drama: rhymed tetrameter couplets, with varying numbers of
    unstressed syllables.
5 *ere we pass* before we are finished

For know, here [*Indicating* ANDROGYNO] is enclosed the
    soul of Pythagoras,
That juggler divine, as hereafter shall follow;
    Which Soul (fast, and loose, sir) came first from Apollo,
And was breathed into Aethalides, Mercurius his son,
    Where it had the gift to remember all that ever was done.   10
From thence it fled forth, and made quick transmigration
    To goldy-locked Euphorbus, who was killed, in good
        fashion,
At the siege of old Troy, by the cuckold of Sparta.
    Hermotimus was next (I find it, in my charta)
To whom it did pass, where no sooner it was missing,   15
    But with one Pyrrhus of Delos, it learned to go a-fishing:
And thence did it enter the Sophist of Greece.
    From Pythagore, she went into a beautiful piece,
Hight Aspasia, the meretrix; and the next toss of her
    Was, again, of a whore, she became a philosopher,   20

6 *Pythagoras* a famous ancient Greek philosopher, whose followers believed in
   reincarnation, including across species. The cynical version Volpone's freakish
   servants perform here echoes Lucian's parody of those beliefs in *The Dream, or
   The Cock* – a parody which warns against worshipping wealth. So there is a
   warning for Volpone here, especially since people degrade themselves into lower
   animals throughout this play. The rest of the speech echoes many Pythagorean
   doctrines, including the musical order of the cosmos, and the silence and bean-
   free vegetarianism he demanded from his followers (lines 26–40) (Parker).
7 *juggler* Often a pejorative term for any kind of cheater in this period, though
   juggling in the modern sense would fit the tricky series of hand-offs that follows.
8 *fast, and loose* hard to pin down; based on a tricky game of guessing whether a
   belt was actually knotted around a dagger, and hence held fast, or could simply
   be pulled loose.
9 *Aethalides, Mercurius his son* the herald for Jason's argonauts, Mercury's son
   (Jonson liked this form of the possessive, though it is based on a false etymol-
   ogy).
12 *goldy-locked Euphorbus* According to *The Iliad*, the Trojan Euphorbus bound
    up his hair with gold, wounded Patroclus, and was killed by the Spartan king
    Menelaus (the theft of whose wife provoked the Trojan wars).
14 *Hermotimus* ancient Greek philosopher who probably lived shortly after
    Pythagoras
    charta charter, written script or history
16 *Pyrrhus* perhaps the Greek philosopher who was 'a fisherman of Delos' (Parker)
17 *Sophist of Greece* Pythagoras
19 *Hight Aspasia, the meretrix* Called Aspasia the courtesan; she was the mistress
    of the ancient Greek king Pericles.
20 *again* This may refer ahead syntactically to becoming again a philosopher.

Crates the Cynic (as itself doth relate it);
   Since, kings, knights, and beggars, knaves, lords and
     fools gat it,
Besides, ox, and ass, camel, mule, goat, and brock,
   In all which it hath spoke, as in the cobbler's cock.
But I come not here to discourse of that matter,   25
   Or his one, two, or three, or his great oath, 'by quater',
His musics, his trigon, his golden thigh,
   Or his telling how elements shift; but I
Would ask, how of late, thou hast suffered translation,
   And shifted thy coat, in these days of reformation?   30
ANDROGYNO
   Like one of the reformèd, a fool, as you see,
   Counting all old doctrine heresy.
NANO
   But not on thine own forbid meats hast thou ventured?
ANDROGYNO
   On fish, when first a Carthusian I entered.
NANO
   Why, then thy dogmatical silence hath left thee?   35
ANDROGYNO
   Of that an obstreperous lawyer bereft me.
NANO
   O wonderful change! When Sir Lawyer forsook thee,
   For Pythagore's sake, what body then took thee?

21 *Crates* a student of Diogenes, who disdained material pleasures
    itself The neuter pronoun here may refer to the soul itself, the source text, the
    cock narrator in Lucian, or Androgyno, whose name indicates mixed gender.
22 *gat it* temporarily held this soul
23 *brock* badger
24 *the cobbler's cock* In the Lucian text, a rooster tells its tale to a greedy shoe-
    maker.
26 *quater* Pythagoras's musical and mathematical model of the universe was based
    on symmetrical permutations of the numbers 1–4, as in the balanced triangle
    (the 'trigon' of the next line).
27 *golden thigh* a legend about Pythagoras's body
30 *shifted ... reformation* changed allegiance (hence the expression 'turn-coat' for
    a traitor) since Protestantism gained power
31 *reformèd, a fool* One of Jonson's many attacks on the radical Protestants, now
    known as Puritans, whom he would have hated as enemies of three things very
    important to him at this time: theatre, bodily pleasures, and Catholicism.
32 *Counting* Considering
34 *Carthusian* an austere order of monks, forbidden meat and speech, but allowed
    fish

ANDROGYNO
    A good dull mule.
NANO   And how! by that means,
    Thou wert brought to allow of the eating of beans?   40
ANDROGYNO
    Yes.
NANO But, from the mule, into whom didst thou pass?
ANDROGYNO
    Into a very strange beast, by some writers called an ass;
    By others, a precise, pure, illuminate brother,
        Of those devour flesh, and sometimes one another,
    And will drop you forth a libel, or a sanctified lie,   45
        Betwixt every spoonful of a Nativity pie.
NANO
    Now quit thee, for heaven, of that profane nation;
    And gently report thy next transmigration.
ANDROGYNO
    To the same that I am.
NANO   A creature of delight?
    And (what is more than a fool) an hermaphrodite?   50
    Now 'pray thee, sweet soul, in all thy variation,
        Which body wouldst thou choose, to take up thy station?
ANDROGYNO
    Troth, this I am in, even here would I tarry.
NANO
    'Cause here, the delight of each sex thou canst vary?
ANDROGYNO
    Alas, those pleasures be stale, and forsaken;   55
        No, it is your fool wherewith I am so taken,
    The only one creature that I can call blessed,
        For all other forms I have proved most distressed.
NANO
    Spoke true, as thou wert in Pythagoras still.
    This learnèd opinion we celebrate will,   60
    Fellow eunuch, as behooves us, with all our wit, and art,

---

39 *how!* an exclamation of surprise and inquiry
43 *precise, pure, illuminate brother* a Puritan, one who claims to have seen the light
44 *those* those who; cf. Galatians V.14–15
46 *Nativity* an alternative term for Christmas used by Puritans, who mistrusted any
    residue of the term 'Mass'
47 *quit thee* get out
    for heaven for heaven's sake
51 *'pray thee* [I] prithee tell me
52 *take up thy station* stay in
53 *Troth* I swear by my honesty

To dignify that, whereof ourselves are so great, and
  special a part.
VOLPONE
  Now very, very pretty! Mosca, this
  Was thy invention?
MOSCA   If it please my patron,
  Not else.
VOLPONE It doth, good Mosca.
MOSCA   Then it was, sir.   65

Song

  Fools, they are the only nation
  Worth men's envy, or admiration;
  Free from care, or sorrow-taking,
  Themselves, and others merry making;
  All they speak, or do, is sterling.   70
  Your Fool, he is your great man's dearling,
  And your lady's sport, and pleasure:
  Tongue and bable are his treasure.
  His very face begetteth laughter,
  And he speaks truth, free from slaughter;   75
  He's the grace of every feast,
  And, sometimes, the chiefest guest;
  Hath his trencher, and his stool,
  When wit shall wait upon the Fool:
    O, who would not be   80
    He, he, he?

One knocks without

VOLPONE
  Who's that? Away, look Mosca.

[Exit NANO *and* CASTRONE*]*

---

62 *that* the folly
65 s.d. *Song* probably sung by Nano and Castrone in high-pitched eunuch voices
70 *sterling* excellent, valuable
73 *bable* both the fool's sceptre (called a bauble) with its clear phallic suggestions,
    and babble, rapid meaningless speech
75 *free from slaughter* immune from punishment; Jonson's rival Marston mocked
    this eye-rhyme in *The Fawn*, IV.i (Brockbank).
78 *trencher* plate for eating
79 *wait upon* several simultaneous meanings: serves as a food-waiter for, acts as a
    subservient courtier to, and waits for his turn after
81 s.d. *without* outside, offstage

MOSCA   Fool, be gone,

[*Exit* ANDROGYNO]

'Tis Signior Voltore, the advocate,
I know him by his knock.
VOLPONE   Fetch me my gown,
My furs, and night-caps. Say, my couch is changing,   85
And let him entertain himself, awhile,
Within i' th' gallery.

[*Exit* MOSCA]

                     Now, now, my clients
Begin their visitation! Vulture, kite,
Raven, and gorcrow, all my birds of prey,
That think me turning carcass, now they come;   90
I am not for 'em yet.

[*Enter* MOSCA *carrying* VOLPONE's *disguise*]

                     How now? The news?
MOSCA
   A piece of plate, sir.
VOLPONE   Of what bigness?
MOSCA   Huge,
   Massy, and antique, with your name inscribed,
   And arms engraven.
VOLPONE   Good! And not a fox
   Stretched on the earth, with fine delusive sleights,   95
   Mocking a gaping crow? ha, Mosca?
MOSCA   Sharp, sir.
VOLPONE
   Give me my furs. Why dost thou laugh so, man?
MOSCA
   I cannot choose, sir, when I apprehend
   What thoughts he has within now, as he walks:
   That this might be the last gift he should give;   100
   That this would fetch you; if you died today,
   And gave him all, what he should be tomorrow;

OMG!
Mosca has
been playing
him

---

85 *couch is changing* bed is being made
89 *gorcrow* flesh-eating crow
91 *not for* not ready for – not yet disguised, but also, not yet decayed
93 *Massy* Massive, Heavy
94–6 *And not ... crow?* Volpone jokes that the coat of arms engraved on the plate
      ought to refer to the tactics (such as playing dead) by which the fox consumes
      the crow who was hoping to consume him.
98 *choose* resist

What large return would come of all his ventures;
How he should worshipped be, and reverenced;
Ride, with his furs, and foot-cloths; waited on   105
By herds of fools, and clients; have clear way
Made for his mule, as lettered as himself;
Be called the great and learnèd advocate:
And then concludes, there's nought impossible.

VOLPONE
Yes, to be learnèd, Mosca.

MOSCA   O no: rich   110
Implies it. Hood an ass with reverend purple,
So you can hide his two ambitious ears,
And he shall pass for a cathedral doctor.

VOLPONE
My caps, my caps, good Mosca, fetch him in.

MOSCA
Stay, sir, your ointment for your eyes.

VOLPONE   That's true;   115
Dispatch, dispatch: I long to have possession
Of my new present.

MOSCA   That, and thousands more,
I hope, to see you lord of.

VOLPONE   Thanks, kind Mosca.

MOSCA
And that, when I am lost in blended dust,
And hundred such as I am, in succession –   120

VOLPONE
Nay, that were too much, Mosca.

MOSCA   You shall live,
Still, to delude these harpies.

VOLPONE   Loving Mosca,
'Tis well, my pillow now, and let him enter.

                                        Exit MOSCA

---

103 *What large … ventures* What a profit he would make on his investment in
    expensive gifts designed to win the dying man's favour
105 *foot-cloths* richly ornamented fabric draped over an aristocrat's horse
107 *lettered* learned
111–13 Erasmus makes this joke repeatedly in *Praise of Folly*, based on the purple
    hood worn by Doctors of Philosophy.
114 *caps* nightcaps; but perhaps with an unwitting ironic resemblance to the ass's
    hood in the previous lines
116 *Dispatch* Hurry
122 *harpies* mythological creatures with the face of a woman and the body of a fierce
    bird of prey

Now, my feigned cough, my phthisic, and my gout,
My apoplexy, palsy, and catarrh,   125
Help, with your forcèd functions, this my posture,
Wherein, this three year, I have milked their hopes.
He comes, I hear him – uh, uh, uh, uh – oh.

Act I, Scene iii

MOSCA *[brings in]* VOLTORE *[clutching the plate]*

MOSCA
  You still are, what you were, sir. Only you,
  Of all the rest, are he, commands his love;
  And you do wisely to preserve it, thus,
  With early visitation, and kind notes
  Of your good meaning to him, which, I know,   5
  Cannot but come most grateful. *[To* VOLPONE*]* Patron, sir.
  Here's Signior Voltore is come –
VOLPONE   What say you?
MOSCA
  Sir, Signior Voltore is come, this morning,
  To visit you.
VOLPONE   I thank him.
MOSCA   And hath brought
  A piece of antique plate, bought of St Mark,   10
  With which he here presents you.
VOLPONE   He is welcome.
  Pray him, to come more often.
MOSCA   Yes.
VOLTORE   What says he?
MOSCA
  He thanks you, and desires you see him often.

124 *phthisic* tuberculosis, or possibly asthma
125 *apoplexy, palsy, and catarrh* stroke or seizure, paralysis or quivering, and mucus
    flow
126 *forcèd* feigned
    posture imposture, deluding performance (though perhaps referring directly to
    his sickly sprawl in the bed)
128 *uh* Jonson probably intended the 'h' to sound like the German guttural 'ch', sim-
    ulating a shallow cough (Parker).
  2 *he ... love* the man who has Volpone's favour
  6 *Cannot ... grateful* Must be very welcome
 10 *St Mark* Venice's Piazza di San Marco was famous for its goldsmiths.

VOLPONE
  Mosca.
MOSCA   My patron?
VOLPONE   Bring him near, where is he?
  I long to feel his hand.
MOSCA [*Guiding his hand*] The plate is here, sir.   15
VOLTORE
  How fare you, sir?
VOLPONE   I thank you, Signior Voltore.
  Where is the plate? Mine eyes are bad.
VOLTORE [*Putting the plate in* VOLPONE'*s hands*] I am sorry,
  To see you still thus weak.
MOSCA   [*Aside*] That he is not weaker.
VOLPONE
  You are too munificent.
VOLTORE   No, sir, would to heaven
  I could as well give health to you, as that plate.   20
VOLPONE
  You give, sir, what you can. I thank you. Your love
  Hath taste in this, and shall not be unanswered.
  I pray you see me often.
VOLTORE   Yes, I shall, sir.
VOLPONE
  Be not far from me.
MOSCA [*Aside to* VOLTORE] Do you observe that, sir?
VOLPONE
  Hearken unto me, still. It will concern you.   25
MOSCA
  [*Aside to* VOLTORE] You are a happy man, sir, know your
     good.
VOLPONE
  I cannot now last long.
MOSCA [*Aside to* VOLTORE] You are his heir, sir.
VOLTORE
  [*Aside to* MOSCA] Am I?
VOLPONE   I feel me going – uh,uh,uh,uh –
  I am sailing to my port – uh,uh,uh,uh! –
  And I am glad I am so near my haven.   30
MOSCA
  Alas, kind gentleman, well, we must all go.

22 *Hath taste* Can be sensed

VOLTORE
  But, Mosca.
MOSCA   Age will conquer.
VOLTORE   'Pray thee hear me.
  Am I inscribed his heir, for certain?
MOSCA   Are you?
  I do beseech you, sir, you will vouchsafe
  To write me i' your family. All my hopes   35
  Depend upon your worship: I am lost,
  Except the rising sun do shine on me.
VOLTORE
  It shall both shine, and warm thee, Mosca.
MOSCA   Sir.
  I am a man that have not done your love
  All the worst offices: here I wear your keys,   40
  See all your coffers, and your caskets locked,
  Keep the poor inventory of your jewels,
  Your plate, and monies, am your steward, sir.
  Husband your goods here.
VOLTORE   But am I sole heir?
MOSCA
  Without a partner, sir, confirmed this morning;   45
  The wax is warm yet, and the ink scarce dry
  Upon the parchment.
VOLTORE   Happy, happy me!
  By what good chance, sweet Mosca?
MOSCA   Your desert, sir;
  I know no second cause.
VOLTORE   Thy modesty
  Is loath to know it; well, we shall requite it.   50
MOSCA
  He ever liked your course, sir: that first took him.
  I oft have heard him say, how he admired
  Men of your large profession, that could speak

---

35 *write ... family* include me in your household (when Volpone's death ends my
    employment there)
37 *rising sun* This plays on Voltore's hope to become an inheriting 'son' to Volpone,
    and Mosca's hope to become 'son' to Voltore (as well as recalling the play's
    opening lines).
39–40 *that have ... offices* who has not rewarded your kindness with such bad ser-
    vices
44 *Husband* Manage prudently
46 *wax* the stamped sealing wax that marked the will as legitimate
51 *He ever ... him* He always liked your manner, or path of life; that was what first
    won his affection

To every cause, and things mere contraries,
Till they were hoarse again, yet all be law;   55
That, with most quick agility, could turn,
And return; make knots, and undo them;
Give forkèd counsel; take provoking gold
On either hand, and put it up. These men,
He knew, would thrive, with their humility.   60
And (for his part) he thought, he should be blest
To have his heir of such a suffering spirit,
So wise, so grave, of so perplexed a tongue,
And loud withal, that would not wag, nor scarce
Lie still, without a fee; when every word   65
Your worship but lets fall, is a chequin.

                                        Another knocks

Who is that? One knocks, I would not have you seen, sir.
And yet – pretend you came, and went in haste;
I'll fashion an excuse. And, gentle sir,
When you do come to swim, in golden lard,   70
Up to the arms, in honey, that your chin
Is borne up stiff with fatness of the flood,
Think on your vassal; but remember me:
I have not been your worst of clients.
VOLTORE   Mosca –
MOSCA
When will you have your inventory brought, sir?   75
Or see a copy of the will? [*More knocking, and* MOSCA
    shouts toward the door] Anon!
[*To* VOLTORE] I'll bring 'em to you, sir. Away, be gone,
Put business i' your face.

                                        [*Exit* VOLTORE]

                    [VOLPONE *sits up in bed*]
VOLPONE   Excellent, Mosca!
Come hither, let me kiss thee.

54 *mere contraries* totally contradictory
58 *forkèd* ambiguous; but the term has diabolical associations. Mosca keeps thinly
    disguising his insults.
59 *On . . . up* From both sides, and pocket it (as if for safe-keeping)
62 *suffering* patiently enduring
63 *perplexed* intricate, with an implication of double-dealing
66 *chequin* a gold coin used in Renaissance Venice
76 *Anon!* In just a moment (to the person knocking)
78 *Put . . . face* Look hurried, and/or look as if you were here on business

MOSCA   Keep you still, sir.
Here is Corbaccio.
VOLPONE   Set the plate away,   80
The vulture's gone, and the old raven's come.

Act I, Scene iv

MOSCA
[*To* VOLPONE] Betake you to your silence, and your sleep;
[*To the silver plate*] Stand there, and multiply. Now shall
     we see
A wretch, who is, indeed, more impotent,
Than this can feign to be; yet hopes to hop
Over his grave.

[*Enter* CORBACCIO]

                    Signior Corbaccio   5
You're very welcome, sir.
CORBACCIO   How does your patron?
MOSCA
Troth, as he did, sir, no amends.
CORBACCIO   What? Mends he?
MOSCA
No, sir: he is rather worse.
CORBACCIO   That's well. Where is he?
MOSCA
Upon his couch sir, newly fall'n asleep.
CORBACCIO
Does he sleep well?
MOSCA   No wink, sir, all this night,   10
Nor yesterday, but slumbers.
CORBACCIO   Good! He should take
Some counsel of physicians: I have brought him
An opiate here, from mine own doctor –
MOSCA
He will not hear of drugs.
CORBACCIO   Why? I myself
Stood by while't was made; saw all th' ingredients;   15

___

  2 *multiply* Mosca encourages the precious metal to breed more like itself, as he is
    about to make it do; the way greed replaces natural human reproduction with
    unnatural or perverted reproduction is a persistent theme of the play.
  4 *this* Volpone
 11 *but slumbers* only dozes

And know, it cannot but most gently work.
My life for his, 'tis but to make him sleep.
VOLPONE
[*Aside*] Ay, his last sleep, if he would take it.
MOSCA   Sir,
He has no faith in physic.
CORBACCIO   Say you? Say you?
MOSCA
He has no faith in physic: he does think   20
Most of your doctors are the greater danger,
And worse disease, t' escape. I often have
Heard him protest that your physician
Should never be his heir.
CORBACCIO   Not I his heir?
MOSCA
Not your physician, sir.
CORBACCIO   O, no, no, no,   25
I do not mean it.
MOSCA   No sir, nor their fees
He cannot brook: he says, they flay a man,
Before they kill him.
CORBACCIO   Right, I conceive you.
MOSCA
And then, they do it by experiment,
For which the law not only doth absolve them,   30
But gives them great reward; and, he is loath
To hire his death so.
CORBACCIO   It is true, they kill
With as much licence as a judge.
MOSCA   Nay, more;
For he but kills, sir, where the law condemns,
And these can kill him, too.
CORBACCIO   Ay, or me;   35
Or any man. How does his apoplex?
Is that strong on him, still?

---

19 *physic* medicine
21 *your doctors* doctors in general (a common Renaissance construction); the com-
    plaints against this profession that follow, like those against lawyers in the pre-
    vious scene, were familiar from classical as well as Renaissance commentators.
27 *brook* tolerate
    flay take the skin off
28 *conceive* understand
29 *by experiment* by trying out medicines on their patients
35 *these can kill him* doctors can safely kill a judge

MOSCA   Most violent.
  His speech is broken, and his eyes are set,
  His face drawn longer, than 'twas wont –
CORBACCIO   How? how?
  Stronger, than he was wont?
MOSCA   No, sir: his face   40
  Drawn longer, than 'twas wont.
CORBACCIO   O, good.
MOSCA   His mouth
  Is ever gaping, and his eyelids hang.
CORBACCIO   Good.
MOSCA
  A freezing numbness stiffens all his joints,
  And makes the colour of his flesh like lead.
CORBACCIO   'Tis good.
MOSCA
  His pulse beats slow, and dull.
CORBACCIO   Good symptoms, still.   45
MOSCA
  And, from his brain –
CORBACCIO   Ha? How? Not from his brain?
MOSCA
  Yes, sir, and from his brain –
CORBACCIO   I conceive you, good.
MOSCA
  Flows a cold sweat, with a continual rheum,
  Forth the resolvèd corners of his eyes.
CORBACCIO
  Is't possible? Yet I am better, ha!   50
  How does he, with the swimming of his head?
MOSCA
  O, sir, 'tis past the scotomy: he now
  Hath lost his feeling, and hath left to snort;
  You hardly can perceive him, that he breathes.
CORBACCIO
  Excellent, excellent, sure I shall outlast him: 55

---

39 *wont* formerly accustomed to being
40 Q gives this line to Mosca, but that is clearly a technical error, corrected by F.
46 *from his brain* Though the hard-of-hearing Corbaccio again misunderstands at
      first, thinking perhaps Mosca is talking about whether Volpone is out of his
      mind, he soon gleefully recognizes that Mosca is describing the final stages of
      apoplexy, in which the drainage of brain fluid was thought to lead to death.
49 *resolvèd* drooping and/or watery
50 *Yet I am better* I am even better off (because Volpone is even worse)
52 *scotomy* dizziness, accompanied by dimness of sight (OED)
53 *left* ceased

This makes me young again, a score of years.

MOSCA
I was a-coming for you, sir.

CORBACCIO   Has he made his will?
What has he giv'n me?

MOSCA   No, sir.

CORBACCIO   Nothing? ha?

MOSCA
He has not made his will, sir.

CORBACCIO   Oh, oh, oh.
But what did Voltore, the lawyer, here?   60

MOSCA
He smelled a carcass, sir, when he but heard
My master was about his testament;
As I did urge him to it, for your good –

CORBACCIO
He came unto him, did he? I thought so.

MOSCA
Yes, and presented him this piece of plate.   65

CORBACCIO
To be his heir?

MOSCA   I do not know, sir.

CORBACCIO   True,
I know it too.

MOSCA   By your own scale, sir.

CORBACCIO   Well,
I shall prevent him, yet. See, Mosca, look,
Here, I have brought a bag of bright chequins,
Will quite weigh down his plate.

MOSCA   Yea, marry, sir.   70
This is true physic, this your sacred medicine,
No talk of opiates, to this great elixir.

CORBACCIO
'Tis *aurum palpabile*, if not *potabile*.

MOSCA
It shall be ministered to him, in his bowl?

---

62 *about his testament* working on composing his will
70 *weigh down* outweigh
      marry indeed (a common form of the oath, '[I swear by the Virgin] Mary')
72 *No talk ... elixir* Opiates can't compare to this great medicine, gold, which is
      like the alchemists' elixir, the 'philosopher's stone', that was rumoured to bestow
      eternal life
73 *'Tis ... potabile* It is gold which can be felt, if not drunk. A liquid solution of
      gold was widely believed to be a health-giving miracle drug.

CORBACCIO
  Ay, do, do, do.
MOSCA   Most blessed cordial,   75
  This will recover him.
CORBACCIO   Yes, do, do, do.
MOSCA
  I think, it were not best, sir.
CORBACCIO   What?
MOSCA   To recover him.
CORBACCIO
  O, no, no, no; by no means.
MOSCA   Why, sir, this
  Will work some strange effect if he but feel it.
CORBACCIO
  'Tis true, therefore forbear; I'll take my venture: 80
  Give me't again.
MOSCA   At no hand, pardon me;
  You shall not do your self that wrong, sir. I
  Will so advise you, you shall have it all.
CORBACCIO
  How!
MOSCA All, sir, 'tis your right, your own; no man
  Can claim a part; 'tis yours, without a rival,   85
  Decreed by destiny.
CORBACCIO   How? How, good Mosca?
MOSCA
  I'll tell you, sir. This fit he shall recover –
CORBACCIO
  I do conceive you.
MOSCA   And, on first advantage
  Of his gained sense, will I re-importune him
  Unto the making of his testament;   90
  And show him this. [Indicates the money]
CORBACCIO   Good, good.
MOSCA   'Tis better yet,
  If you will hear, sir.

75 cordial medicine for the heart
80 venture speculative investment, in this case the gold he brought Volpone
81 At no hand By no means
84 How! Perhaps a question, as two lines later, but probably here an exclamation,
    much like the modern 'What!'
88–9 advantage ... sense opportunity of Volpone's recovering consciousness

CORBACCIO   Yes, with all my heart.
MOSCA
  Now, would I counsel you, make home with speed;
  There, frame a will; whereto you shall inscribe
  My master your sole heir.
CORBACCIO   And disinherit   95
  My son?
MOSCA   O, sir, the better: for that colour
  Shall make it much more taking.
CORBACCIO   O, but colour?
MOSCA
  This will, sir, you shall send it unto me.
  Now, when I come to enforce (as I will do)
  Your cares, your watchings, and your many prayers,   100
  Your more than many gifts, your this day's present,
  And, last, produce your will; where – without thought,
  Or least regard, unto your proper issue,
  A son so brave, and highly meriting –
  The stream of your diverted love hath thrown you   105
  Upon my master, and made him your heir;
  He cannot be so stupid, or stone dead,
  But, out of conscience, and mere gratitude –
CORBACCIO
  He must pronounce me, his?
MOSCA   It is true.
CORBACCIO   This plot
  Did I think on before.
MOSCA   I do believe it.   110
CORBACCIO
  Do you not believe it?
MOSCA   Yes, sir.
CORBACCIO   Mine own project.
MOSCA
  Which when he hath done, sir –
CORBACCIO   Published me his heir?
MOSCA
  And you so certain to survive him.
CORBACCIO   Ay.

---

93 *make* go
96–7 *that colour ... taking* that pretence will make your overall pretence toward
   Volpone much more convincing; a similar trick appears in Lucian's *Dialogues of
   the Dead*, XVIII (Parker).
99 *enforce* emphasize, impress on Volpone
103 *proper issue* own true offspring

MOSCA
  Being so lusty a man.
CORBACCIO   It is true.
MOSCA   Yes, sir.
CORBACCIO
  I thought on that too. See, how he should be   115
  The very organ to express my thoughts!
MOSCA
  You have not only done yourself a good –
CORBACCIO
  But multiplied it on my son?
MOSCA   It is right, sir.
CORBACCIO
  Still, my invention.
MOSCA   'Las, sir, heaven knows,
  It hath been all my study, all my care –   120
  I e'en grow grey withal – how to work things –
CORBACCIO
  I do conceive, sweet Mosca.
MOSCA   You are he,
  For whom I labour, here.
CORBACCIO   Ay, do, do, do:
  I'll straight about it.
MOSCA   Rook go with you, raven.
CORBACCIO
  I know thee honest.
MOSCA   You do lie, sir.
CORBACCIO   And –   125
MOSCA
  Your knowledge is no better than your ears, sir.
CORBACCIO
  I do not doubt, to be a father to thee.
MOSCA
  Nor I, to gull my brother of his blessing.
CORBACCIO
  I may ha' my youth restored to me, why not?

114 *lusty* healthy, robust, energetic
115 *he* Mosca
116 *very organ* true instrument
119 *Still, my invention* This, too, is what I had planned
124 *straight* immediately
       Rook ... raven May you be cheated (with a pun on 'rook', which means both
       'swindle' and 'a kind of raven')
128 *Nor I ... blessing* And I intend to steal, by trickery, this father's legacy. Mosca is
       alluding to Jacob's theft of the paternal blessing from his brother Esau in Genesis.

MOSCA
   Your worship is a precious ass –
CORBACCIO   What say'st thou?   130
MOSCA
   I do desire your worship, to make haste, sir.
CORBACCIO
   'Tis done, 'tis done, I go.   [Exit]
VOLPONE   O, I shall burst;
   Let out my sides, let out my sides –
MOSCA   Contain
   Your flux of laughter, sir: you know, this hope
   Is such a bait, it covers any hook.   135
VOLPONE
   O, but thy working, and thy placing it!
   I cannot hold; good rascal, let me kiss thee;
   I never knew thee in so rare a humour.
MOSCA
   Alas, sir, I but do as I am taught:
   Follow your grave instructions; give 'em words;   140
   Pour oil into their ears; and send them hence.
VOLPONE
   'Tis true, 'tis true. What a rare punishment
   Is avarice, to itself!
MOSCA   Ay, with our help, sir.
VOLPONE
   So many cares, so many maladies,
   So many fears attending on old age,   145
   Yea, death so often called on, as no wish
   Can be more frequent with 'em, their limbs faint,
   Their senses dull, their seeing, hearing, going,
   All dead before them; yea, their very teeth,
   Their instruments of eating, failing them: 150
   Yet this is reckoned life! Nay, here was one,
   Is now gone home, that wishes to live longer!
   Feels not his gout, nor palsy, feigns himself

134 *flux* flood
     this hope the hope of inheriting Volpone's estate
137 *hold* hold back
138 *so rare a humour* so excellent a state of inspired wit
140 *grave* wise
141 *Pour ... ears* Flatter them with pleasing words (from a Latin proverb) (Parker)
142 *'Tis true* Even while laughing at Corbaccio for believing Mosca's flattery,
     Volpone here believes an almost identical flattery – that he is really the one who
     conceived the plots he sees Mosca executing, supposedly on his behalf.
148 *going* walking

Younger, by scores of years, flatters his age,
With confident belying it, hopes he may   155
With charms, like Aeson, have his youth restored,
And with these thoughts so battens, as if fate
Would be as easily cheated on, as he,
And all turns air!

                                        Another knocks
                Who's that, there, now? A third?
MOSCA
    Close, to your couch again; I hear his voice.   160
    It is Corvino, our spruce merchant.
VOLPONE   [*Lying down*] Dead.
MOSCA
    Another bout, sir, with your eyes. [*Applies more ointment*]
                                        Who's there?

Act I, Scene v

                        [*Enter*] CORVINO

MOSCA
    Signior Corvino! Come most wished for! O,
    How happy were you, if you knew it, now!
CORVINO
    Why? What? Wherein?
MOSCA   The tardy hour is come, sir.
CORVINO
    He is not dead?
MOSCA   Not dead, sir, but as good;
    He knows no man.

155 *belying* denying
156 *Aeson* The evil magic of Medea restored the youth of Aeson, the father of Jason
    (see the note to I.ii.9 above).
157 *battens* feeds himself into fatness
159 *And all turns air* Though all his hopes will turn out to be empty; or perhaps, As
    if the material fact of Corbaccio's decaying body meant nothing.
160 *Close* Hush, resume your secrecy
161 *spruce* trim, dapper
162 *bout* dose (of the substance used to make Volpone's eyes appear sickly)
  1 *Come* You have come when you were

CORVINO   How shall I do then?
MOSCA   Why, sir?   5
CORVINO
I have brought him, here, a pearl.
MOSCA   Perhaps he has
So much remembrance left, as to know you, sir;
He still calls on you: nothing but your name
Is in his mouth. Is your pearl orient, sir?
CORVINO
Venice was never owner of the like.   10
VOLPONE
[*Faintly*] Signior Corvino.
MOSCA   Hark.
VOLPONE   Signior Corvino.
MOSCA
He calls you, step and give it him. [*Aloud to* VOLPONE] He's
    here, sir,
And he has brought you a rich pearl.
CORVINO   How do you, sir?
Tell him, it doubles the twelfth carat.
MOSCA   Sir,
He cannot understand, his hearing's gone;   15
And yet it comforts him, to see you –
CORVINO   Say,
I have a diamond for him, too.
MOSCA   Best show't, sir,
Put it into his hand: 'tis only there
He apprehends; he has his feeling, yet.

                    [VOLPONE *seizes the pearl*]

See, how he grasps it!
CORVINO   'Las, good gentleman!   20
How pitiful the sight is!
MOSCA   Tut, forget, sir.
The weeping of an heir should still be laughter,
Under a visor.

---

8 *still* always
9 *orient* The most lustrous and hence valuable pearls came from the East. Since
   'stones' was common slang for testicles, the fact that Corvino here gives Volpone
   two stones may foreshadow the sexual advantage he will give Volpone later.
14 *doubles ... carat* The pearl measures twenty-four carats, hence extremely valuable.
23 *visor* mask – in this case, of feigned mourning

CORVINO   Why, am I his heir?

MOSCA
Sir, I am sworn, I may not show the will,
Till he be dead. But, here has been Corbaccio,   25
Here has been Voltore, here were others too,
I cannot number 'em, they were so many,
All gaping here for legacies; but I,
Taking the vantage of his naming you –
[*Mimicking* VOLPONE] 'Signior Corvino, Signior Corvino' –
took   30
Paper, and pen, and ink, and there I asked him,
Whom he would have his heir? Corvino. Who
Should be executor? Corvino. And,
To any question he was silent to,
I still interpreted the nods he made   35
Through weakness for consent; and sent home th' others,
Nothing bequeathed them, but to cry, and curse.

CORVINO
O, my dear Mosca.

                                        They embrace

                    Does he not perceive us?

MOSCA
No more than a blind harper. He knows no man,
No face of friend, nor name of any servant,   40
Who't was that fed him last, or gave him drink;
Not those he hath begotten, or brought up
Can he remember.

CORVINO   Has he children?

MOSCA   Bastards,
Some dozen, or more, that he begot on beggars,
Gypsies, and Jews, and black-moors, when he was drunk.   45
Knew you not that, sir? 'Tis the common fable.
The dwarf, the fool, the eunuch are all his:
He's the true father of his family,
In all, save me; but he has giv'n 'em nothing.

CORVINO
That's well, that's well. Art sure he does not hear us?   50

MOSCA
Sure, sir? Why look you, credit your own sense.

---

39 *blind harper* Proverbial for insensibility: cf. Tilley H175, 176.
46 *'Tis the common fable* This is widely known. Again the play stresses the perver-
     sion of Volpone's reproductive powers.
51 *credit* believe

[*Aloud to* VOLPONE] The pox approach, and add to your
   diseases,
If it would send you hence the sooner, sir.
For, your incontinence, it hath deserved it
Throughly, and throughly, and the plague to boot.   55
[*To* CORVINO] You may come near, sir. [*Aloud to* VOLPONE]
   Would you would once close
Those filthy eyes of yours, that flow with slime,
Like two frog-pits; and those same hanging cheeks,
Covered with hide, instead of skin, [*To* CORVINO] Nay,
   help, sir,
[*Aloud to* VOLPONE] That look like frozen dish-clouts, set
   on end.   60
CORVINO
Or, like an old smoked wall, on which the rain
Ran down in streaks.
MOSCA   Excellent, sir, speak out;
You may be louder yet: a culverin,
Dischargèd in his ear would hardly bore it.
CORVINO
His nose is like a common sewer, still running.   65
MOSCA
'Tis good! And, what his mouth?
CORVINO   A very draught.
MOSCA
[*Taking up a pillow to smother* VOLPONE]
O stop it up –
CORVINO   By no means.
MOSCA   'Pray you let me.
Faith, I could stifle him, rarely, with a pillow,

---

52 *pox* either smallpox or (as line 54 hints) syphilis. The series of insults that follow
   offers several layers of irony, as Corvino thinks they are making fun of Volpone,
   Volpone thinks they are actually making fun of that delusion of Corvino's, and
   Mosca may actually be taking advantage of the situation to insult Volpone after
   all.
53 *send you hence* kill you off
54 *your incontinence ... deserved it* your sexual promiscuity and other indulgences
   should have earned you the pox
58 *frog-pits* stagnant puddles, or possibly 'frogspit', the froth around insect larvae
60 *clouts* rags
63–4 *culverin, / Dischargèd* handgun fired
66 *draught* sewer drain, or possibly, chimney flue
68 *Faith* a common condensation of the oath, '[I swear by my] faith'
   rarely skilfully

As well as any woman that should keep him.
CORVINO
Do as you will, but I'll be gone.
MOSCA   Be so: 70
It is your presence makes him last so long.
CORVINO
I pray you, use no violence.
MOSCA   No, sir? Why?
Why should you be thus scrupulous? 'Pray you, sir.
CORVINO
Nay, at your discretion.
MOSCA   Well, good sir, be gone.
CORVINO
I will not trouble him now, to take my pearl?   75
MOSCA
Puh, nor your diamond. [*Taking the jewels*] What a
    needless care
Is this afflicts you? Is not all, here, yours?
Am not I here? whom you have made? your creature?
That owe my being to you?
CORVINO   Grateful Mosca!
Thou art my friend, my fellow, my companion,   80
My partner, and shalt share in all my fortunes.
MOSCA
Excepting one.
CORVINO   What is that?
MOSCA   Your gallant wife, sir.

                    [*Exit* CORVINO *hurriedly*]

Now is he gone: we had no other means,
To shoot him hence, but this.
VOLPONE   My divine Mosca!
Thou hast today outgone thyself.

                              Another knocks

                    Who's there?   85
I will be troubled with no more. Prepare
Me music, dances, banquets, all delights:

---

69 *that should keep him* who would be his caretaker
73 *'Pray you* I ask you, pray tell me
74 *Nay ... discretion* Well, I'll leave it up to you
83–4 *we had ... but this* the only way to get him to leave was to remind him that he
    has left his wife alone
85 *outgone* outdone

The Turk is not more sensual, in his pleasures,
Than will Volpone.

                                              [*Exit* MOSCA]

                    Let me see, a pearl?
A diamond? Plate? Chequins? Good morning's purchase!   90
Why this is better than rob churches, yet;
Or fat, by eating, once a month, a man.

                         [*Enter* MOSCA]

Who is't?
MOSCA   The beauteous Lady Would-Be, sir,
Wife to the English knight, Sir Politic Would-Be,
(This is the style, sir, is directed me),   95
Hath sent to know, how you have slept tonight,
And if you would be visited.
VOLPONE   Not now.
Some three hours hence –
MOSCA   I told the squire so much.
VOLPONE
When I am high with mirth, and wine: then, then.
'Fore heaven, I wonder at the desperate valour   100
Of the bold English, that they dare let loose
Their wives, to all encounters!
MOSCA   Sir, this knight
Had not his name for nothing, he is politic,
And knows, howe'er his wife affect strange airs,
She hath not yet the face to be dishonest.   105
But had she Signior Corvino's wife's face –
VOLPONE
Has she so rare a face?
MOSCA   O, sir, the wonder,
The blazing star of Italy! A wench

---

88   *The Turk* Either Turks in general, or Mahomet III, Sultan of the Ottoman
     empire; in either case, a person devoted to sensual pleasures.
90   *Good morning's purchase!* A profitable morning!
92   *fat* grow fat
95   *This is ... directed me* That is how she told me to identify her
98   *squire* attendant, but sometimes with a suggestion of 'pimp'
101 *bold English* By Venetian standards, English husbands gave their wives an
     unusual and risky degree of freedom.
104 *affect strange airs* probably a pun on 1) visiting foreign countries, 2) putting on
     pretentious behaviour, and possibly 3) producing unusual odours
105 *She hath ... dishonest* She is no longer pretty enough to commit adultery, and/or,
     She nonetheless lacks the nerve to commit adultery

O' the first year, a beauty, ripe, as harvest!
Whose skin is whiter then a swan, all over!   110
Than silver, snow, or lilies! A soft lip,
Would tempt you to eternity of kissing!
And flesh, that melteth, in the touch, to blood!
Bright as your gold, and lovely, as your gold!
VOLPONE
Why had not I known this, before?
MOSCA   Alas, sir.   115
Myself but yesterday discovered it.
VOLPONE
How might I see her?
MOSCA   O, not possible:
She's kept as warily as is your gold;
Never does come abroad, never takes air,
But at a window. All her looks are sweet,   120
As the first grapes, or cherries; and are watched
As near as they are.
VOLPONE   I must see her –
MOSCA   Sir.
There is a guard, of ten spies thick, upon her:
All his whole household, each of which is set
Upon his fellow, and have all their charge –   125
When he goes out, when he comes in – examined.
VOLPONE
I will go see her, though but at her window.
MOSCA
In some disguise, then?

109 *O' the first year* Of the best vintage, and/or, In the innocent first bloom of wom-
    anhood
113 *melteth ... to blood* blushes when touched, or responds with passionate heat to
    touch, or is as yielding to the touch as warm liquid. 'Touch' was also a term for
    testing the quality of gold, and so leads to Mosca's next line, which shows his
    understanding of Volpone's deepest desires.
119 *abroad* outside
122 *near* closely. The fruit comparisons recall Aesop's fable of the fox and the grapes,
    and Volpone's earlier reference to the game of bob-cherry; Volpone again fails
    to notice that Mosca is doing to him what he does to the legacy-hunters.
124–6 *each ... examined* each of whom is assigned to spy on the others, and is inter-
    rogated about his responsibilities (or, about Corvino's wife) every time Corvino
    departs or returns home

VOLPONE   That is true, I must
Maintain mine own shape, still, the same: we'll think.

                                                   [*Exeunt*]

Act II, Scene i

[*Enter Sir*] POLITIC WOULD-BE, PEREGRINE

SIR POLITIC
    Sir, to a wise man, all the world's his soil.
It is not Italy, nor France, nor Europe,
That must bound me, if my fates call me forth.
Yet, I protest, it is no salt desire
Of seeing countries, shifting a religion,   5
Nor any disaffection to the state
Where I was bred and unto which I owe
My dearest plots, hath brought me out; much less,
That idle, antique, stale, grey-headed project
Of knowing men's minds and manners, with Ulysses;   10
But, a peculiar humour of my wife's,
Laid for this height of Venice, to observe,
To quote, to learn the language, and so forth –
I hope you travel, sir, with licence?

129 *Maintain mine own shape* Maintain the appearance that I am confined to my
    death-bed
  4 *salt* intense, with connotations of sexual appetite and a possible pun on the salti-
    ness of sea voyages
  5 *shifting* changing; recusant Englishmen (and Jonson may have been one) sometimes
    fled that Protestant country so that they could practice openly in Catholic Italy.
  8 *plots* plans (of which Sir Pol has many)
 10 *knowing ... Ulysses* The opening lines of Homer's *Odyssey* describe the hero as
    one who 'learned the minds of many distant men' (trans. Robert Fitzgerald).
 11 *humour* whim or obsession; Jonson wrote two comedies about characters con-
    trolled by 'humours' – four bodily fluids whose balance was believed to dictate
    psychological tendencies.
 12 *Laid for this height* Aimed for this place; 'height' may refer to latitude, it may
    reflect Pol's folly, since Venice is decidedly at sea-level, or it may refer to the
    famous arched bridge of the Rialto (from *rivo alto*) where (as a common meet-
    ing-place) this scene may be set.
 13 *quote* take note of things, whether mentally or in writing
 14 *licence* a kind of passport or visa, required by the Privy Council for overseas
    travel, and often excluding Catholic countries as dangerous to the traveller's soul
    and England's safety

PEREGRINE   Yes.
SIR POLITIC
  I dare the safelier converse – How long, sir,   15
  Since you left England?
PEREGRINE   Seven weeks.
SIR POLITIC   So lately!
  You ha' not been with my lord ambassador?
PEREGRINE
  Not yet, sir.
SIR POLITIC 'Pray you, what news, sir, vents our climate?
  I heard, last night, a most strange thing reported
  By some of my lord's followers, and I long   20
  To hear how 'twill be seconded!
PEREGRINE   What was't, sir?
SIR POLITIC
  Marry, sir, of a raven, that should build
  In a ship royal of the King's.
PEREGRINE   [Aside] This fellow,
  Does he gull me, trow? or is gulled? [To SIR POLITIC] Your
    name, sir?
SIR POLITIC
  My name is Politic Would-Be.
PEREGRINE   [Aside] O, that speaks him.   25
  [To SIR POLITIC] A knight, sir?
SIR POLITIC   A poor knight, sir.
PEREGRINE   Your lady
  Lies here in Venice for intelligence
  Of tires, and fashions, and behaviour,
  Among the courtesans? The fine Lady Would-Be?

---

17 *my lord ambassador* Sir Pol may be partly a caricature of England's crafty
    ambassador to Venice in this period, Sir Henry Wotton, a close friend of John
    Donne's.
18 *vents our climate* blows in from our home country, or is breathily reported about it
21 *seconded* confirmed by some other source
22 *Marry ... build* I swear by Mary, news of a raven that was said to build (birds
    building nests were bad omens on a ship, as Shakespeare suggests at IV.xii.4 of
    Antony and Cleopatra)
24 *Does ... gulled?* Is he trying to make a fool of me, I wonder, or is he fooled him-
    self (by this grandiose gossip)?
25 *speaks* defines
27 *Lies* Stays (but with possible sexual connotations)
    for intelligence to gather information
28 *Of tires* About attire, clothing
29 *courtesans* high-class prostitutes, for which Venice was famous

SIR POLITIC
Yes, sir: the spider and the bee, ofttimes,   30
Suck from one flower.
PEREGRINE   Good Sir Politic!
I cry you mercy: I have heard much of you.
'Tis true, sir, of your raven.
SIR POLITIC   On your knowledge?
PEREGRINE
Yes, and your lion's whelping, in the Tower.
SIR POLITIC
Another whelp?
PEREGRINE   Another, sir.
SIR POLITIC   Now heaven!   35
What prodigies be these? The fires at Berwick!
And the new star! These things concurring, strange!
And full of omen! Saw you those meteors?
PEREGRINE
I did, sir.
SIR POLITIC Fearful! 'Pray you, sir, confirm me:
Were there three porpoises seen, above the bridge,   40
As they give out?
PEREGRINE   Six, and a sturgeon, sir.
SIR POLITIC
I am astonished.

30–1 *the spider ... flower* A common proverb (Tilley, B208); Sir Pol means that, as
one kind of creature can draw sweetness from the same place another kind draws
poison, so his wife could use virtuously the Venetian arts the courtesans use sin-
fully.
32 *I cry you mercy* I beg your pardon (for not recognizing you sooner)
33 *your raven* the aforementioned raven; as in the next line, the 'your' is impersonal
34 *lion's whelping* A lioness kept in the Tower of London bore cubs in 1604 and
1605.
36 *fires at Berwick* Armies were reported seen fighting in the sky near Scotland in
1604, perhaps an effect of the *aurora borealis*.
37 *the new star* a supernova observed by Kepler in 1604
38 *meteors* Meteors were believed ominous, since they evinced disruption in the
heavens.
40 *porpoises* According to Stow's *Annals*, early in 1606 'a great Porpus was taken
alive at Westham ... and within a few dayes after, a very great whale came up
within 8 mile of London'; this reference suggests that Jonson did not finish
Volpone until 1606.
the bridge London Bridge
41 *sturgeon* Peregrine is making fun of Sir Pol here, since sturgeon were common in
the Thames (Parker).

PEREGRINE   Nay, sir, be not so:
I'll tell you a greater prodigy than these –
SIR POLITIC
What should these things portend!
PEREGRINE   The very day
(Let me be sure) that I put forth from London,   · 45
There was a whale discovered, in the river,
As high as Woolwich, that had waited there,
Few know how many months, for the subversion
Of the Stode fleet.
SIR POLITIC   Is't possible? Believe it,
'Twas either sent from Spain, or the Archdukes!   50
Spinola's whale, upon my life, my credit!
Will they not leave these projects? Worthy sir,
Some other news.
PEREGRINE   Faith, Stone, the fool, is dead;
And they do lack a tavern fool, extremely.
SIR POLITIC
Is Mas' Stone dead?
PEREGRINE   He's dead sir; why? I hope   55
You thought him not immortal? [Aside] O this knight,
Were he well known, would be a precious thing
To fit our English stage. He that should write
But such a fellow should be thought to feign
Extremely, if not maliciously.
SIR POLITIC   Stone dead?   60
PEREGRINE
Dead. Lord, how deeply, sir, you apprehend it!
He was no kinsman to you?
SIR POLITIC   That I know of.
Well; that same fellow was an unknown fool.

49 *the Stode fleet* the ships of the English Merchant Adventurers, near the mouth of
the Elbe river
51 *Spinola* a Spanish general feared in England for his ingenious secret weapons,
including a whale 'hir'd to have drown'd London by snuffling up the Thames
and spouting it upon the City' (Charles Herle, *Worldly Policy and Moral
Prudence* [1654])
53 *Stone* a London clown who had been whipped in 1605 for 'a blasphemous
speech'
55 *Stone dead* Here, and again at line 60, playing off the sense 'completely dead';
see I.iv.107.
62 *That I know of* Not that I know of
63 *that . . . unknown fool* Stone's actual cleverness was successfully concealed; ironically, Sir Pol, who is a fool fancying himself a clever spy, believes Stone was a
clever spy masquerading as a fool.

PEREGRINE
  And yet you know him, it seems?
SIR POLITIC   I did so. Sir,
  I knew him one of the most dangerous heads   65
  Living within the state, and so I held him.
PEREGRINE
  Indeed, sir?
SIR POLITIC While he lived, in action.
  He has received weekly intelligence,
  Upon my knowledge, out of the Low Countries,
  For all parts of the world, in cabbages;   70
  And those dispensed again t' ambassadors,
  In oranges, musk-melons, apricots,
  Lemons, pome-citrons, and such-like; sometimes,
  In Colchester oysters, and your Selsey cockles.
PEREGRINE
  You make me wonder!
SIR POLITIC   Sir, upon my knowledge.   75
  Nay, I have observed him, at your public ordinary,
  Take his advertisement from a traveller
  (A concealed statesman) in a trencher of meat;
  And, instantly, before the meal was done,
  Convey an answer in a toothpick.
PEREGRINE   Strange!   80
  How could this be, sir?
SIR POLITIC   Why, the meat was cut
  So like his character, and so laid, as he
  Must easily read the cipher.
PEREGRINE   I have heard,
  He could not read, sir.
SIR POLITIC   So 'twas given out,
  In polity, by those that did employ him;   85
  But he could read, and had your languages,
  And to't, as sound a noddle –

66 *held* considered
67 *in action* while active, or, in actuality
70 *cabbages* England imported cabbage from Holland; Sir Pol's paranoid fantasies
    echo many that were produced by the failed Gunpowder Plot of 1605.
76 *ordinary* tavern/restaurant
77 *advertisement* information, instructions
82 *character* writing or code; Shakespeare's *Cymbeline* IV.ii.49 describes a similarly
    intricate cutting of food.
87 *And to't, as sound a noddle* And in addition to that ability, he had as healthy a
    brain

PEREGRINE   I have heard, sir,
That your baboons were spies; and that they were
A kind of subtle nation, near to China.
SIR POLITIC
Ay, ay, your *Mamaluchi*. Faith, they had   90
Their hand in a French plot, or two; but they
Were so extremely given to women, as
They made discovery of all. Yet I
Had my advices here, on Wednesday last,
From one of their own coat, they were returned,   95
Made their relations (as the fashion is)
And now stand fair, for fresh employment.
PEREGRINE   [*Aside*] 'Heart!
This Sir Pol will be ignorant of nothing.
[*To* SIR POLITIC] It seems, sir, you know all?
SIR POLITIC   Not all, sir. But,
I have some general notions; I do love   100
To note, and to observe; though I live out,
Free from the active torrent, yet I'd mark
The currents, and the passages of things,
For mine own private use; and know the ebbs,
And flows of state.
PEREGRINE   Believe it, sir, I hold   105
Myself, in no small tie, unto my fortunes,
For casting me thus luckily, upon you;
Whose knowledge, if your bounty equal it,
May do me great assistance, in instruction
For my behaviour, and my bearing, which   110
Is yet so rude, and raw –

---

89 *subtle* crafty
90 *Mamaluchi* slaves who seized power in Egypt in the thirteenth century; the irrel-
     evance emphasizes Sir Pol's ridiculous efforts to sound knowledgeable.
91 *hand in a French plot* role in a French conspiracy, but probably with an unwit-
     ting sexual implication
92 *given* susceptible (Topsell claimed baboons were so 'lustful' that they tried 'to
     defile all sorts of women' [Parker]).
93 *made discovery of all* disclosed all their secrets
94 *advices* news dispatches
95 *coat* faction
96 *relations* reports
97 *stand ... employment* are ready to resume their spying
     'Heart! I swear by God's heart
105–7 *I hold ... upon you* I count myself very lucky to have run into you
108 *bounty* generosity

SIR POLITIC   Why, came you forth
Empty of rules for travel?
PEREGRINE   Faith, I had
Some common ones, from out that vulgar grammar,
Which he that cried Italian to me taught me.
SIR POLITIC
Why, this it is that spoils all our brave bloods,   115
Trusting our hopeful gentry unto pedants,
Fellows of outside, and mere bark. You seem
To be a gentleman, of ingenuous race –
I not profess it, but my fate hath been
To be where I have been consulted with,   120
In this high kind, touching some great men's sons,
Persons of blood, and honour –
PEREGRINE   Who be these, sir?

Act II, Scene ii

[Enter MOSCA *and* NANO, *disguised as mountebank's
assistants and carrying the makings of a scaffold stage,
followed by a* CROWD]

MOSCA
Under that window, there't must be. The same.
SIR POLITIC
Fellows to mount a bank! Did your instructor
In the dear tongues never discourse to you
Of the Italian mountebanks?
PEREGRINE   Yes, sir.
SIR POLITIC   Why,
Here shall you see one.

114 *cried* taught
115 *brave bloods* aristocratic young men
116 *hopeful* promising
118 *ingenuous race* noble lineage
121 *touching* concerning
122 *blood* noble birth
  2 *mount a bank* 'An itinerant quack who from an elevated platform appealed to
    his audience by means of stories, tricks, juggling, and the like' (OED). Such fig-
    ures were common in Venice, and had probably appeared in London as well. The
    travelling show dispensing patent medicines in rural America was a more recent
    equivalent. This set-up also strongly resembles the travelling scaffold stage on
    which most English drama had been performed in Jonson's youth (Kernan).
  3 *dear* valuable

PEREGRINE   They are quacksalvers,   5
Fellows that live by venting oils, and drugs?
SIR POLITIC
Was that the character he gave you of them?
PEREGRINE
As I remember.
SIR POLITIC   Pity his ignorance.
They are the only knowing men of Europe!
Great, general scholars, excellent physicians,   10
Most admired statesmen, professed favourites,
And cabinet counsellors, to the greatest princes!
The only languaged men of all the world!
PEREGRINE
And, I have heard, they are most lewd impostors;
Made all of terms, and shreds; no less beliers   15
Of great men's favours, than their own vile med'cines;
Which they will utter upon monstrous oaths,
Selling that drug for two pence, ere they part,
Which they have valued at twelve crowns, before.
SIR POLITIC
Sir, calumnies are answered best with silence: 20
Yourself shall judge. [*To* MOSCA *and* NANO] Who is it
mounts, my friends?
MOSCA
Scoto of Mantua, sir.
SIR POLITIC   Is't he? Nay, then
I'll proudly promise, sir, you shall behold
Another man than has been fant'sied to you.
I wonder, yet, that he should mount his bank   25
Here, in this nook, that has been wont t' appear
In face of the Piazza! Here, he comes.

6 *venting* advertising and selling (vending)
7 *Was that ... them?* Was that how your instructor characterized mountebanks?
9 *knowing* truly knowledgeable
12 *cabinet* private
15 *terms, and shreds* impressive jargon, and bits of undigested learning
15–16 *no less ... med'cines* as dishonest in claiming great patrons as in claiming that
their disgusting potions are healthy (or, possibly, as treacherous to their great
patrons as the supposed medicines are)
17 *utter* offer for sale
19 *crowns* silver coins stamped with a crown (Parker)
22 *Scoto of Mantua* A famous Italian juggler and sleight-of-hand performer who
visited Elizabethan England, and whose name became a by-word for a skilful
deceiver.
26 *wont* accustomed. Sir Pol believes Scoto normally rates a grander setting.

[*Enter* VOLPONE, *disguised as a mountebank*]

VOLPONE
[*To* NANO] Mount, zany.

CROWD   Follow, follow, follow, follow,
                                                  follow.

SIR POLITIC
See how the people follow him! He's a man
May write ten thousand crowns, in bank, here.

[VOLPONE *climbs onto the platform*]

                                    Note,   30
Mark but his gesture; I do use to observe
The state he keeps, in getting up!

PEREGRINE   'Tis worth it, sir.

VOLPONE
Most noble gentlemen and my worthy patrons, it may seem
strange, that I, your Scoto Mantuano, who was ever wont
to fix my bank in face of the public Piazza, near the shelter   35
of the portico to the *Procuratía*, should, now, after eight
months absence from this illustrious city of Venice, humbly
retire myself into an obscure nook of the Piazza.

SIR POLITIC
Did not I, now, object the same?

28   *zany* the clownish assistant of a performer
31–2 *I do use ... getting up* I always admire the dignity Scoto maintains in climbing
        onto the stage
33–248 Throughout this scene, Jonson not only builds on standard episodes from
        the beast-fable and *commedia dell'arte* traditions, but also builds an extended
        metaphor that makes Volpone/Scoto a playful parody of Jonson himself (as
        Kernan has shown): a proud intellectual selling his goods now at a lower price
        to a public audience (at the Globe) instead of his usual aristocratic private one
        (at Blackfriars), after being jailed for offending a powerful man (Jonson
        angered King James, a Scot, by satirizing Scots in *Eastward Ho!*). Scoto and
        Jonson alike scorn their less scholarly competitors (whom they dismiss as poor
        imitators of their work, and purveyors of stale material), while trying to argue
        that their products have the power to cure his audience (notice the ways
        Jonson's boastful Prologue and Epistle resemble Scoto's sales-pitch). Many of
        the Londoners from whom Jonson was now trying to coax the occasional six-
        pence (the likely cost of admission to *Volpone*) would surely have appreciated
        the in-joke.
36   *portico to the Procuratía* arcade of the residence of senior Venetian officials on
        the Piazza di San Marco

PEREGRINE   Peace, sir.

VOLPONE

Let me tell you: I am not (as your Lombard proverb saith)   40
cold on my feet, or content to part with my commodities at
a cheaper rate than I accustomed: look not for it. Nor, that
the calumnious reports of that impudent detractor, and
shame to our profession (Alessandro Buttone, I mean) who
gave out, in public, I was condemned *a sforzato* to the gal-   45
leys, for poisoning the Cardinal Bembo's – cook, hath at all
attached, much less dejected me. No, no, worthy gentlemen, to tell you true, I cannot endure to see the rabble of
these ground *ciarlitani*, that spread their cloaks on the
pavement, as if they meant to do feats of activity, and then   50
come in, lamely, with their mouldy tales out of Boccaccio,
like stale Tabarin, the fabulist; some of them discoursing
their travels, and of their tedious captivity in the Turk's galleys, when indeed, were the truth known, they were the
Christian's galleys, where very temperately they ate bread,   55
and drunk water, as a wholesome penance, enjoined them
by their confessors, for base pilferies.

SIR POLITIC

Note but his bearing, and contempt of these.

VOLPONE

These turdy-facey-nasty-patey-lousy-fartical rogues, with
one poor groatsworth of unprepared antimony, finely   60
wrapped up in several *scartoccios*, are able, very well, to
kill their twenty a week, and play; yet these meagre starved
spirits, who have half stopped the organs of their minds

---

41 *cold on my feet* stage-frightened, or, desperate to sell
45 *a sforzato* by force (into enslavement)
46 *Cardinal Bembo's – cook* Bembo was a great Venetian Renaissance humanist;
    the dash suggests a hesitation about naming a more scandalous relationship (per-
    haps, 'mistress').
49 *ground ciarlitani* lowly charlatans who lack a bank or bench to mount
50 *feats of activity* gymnastics
51 *Boccaccio* fourteenth-century author whose *Decameron* provided plots for many
    later writers, including Shakespeare
52 *Tabarin, the fabulist* a travelling Venetian zany, contemporary with Scoto, here
    identified as a story-teller as well as comic performer; also a stock minor char-
    acter in the *commedia*
56 *enjoined them* prescribed for them
60 *groatsworth of unprepared antimony* fourpence worth of native trisulphide
    (known as monksbane)
61 *several scartoccios* separate paper bins
62 *play* keep their show running

with earthy oppilations, want not their favourers among
your shrivelled, salad-eating artisans, who are overjoyed   65
that they may have their half-pe'rth of physic, though it
purge them into another world, makes no matter.

SIR POLITIC
Excellent! Ha' you heard better language, sir?

VOLPONE
Well, let 'em go. And gentlemen, honourable gentlemen,
know, that for this time, our bank, being thus removed   70
from the clamours of the *canaglia*, shall be the scene of
pleasure, and delight; for I have nothing to sell, little or
nothing to sell.

SIR POLITIC
I told you, sir, his end.

PEREGRINE   You did so, sir.

VOLPONE
I protest, I and my six servants are not able to make of this   75
precious liquor so fast as it is fetched away from my lodging, by gentlemen of your city; strangers of the *terra-firma*;
worshipful merchants; ay, and senators too – who, ever
since my arrival, have detained me to their uses, by their
splendidous liberalities. And worthily. For what avails your   80
rich man to have his magazines stuffed with *moscadelli*, or
the purest grape, when his physicians prescribe him (on
pain of death) to drink nothing but water, cocted with
anise-seeds? O health! health! the blessing of the rich, the
riches of the poor! Who can buy thee at too dear a rate,   85
since there is no enjoying this world, without thee? Be not
then so sparing of your purses, honourable gentlemen, as to
abridge the natural course of life –

PEREGRINE
You see his end?

SIR POLITIC   Ay, is't not good?

VOLPONE
For, when a humid flux, or catarrh, by the mutability of air,   90

---

64 *earthy oppilations* mundane thoughts, which function like constipating foods
66 *half-pe'rth of physic* half-penny worth of medicine
71 *canaglia* rabble
77 *terra-firma* mainland, especially the parts owned by Venice
81 *magazines* storehouses
    moscadelli muscatel wines
83 *cocted* boiled
90 *humid flux* Scoto/Volpone here uses the Renaissance theory of 'humours', which
    linked bodily and spiritual conditions to the balance of four fluids, to warn that
    inclement weather could send dampness from the head down into the body.

falls from your head, into an arm or shoulder, or any other
part, take you a ducat, or your chequin of gold, and apply
to the place affected: see what good effect it can work. No,
no, 'tis this blessed *unguento*, this rare extraction, that hath
only power to disperse all malignant humours, that pro-   95
ceed, either of hot, cold, moist or windy causes –

PEREGRINE
I would he had put in dry too.

SIR POLITIC   'Pray you, observe.

VOLPONE
To fortify the most indigest, and crude stomach – ay, were
it of one that, through extreme weakness, vomited blood –
applying only a warm napkin to the place, after the unc-   100
tion, and fricace; for the *vertigine* in the head, putting but
a drop into your nostrils, likewise, behind the ears; a most
sovereign and approved remedy: the *mal caduco*, cramps,
convulsions, paralyses, epilepsies, *tremor cordia*, retired
nerves, ill vapours of the spleen, stoppings of the liver, the 105
stone, the strangury, *hernia ventosa, iliaca passio*; stops a
dysenteria, immediately; easeth the torsion of the small
guts; and cures *melancholia hypocondriaca*, being taken
and applied, according to my printed receipt. (*Pointing to
his bill and his glass*.) For, this is the physician, this the   110
medicine; this counsels, this cures; this gives the direction,
this works the effect; and, in sum, both together may be
termed an abstract of the theoric and practic in the
Aesculapian art. 'Twill cost you eight crowns. [*Aloud to
NANO*] And, Zan Fritada, 'pray thee sing a verse, extem-   115
pore, in honour of it.

SIR POLITIC
How do you like him, sir?

PEREGRINE   Most strangely, I!

94 *unguento* ointment
101–6 *fricace* massage
   Scoto/Volpone claims to cure a variety of common medical problems: *vertigine*:
   vertigo, dizziness; *mal caduco*: epilepsy; *tremor cordia*: heart palpitations; *retired
   nerves*: shrunken sinews; *stone*: kidney stone; *strangury*: difficult urination; *iliaca
   passio*: intestinal cramps.
109 *receipt* recipe, prescription
110 *his bill and his glass* Volpone points alternately to his prescription list and his
   beaker of medicinal oil.
114 *the Aesculapian art* medicine, of which Aesculapius was the classical god
115 *Zan Fritada* Volpone calls on Nano by the name of a well-known zany.
117 *strangely* exceptionally, but not necessarily in a positive sense

SIR POLITIC
  Is not his language rare?
PEREGRINE   But alchemy,
  I never heard the like; or Broughton's books.

           Song [by VOLPONE'S SERVANTS]

  Had old Hippocrates, or Galen,   120
  That to their books put med'cines all in,
  But known this secret, they had never
  (Of which they will be guilty ever)
  Been murderers of so much paper,
  Or wasted many a hurtless taper;   125
  No Indian drug had e'er been famèd,
  Tobacco, sassafras not namèd;
  Ne yet, of guacum one small stick, sir,
  Nor Raymond Lully's great elixir;
  Ne had been known the Danish Gonswart,   130
  Or Paracelsus, with his long-sword.

PEREGRINE
  All this, yet, will not do: eight crowns is high.
VOLPONE
  No more. Gentlemen, if I had but time to discourse to you
  the miraculous effects of this my oil, surnamed *Oglio del*
  Scoto, with the countless catalogue of those I have cured   135
  of th' aforesaid, and many more diseases, the patents and
  privileges of all the princes and commonwealths of

119 *Broughton* Hugh Broughton, a scholarly Puritan minister whose eccentric works
    Jonson mocks in *The Alchemist* (II.iii.237, IV.v.1–32)
119 s.d. *Song* This song, and the one at line 192, are sung by some combination of
    Nano, as the zany, and perhaps Mosca (since Volpone refers to their 'voices'); it
    is also possible that Castrone appears and sings, since a primary purpose of cas-
    tration was to preserve a pure soprano singing-voice.
120 *Hippocrates, or Galen* revered masters of ancient medicine, and inventor and
    propagator respectively, of the theory of humours
128 *guacum* The wood and resin of the West Indian guaiacum tree were used med-
    ically.
129 *Lully* a Medieval astrologer later rumoured to have discovered the alchemical
    elixir of life
131 *Paracelsus* a revolutionary Renaissance theorist of the body-chemistry of health,
    said to keep his medicines inside a sword handle
134–5 *Oglio del Scoto* Scoto's Oil

Christendom; or but the depositions of those that appeared
on my part, before the signiory of the *Sanità*, and most
learned college of physicians, where I was authorized, upon   140
notice taken of the admirable virtues of my medicaments,
and mine own excellency in matter of rare and unknown
secrets, not only to disperse them publicly in this famous
city, but in all the territories that happily joy under the government of the most pious and magnificent states of Italy.   145
But may some other gallant fellow say, 'O, there be divers,
that make profession to have as good, and as experimented
receipts, as yours.' Indeed, very many have assayed, like
apes, in imitation of that which is really and essentially in
me, to make of this oil; bestowed great cost in furnaces,   150
stills, alembics, continual fires, and preparation of the
ingredients, (as indeed there goes to it six hundred several
simples, beside some quantity of human fat, for the conglutination, which we buy of the anatomists); but, when
these practitioners come to the last decoction, blow, blow,   155
puff, puff, and all flies *in fumo*: ha, ha, ha! Poor wretches!
I rather pity their folly, and indiscretion, than their loss of
time, and money; for those may be recovered by industry,
but to be a fool born is a disease incurable. For myself, I
always from my youth have endeavoured to get the rarest   160
secrets, and book them, either in exchange or for money; I
spared nor cost, nor labour, where anything was worthy to
be learned. And gentlemen, honourable gentlemen, I will
undertake, by virtue of chemical art, out of the honourable
hat that covers your head, to extract the four elements; that   165
is to say, the fire, air, water, and earth, and return you your
felt without burn or stain. For, whilst others have been at
the *balloo*, I have been at my book; and am now past the
craggy paths of study, and come to the flowery plains of
honour, and reputation.   170

SIR POLITIC
I do assure you, sir, that is his aim.

139 *signiory of the Sanità* Venetian medical board
146 *divers* many other people
152–3 *several simples* separate herbs
153–4 *conglutination* gluing together
155 *decoction* boiling down
155–6 *blow, blow, puff, puff* Volpone imitates alchemists trying to increase the heat
     of their fires with breath or bellows.
156 *in fumo* up in smoke; a similar catastrophe is reported in *The Alchemist*.
168 *balloo* a Venetian ball-game

VOLPONE
But, to our price.
PEREGRINE   And that withal, Sir Pol.
VOLPONE
You all know, honourable gentlemen, I never valued this
ampulla, or vial, at less than eight crowns, but for this time,
I am content to be deprived of it for six: six crowns is the   175
price, and less in courtesy I know you cannot offer me; take
it, or leave it, howsoever, both it, and I am at your service.
I ask you not as the value of the thing, for then I should
demand of you a thousand crowns: so the Cardinals
Montalto, Fernese, the great Duke of Tuscany, my gossip,   180
with divers other princes have given me; but I despise
money. Only to show my affection to you, honourable gentlemen, and your illustrious state here, I have neglected the
messages of these princes, mine own offices, framed my
journey hither, only to present you with the fruits of my   185
travels. Tune your voices once more, to the touch of your
instruments, and give the honourable assembly some
delightful recreation.
PEREGRINE
What monstrous, and most painful circumstance
Is here, to get some three or four gazets?   190
Some threepence, i' th' whole; for that 'twill come to.

Song [*by* VOLPONE'S SERVANTS,
during which CELIA *appears at a window above*]

You that would last long, list to my song,
Make no more coil, but buy of this oil.
Would you be ever fair? and young?
Stout of teeth? and strong of tongue?   195
Tart of palate? quick of ear?
Sharp of sight? of nostril clear?
Moist of hand? and light of foot?
Or – I will come nearer to't –

---

172   *that withal* Peregrine points out that Scoto is also aiming at money.
180   *Montalto, Fernese* sixteenth-century popes; but Jonson may also be alluding to
        the contrast between the inexpensive tickets to *Volpone* and his well-paid work
        writing single-performance masques for powerful Jacobean courtiers.
        gossip godfather or close friend
184   *offices* duties
189   *painful circumstance* careful and elaborate set-up
190   *gazets* Venetian pennies
193   *coil* fuss
196   *Tart* Keen

Would you live free from all diseases?   200
Do the act your mistress pleases;
Yet fright all aches from your bones?
Here's a med'cine, for the nones.

VOLPONE
Well, I am in a humour, at this time, to make a present of
the small quantity my coffer contains: to the rich, in cour-   205
tesy, and to the poor, for God's sake. Wherefore, now
mark: I asked you six crowns, and six crowns, at other
times, you have paid me. You shall not give me six crowns;
nor five, nor four, nor three, nor two, nor one; nor half a
ducat; no, nor a *moccenigo*. Six pence it will cost you, or   210
six hundred pound – expect no lower price, for by the
banner of my front, I will not bate a *bagatine*, that I will
have, only, a pledge of your loves, to carry something from
amongst you, to show I am not contemned by you.
Therefore, now, toss your handkerchiefs, cheerfully, cheer-   215
fully; and be advertised, that the first heroic spirit, that
deigns to grace me with a handkerchief, I will give it a little
remembrance of something, beside, shall please it better
than if I had presented it with a double pistolet.

PEREGRINE
Will you be that heroic spark, Sir Pol?   220

CELIA *at the window throws down her handkerchief*

O, see! The window has prevented you.

VOLPONE
Lady, I kiss your bounty; and, for this timely grace you
have done your poor Scoto of Mantua, I will return you,

---

202 *aches from your bones* possibly arthritis, but more likely venereal disease; 'aches'
is two syllables, probably pronounced 'aitches'.
203 *nones* nonce, occasion
210 *moccenigo* small Venetian coin
212 *banner of my front* a sheet advertising the mountebank's cures
bate a bagatine drop the price by even the tiniest amount
214 *contemned* scorned
215 *handkerchiefs* Payments were often tossed to mountebanks, and the purchase
tossed back, in tied handkerchiefs. But – as Shakespeare's *Othello* demonstrates
– handkerchiefs could also serve as symbols of erotic interest.
219 *pistolet* valuable Spanish coin
220 *spark* gallant
221 *The window has prevented you* Someone above has beaten you to it; the
Jacobean stage set had an upper level where (at some unspecified point) Celia
appears at a window.

over and above my oil, a secret of that high and inestimable
nature, shall make you for ever enamoured on that minute   225
wherein your eye first descended on so mean (yet not
altogether to be despised) an object. Here is a powder, concealed in this paper, of which, if I should speak to the
worth, nine thousand volumes were but as one page, that
page as a line, that line as a word; so short is this pilgrim-   230
age of man (which some call life) to the expressing of it.
Would I reflect on the price? Why, the whole world were
but as an empire, that empire as a province, that province
as a bank, that bank as a private purse, to the purchase of
it. I will only tell you: it is the powder that made Venus a   235
goddess, given her by Apollo, that kept her perpetually
young, cleared her wrinkles, firmed her gums, filled her
skin, coloured her hair; from her, derived to Helen, and at
the sack of Troy, unfortunately, lost; till now, in this our
age, it was as happily recovered, by a studious antiquary,   240
out of some ruins of Asia, who sent a moiety of it to the
Court of France (but much sophisticated) wherewith the
ladies there now colour their hair. The rest, at this present,
remains with me, extracted, to a quintessence; so that,
wherever it but touches, in youth it perpetually preserves,   245
in age restores the complexion; seats your teeth, did they
dance like virginal jacks, firm as a wall; makes them white,
as ivory, that were black, as –

Act II, Scene iii

[Enter] CORVINO [shouting up to CELIA]

CORVINO
  Blood of the devil, and my shame! Come down, here;
  Come down! No house but mine to make your scene?
  Signior Flaminio, will you down, sir? down?

235–43 *made Venus ... colour their hair* The decreasing dignity of the powder's roles
    parallels the history of Pythagoras's soul in I.ii.
240 *antiquary* scholar who studies the ancient world
241 *moiety* portion
242 *sophisticated* adulterated
246–7 *did they dance like virginal jacks* even if they danced like little piano keys
  1 Corvino's line plausibly completes Scoto/Volpone's phrase, 'black as'; F reads,
    'Spite of the devil', meaning the seducible woman, the devil's spite against man.
3–8 *Flaminio ... Besogniosi* Among the play's many references to the *commedia dell'
    arte* tradition, these names of actors and stock characters reflect Corvino's fear
    that he has been put in the role of laughable old cuckold.

He beats away the mountebank, etc.

What, is my wife your Franciscina? sir?
No windows on the whole Piazza, here,   5
To make your properties, but mine? but mine?
Heart! ere tomorrow, I shall be new christened,
And called the *Pantalone di Besogniosi*,
About the town.   [*Exit*]
PEREGRINE   What should this mean, Sir Pol?
SIR POLITIC
Some trick of state, believe it. I will home.   10
PEREGRINE
It may be some design on you.
SIR POLITIC   I know not.
I'll stand upon my guard.
PEREGRINE   'Tis your best, sir.
SIR POLITIC
This three weeks, all my advices, all my letters,
They have been intercepted.
PEREGRINE   Indeed, sir?
Best have a care.
SIR POLITIC   Nay, so I will.   [*Exit*]
PEREGRINE   This knight,   15
I may not lose him, for my mirth, till night.   [*Exit*]

Act II, Scene iv

[*Enter*] VOLPONE, MOSCA

VOLPONE
O, I am wounded.
MOSCA   Where, sir?
VOLPONE   Not without:
Those blows were nothing; I could bear them ever.
But angry Cupid, bolting from her eyes,

---

6 *properties* stage props, but punning on the way Scoto has impinged on Corvino's
  property – his house, and perhaps also his wife
11 *design on* plot against
 1 *without* on the outside
 3 *bolting* shooting like an arrow, often called a 'bolt'; cf. Anacreon's Odes 14 and
   16.

Hath shot himself into me, like a flame;
Where, now, he flings about his burning heat,   5
As in a furnace, some ambitious fire,
Whose vent is stopped. The fight is all within me.
I cannot live, except thou help me, Mosca:
My liver melts, and I, without the hope
Of some soft air, from her refreshing breath,   10
Am but a heap of cinders.
MOSCA   'Las, good sir,
Would you had never seen her.
VOLPONE   Nay, would thou
Hadst never told me of her.
MOSCA   Sir, 'tis true:
I do confess, I was unfortunate,
And you unhappy; but I am bound in conscience,   15
No less than duty, to effect my best
To your release of torment, and I will, sir.
VOLPONE
Dear Mosca, shall I hope?
MOSCA   Sir, more than dear,
I will not bid you to despair of aught,
Within a human compass.
VOLPONE   O, there spoke   20
My better angel. Mosca, take my keys,
Gold, plate, and jewels, all's at thy devotion;
Employ them, how thou wilt; nay, coin me, too;
So thou, in this, but crown my longings. Mosca?
MOSCA
Use but your patience.
VOLPONE   So I have.
MOSCA   I doubt not   25
To bring success to your desires.
VOLPONE   Nay, then,
I not repent me of my late disguise.
MOSCA
If you can horn him, sir, you need not.

9 *liver* believed to be the location of violent emotions
19–20 *aught, / Within a human compass* anything within human reach (or imagination)
24 *So ... longings* If you can fulfil my desires in this regard
28 *horn* cuckold (betrayed husbands were said to grow horns)

VOLPONE   True;
  Besides, I never meant him for my heir.
  Is not the colour of my beard, and eyebrows,   30
  To make me known?
MOSCA   No jot.
VOLPONE   I did it well.
MOSCA
  So well, would I could follow you in mine,
  With half the happiness; and, yet, I would
  Escape your epilogue.
VOLPONE   But, were they gulled
  With a belief, that I was Scoto?
MOSCA   Sir,   35
  Scoto himself could hardly have distinguished!
  I have not time to flatter you, we'll part;
  And, as I prosper, so applaud my art.

                                        [*Exeunt*]

Act II, Scene v

[*Enter*] CORVINO, CELIA

CORVINO
  Death of mine honour, with the city's fool?
  A juggling, tooth-drawing, prating mountebank?
  And, at a public window? where whilst he,
  With his strained action, and his dole of faces,
  To his drug-lecture draws your itching ears,   5
  A crew of old, unmarried, noted lechers,
  Stood leering up, like satyrs; and you smile,
  Most graciously! and fan your favours forth,
  To give your hot spectators satisfaction!

29–31 *Besides ... known* Perhaps reminded by his use of the word 'heir', Volpone
       worries that his (fox-red?) hair ruined his disguise.
  31 *No jot* Not in the slightest
  32 *mine* my role in this trickery
33–4 *I would / Escape your epilogue* I would like to avoid the beating you took from
       Corvino. The line is also another oblique signal that Mosca intends to come out
       better than Volpone when their show ends.
   2 *tooth-drawing* Mountebanks sometimes performed dental extractions.
   4 *his strained action ... faces* his exaggerated gestures, and his poor repertoire of
       masks or facial expressions

What, was your mountebank their call? their whistle?   10
Or were you enamoured on his copper rings?
His saffron jewel, with the toad-stone in't?
Or his embroidered suit, with the cope-stitch,
Made of a hearse-cloth? or his old tilt-feather?
Or his starched beard? Well! you shall have him, yes.   15
He shall come home, and minister unto you
The fricace, for the mother. Or, let me see,
I think, you'd rather mount? would you not mount?
Why, if you'll mount, you may; yes truly, you may;
And so, you may be seen, down to th' foot.   20
Get you a cittern, Lady Vanity,
And be a dealer with the virtuous man:
Make one; I'll but protest myself a cuckold,
And save your dowry. I am a Dutchman, I!
For, if you thought me an Italian,   25
You would be damned ere you did this, you whore:
Thou'dst tremble to imagine that the murder
Of father, mother, brother, all thy race,
Should follow, as the subject of my justice.

CELIA
Good sir, have patience.

CORVINO [*Drawing a weapon*] What couldst thou propose   30
Less to thyself, than, in this heat of wrath,
And stung with my dishonour, I should strike

---

10 *their call? their whistle?* Apparently a reference to bird-calls, with hints of prostitution, and resonance in the extended bird-metaphors of the play as a whole.

11–12 *copper rings ... saffron jewel* cheap simulations of the colour of gold
   toad-stone a jewel with magical curative properties believed hidden between the
   eyes of toads

14–15 *hearse-cloth ... starched beard* The Scoto costume was evidently garish, with
   fancy draperies used in funerals, a large feather from a jousting helmet, and a
   fashionably shaped and waxed beard.

17 *fricace, for the mother* massage for hysteria, believed to arise from the womb;
   hence, a thinly disguised metaphor for sexual ministrations

19 *mount* perform as a mountebank, but also implying sexual mounting with the
   mountebank

21 *cittern* zither, sometimes played by mountebanks' assistants or prostitutes
   Lady Vanity a stock sinister character in English morality plays

22 *be a dealer* transact business, presumably prostitution

23 *Make one* Make a deal, join a company, or perform a sexual act

24 *save your dowry* An unfaithful wife legally forfeited her dowry.
   Dutchman Englishmen considered Dutchmen oddly sluggish, apathetic, and tol-
   erant.

This steel into thee, with as many stabs
As thou wert gazed upon with goatish eyes?
CELIA
Alas sir, be appeased: I could not think   35
My being at the window should more, now,
Move your impatience, than at other times.
CORVINO
No? Not to seek and entertain a parley
With a known knave? before a multitude?
You were an actor, with your handkerchief;   40
Which he, most sweetly, kissed in the receipt,
And might, no doubt, return it, with a letter,
And 'point the place where you might meet: your sister's,
Your mother's, or your aunt's might serve the turn.
CELIA
Why, dear sir, when do I make these excuses?   45
Or ever stir abroad but to the church?
And that, so seldom –
CORVINO   Well, it shall be less;
And thy restraint, before, was liberty,
To what I now decree; and therefore, mark me.
First, I will have this bawdy light dammed up;   50
And, till't be done, some two, or three yards off,
I'll chalk a line; o'er which, if thou but chance
To set thy desp'rate foot, more hell, more horror,
More wild, remorseless rage shall seize on thee,
Than on a conjurer, that had heedless left   55
His circle's safety, ere his devil was laid.
Then [*Showing a chastity belt*], here's a lock, which I will
    hang upon thee;
And, now I think on't, I will keep thee backwards:
Thy lodging shall be backwards, thy walks backwards,
Thy prospect – all be backwards; and no pleasure   60

34 *goatish* lustful
38 *parley* conversation or negotiation
40 *actor* an active participant, and perhaps a deceptive one
43 *'point* appoint, designate
44 *turn* purpose
49 *To* Compared to
    mark me listen carefully, mark my words
50 *light* window
55–6 *conjurer ... laid* It was believed that, if a necromancer stepped outside his pro-
    tective chalk-circle before sending the demons he was commanding back to hell,
    they would tear him to pieces.
60 *prospect* future, or, view

That thou shalt know, but backwards. Nay, since you force
My honest nature, know, it is your own
Being too open, makes me use you thus.
Since you will not contain your subtle nostrils
In a sweet room, but, they must snuff the air   65
Of rank and sweaty passengers –

                                        Knock within

                        One knocks.
Away, and be not seen, pain of thy life;
Not look toward the window: if thou dost –

                        [CELIA *begins to exit*]

Nay, stay, hear this – let me not prosper, whore,
But I will make thee an anatomy,   70
Dissect thee mine own self, and read a lecture
Upon thee, to the city, and in public.
Away.

                                        [*Exit* CELIA]

        Who is there?

                        [*Enter* SERVANT]

SERVANT   'Tis Signior Mosca, sir.

                        Act II, Scene vi

CORVINO
Let him come in, his master's dead. There's yet
Some good, to help the bad.

                                [*Exit* SERVANT]

        [*Enter* MOSCA]
                        My Mosca, welcome;
I guess your news.

---

61 *backwards* Corvino vows to keep Celia away from the public edges of his house,
    but by this fifth use, the word has taken on sexual implications, probably related
    to some stage business with the chastity belt.
64 *subtle* crafty (for sniffing out sexual interest), or (sarcastically) delicate
67 *pain* on pain
70 *anatomy* Autopsies became popular public events in this period.

MOSCA   I fear you cannot, sir.
CORVINO
  Is't not his death?
MOSCA   Rather the contrary.
CORVINO
  Not his recovery?
MOSCA   Yes, sir.
CORVINO   I am cursed,   5
  I am bewitched, my crosses meet to vex me.
  How? how? how? how?
MOSCA   Why, sir, with Scoto's oil!
  Corbaccio and Voltore brought of it,
  Whilst I was busy in an inner room –
CORVINO
  Death! that damned mountebank! but for the law,   10
  Now, I could kill the rascal; 't cannot be
  His oil should have that virtue. Ha' not I
  Known him a common rogue, come fiddling in
  To th' *osterìa*, with a tumbling whore,
  And, when he has done all his forced tricks, been glad   15
  Of a poor spoonful of dead wine, with flies in't?
  It cannot be. All his ingredients
  Are a sheep's gall, a roasted bitch's marrow,
  Some few sod earwigs, pounded caterpillars,
  A little capon's grease, and fasting spittle: 20
  I know 'em, to a dram.
MOSCA   I know not, sir;
  But some on't, there, they poured into his ears,
  Some in his nostrils, and recovered him,
  Applying but the fricace.
CORVINO   Pox o' that fricace.
MOSCA
  And since, to seem the more officious,   25
  And flatt'ring of his health, there, they have had,
  At extreme fees, the college of physicians
  Consulting on him how they might restore him;
  Where, one would have a cataplasm of spices,

6 *crosses* afflictions
14 *osterìa* inn
16 *dead* stale
19 *sod* boiled
20 *fasting spittle* the saliva of a starving man – probably Scoto himself
21 *to a dram* down to the most miniscule portion
22 *on't* of it
29 *cataplasm* poultice

Another a flayed ape clapped to his breast,   30
A third would ha' it a dog, a fourth an oil
With wild cats' skins. At last, they all resolved
That, to preserve him, was no other means,
But some young woman must be straight sought out –
Lusty, and full of juice – to sleep by him;   35
And, to this service (most unhappily,
And most unwillingly) am I now employed,
Which, here, I thought to pre-acquaint you with,
For your advice, since it concerns you most,
Because I would not do that thing might cross   40
Your ends, on whom I have my whole dependence, sir.
Yet if I do it not, they may delate
My slackness to my patron, work me out
Of his opinion; and there, all your hopes,
Ventures, or whatsoever, are all frustrate.   45
I do but tell you, sir. Besides, they are all
Now striving, who shall first present him. Therefore –
I could entreat you, briefly, conclude somewhat:
Prevent 'em if you can.
CORVINO   Death to my hopes!
This is my villainous fortune! Best to hire   50
Some common courtesan?
MOSCA   Ay, I thought on that, sir.
But they are all so subtle, full of art,
And age again doting, and flexible,
So as – I cannot tell – we may perchance
Light on a quean may cheat us all.
CORVINO   'Tis true.   55
MOSCA
No, no; it must be one that has no tricks, sir,
Some simple thing, a creature made unto it;
Some wench you may command. Ha' you no kinswoman?
Godso – Think, think, think, think, think, think, think, sir.
One o' the doctors offered, there, his daughter.   60

34–5 *some young woman ... sleep by him* King David is similarly cured in I Kings 1.
    straight immediately
40–1 *cross / Your ends* interfere with your goals
 42 *delate* report
 44 *opinion* favour
 48 *I could ... somewhat* I beg you to make a quick decision
 53 *age ... flexible* old men, moreover, tend to become infatuated and thereby
    manipulated
 55 *quean* whore
 59 *Godso* An exclamatory oath, probably short for 'By God's soul'.

CORVINO
  How!
MOSCA Yes, Signior Lupo, the physician.
CORVINO
  His daughter?
MOSCA   And a virgin, sir. Why? Alas,
  He knows the state of's body, what it is:
  That nought can warm his blood, sir, but a fever;
  Nor any incantation raise his spirit: 65
  A long forgetfulness hath seized that part.
  Besides, sir, who shall know it? Some one, or two –
CORVINO
  I pray thee give me leave. [*Moves away, talking to himself*]
                    If any man
  But I had had this luck – The thing in't self,
  I know, is nothing – Wherefore should not I   70
  As well command my blood, and my affections,
  As this dull doctor? In the point of honour,
  The cases are all one, of wife and daughter.
MOSCA
  [*Aside*] I hear him coming.
CORVINO   She shall do't. 'Tis done.
  'Slight, if this doctor, who is not engaged,   75
  Unless 't be for his counsel (which is nothing)
  Offer his daughter, what should I, that am
  So deeply in? I will prevent him: wretch!
  Covetous wretch! [*To* MOSCA] Mosca, I have determined.
MOSCA
  How, sir?
CORVINO We'll make all sure. The party you wot of,   80
  Shall be mine own wife, Mosca.
MOSCA   Sir. The thing –
  But that I would not seem to counsel you –
  I should have motioned to you at the first;
  And, make your count, you have cut all their throats.
  Why, 'tis directly taking a possession!   85

  61 *Lupo* Italian for a wolf
  73 *all one* equal
  74 *coming* coming around, deciding to cooperate
  75 *'Slight* an exclamatory oath, short for 'I swear by God's light'
      not engaged does not have a monetary investment at stake
  80 *party you wot of* person you were seeking
  83 *motioned* suggested
  84 *make your ... throats* count on it, begin inventory of your grand inheritance,
      because you have thus defeated your rivals for it

And, in his next fit, we may let him go.
'Tis but to pull the pillow from his head,
And he is throttled: 't had been done before,
But for your scrupulous doubts.
CORVINO   Ay, a plague on't,
My conscience fools my wit. Well, I'll be brief,   90
And so be thou, lest they should be before us:
Go home, prepare him, tell him, with what zeal,
And willingness, I do it; swear it was
On the first hearing (as thou mayst do, truly),
Mine own free motion.
MOSCA   Sir, I warrant you,   95
I'll so possess him with it, that the rest
Of his starved clients shall be banished, all;
And only you received. But come not, sir,
Until I send, for I have something else
To ripen, for your good – you must not know't.   100
CORVINO
But do not you forget to send, now.
MOSCA   Fear not. [*Exit* MOSCA]

Act II, Scene vii

CORVINO
Where are you, wife? my Celia? wife?

                    [*Enter* CELIA, *weeping*]

                              What, blubbering?
Come, dry those tears. I think, thou thought'st me in earnest?
Ha? By this light, I talked so but to try thee.
Methinks the lightness of the occasion
Should ha' confirmed thee. Come, I am not jealous.   5
CELIA
No?
CORVINO Faith, I am not, I, nor never was:

---

90 *fools my wit* has caused my intelligence to fail
99–100 *something else / To ripen* a plot to bring to fruition – tricking Corbaccio into
    making Volpone, rather than his own son Bonario, his heir
 3 *try* test
4–5 *the lightness ... confirmed thee* the triviality of the cause of my outburst should
    have assured you I wasn't serious
 6 *Faith* In faith

It is a poor, unprofitable humour.
Do not I know, if women have a will,
They'll do 'gainst all the watches o' the world?
And that the fiercest spies are tamed with gold?   10
Tut, I am confident in thee, thou shalt see't;
And see, I'll give thee cause too, to believe it.
Come, kiss me. Go, and make thee ready straight,
In all thy best attire, thy choicest jewels,
Put 'em all on, and, with 'em, thy best looks: 15
We are invited to a solemn feast,
At old Volpone's, where it shall appear
How far I am free from jealousy or fear.

                                                    [*Exeunt*]

Act III, Scene i

[*Enter*] MOSCA

MOSCA
I fear I shall begin to grow in love
With my dear self, and my most prosp'rous parts,
They do so spring, and burgeon; I can feel
A whimsy i' my blood. I know not how,
Success hath made me wanton. I could skip   5
Out of my skin, now, like a subtle snake,
I am so limber. O! your parasite
Is a most precious thing, dropped from above,
Not bred 'mongst clods and clodpolls here on earth.
I muse the mystery was not made a science,   10
It is so liberally professed! Almost
All the wise world is little else, in nature,
But parasites, or sub-parasites. And yet,

  7 *humour* emotion
  9 *do 'gainst* cheat despite
 11 *Tut* Nonsense, don't be silly
  2 *parts* qualities – but also body-parts and stage-parts
  4 *whimsy* giddiness, or, whirling
  5 *wanton* wild, playful, sensual
  9 *clods and clodpolls* dull, stupid persons
 10 *mystery* craft
    science field of knowledge in higher education

I mean not those, that have your bare town-art,
To know who's fit to feed 'em; have no house,   15
No family, no care, and therefore mould
Tales for men's ears, to bait that sense; or get
Kitchen-invention, and some stale receipts
To please the belly, and the groin; nor those,
With their court-dog-tricks, that can fawn and fleer,   20
Make their revenue out of legs and faces,
Echo my lord, and lick away a moth.
But your fine, elegant rascal, that can rise
And stoop, almost together, like an arrow;
Shoot through the air, as nimbly as a star;   25
Turn short, as doth a swallow; and be here,
And there, and here, and yonder, all at once;
Present to any humour, all occasion;
And change a visor swifter than a thought!
This is the creature had the art born with him;   30
Toils not to learn it, but doth practise it
Out of most excellent nature; and such sparks
Are the true parasites, others but their zanies.

Act III, Scene ii

[Enter] BONARIO

MOSCA
Who's this? Bonario? Old Corbaccio's son?
The person I was bound to seek. Fair sir,
You are happ'ly met.

14 *bare town-art* crude skills of street-hustlers; here and in line 19, the commas after
    'those' are dropped by most modern editors, but they may mark opportunities
    for Mosca to point to members of the audience.
20 *court-dog-tricks* obsequious service, begging favours (as opposed to the more
    practical offerings of town-parasites)
21 *legs and faces* either elaborate bows and smiles, or (as under King James) physi-
    cal attractiveness
22 *moth* any small vermin; minute grooming was a common servile behaviour at
    court, and licking would presumably be an even more dog-like form of that ser-
    vice.
24 *together* simultaneously
28 *Present ... occasion* Ready to respond pleasingly to any mood or event, or,
    Ready to offer justification for any mood, or, Ready to satisfy any whim
29 *visor* mask, facial expression, personality
 2 *bound* on my way

BONARIO   That cannot be, by thee.
MOSCA
  Why sir?
BONARIO   Nay, 'pray thee, know thy way, and leave me:
  I would be loath to interchange discourse   5
  With such a mate as thou art.
MOSCA   Courteous sir,
  Scorn not my poverty.
BONARIO   Not I, by heaven;
  But thou shalt give me leave to hate thy baseness.
MOSCA
  Baseness?
BONARIO   Ay, answer me, is not thy sloth
  Sufficient argument? Thy flattery?   10
  Thy means of feeding?
MOSCA   Heaven, be good to me.
  These imputations are too common, sir,
  And eas'ly stuck on virtue, when she's poor.
  You are unequal to me, and howe'er
  Your sentence may be righteous, yet you are not,   15
  That ere you know me, thus, proceed in censure;
  St Mark bear witness 'gainst you, 'tis inhuman.
BONARIO
  [Aside] What? Does he weep? The sign is soft, and good;
  I do repent me, that I was so harsh.
MOSCA
  'Tis true that, swayed by strong necessity,   20
  I am enforced to eat my careful bread
  With too much obsequy; 'tis true, beside,
  That I am fain to spin mine own poor raiment
  Out of my mere observance, being not born
  To a free fortune; but that I have done   25
  Base offices, in rending friends asunder,
  Dividing families, betraying counsels,
  Whispering false lies, or mining men with praises,
  Trained their credulity with perjuries,
  Corrupted chastity, or am in love   30

   6 *mate* lowly companion
  10 *argument* evidence
  14 *unequal* unfair
       howe'er however much
  21 *careful* full of cares
  23–4 *fain ... observance* obliged to earn the clothes on my back by nothing more
       heroic than dutiful service
  29 *Trained* Led on

With mine own tender ease, but would not rather
Prove the most rugged and laborious course
That might redeem my present estimation,
Let me here perish, in all hope of goodness.

BONARIO
This cannot be a personated passion.   35
I was to blame, so to mistake thy nature;
'Pray thee forgive me, and speak out thy business.

MOSCA
Sir, it concerns you; and though I may seem,
At first, to make a main offence in manners,
And in my gratitude unto my master,   40
Yet, for the pure love which I bear all right,
And hatred of the wrong, I must reveal it.
This very hour, your father is in purpose
To disinherit you –

BONARIO   How!

MOSCA   And thrust you forth,
As a mere stranger to his blood; 'tis true, sir,   45
The work no way engageth me, but as
I claim an interest in the general state
Of goodness, and true virtue, which I hear
T' abound in you; and, for which mere respect,
Without a second aim, sir, I have done it.   50

BONARIO
This tale hath lost thee much of the late trust
Thou hadst with me: it is impossible.
I know not how to lend it any thought,
My father should be so unnatural.

MOSCA
It is a confidence that well becomes   55
Your piety; and formed, no doubt, it is
From your own simple innocence; which makes
Your wrong more monstrous, and abhorred. But, sir,
I now will tell you more. This very minute,

---

32 *Prove* Attempt, Endure
33 *estimation* reputation
35 *personated* impersonated, feigned
41 *bear all right* feel toward the good and just
46 *engageth* holds advantage for
49 *for which mere respect* for this reason only
51 *late* recent
53 *lend it any thought* even imagine the possibility that
56 *piety* filial love (the Latin *pietas*)
58 *Your wrong* The way you are being wronged

It is, or will be doing; and, if you   60
Shall be but pleased to go with me, I'll bring you –
I dare not say where you shall see, but – where
Your ear shall be a witness of the deed:
Hear yourself written bastard, and professed
The common issue of the earth.
BONARIO   I'm mazed.   65
MOSCA
Sir, if I do it not, draw your just sword,
And score your vengeance, on my front, and face:
Mark me your villain. You have too much wrong,
And I do suffer for you, sir. My heart
Weeps blood, in anguish –
BONARIO   Lead. I follow thee.   70

                                                        [*Exeunt*]

Act III, Scene iii

[*Enter*] VOLPONE, NANO, ANDROGYNO, CASTRONE

VOLPONE
Mosca stays long, methinks. Bring forth your sports
And help to make the wretched time more sweet.
NANO
Dwarf, fool, and eunuch, well met here we be.
    A question it were now, whether of us three –
Being, all, the known delicates of a rich man –   5
    In pleasing him, claim the precedency can?
CASTRONE
I claim for myself.
ANDROGYNO   And so doth the fool.
NANO
    'Tis foolish indeed: let me set you both to school.
First, for your dwarf, he's little and witty,
    And everything, as it is little, is pretty;   10
Else, why do men say to a creature of my shape
    So soon as they see him, 'It's a pretty little ape'?

65 *common issue of the earth* child with no acknowledged parent (the Latin *terrae filius*)
4 *whether* which
5 *delicates* favourites; this competition for Volpone's favour parallels that among the legacy-hunters.
8 *set you both to school* instruct you both

And, why a pretty ape, but for pleasing imitation
  Of greater men's action, in a ridiculous fashion?
Beside, this feat body of mine doth not crave   15
  Half the meat, drink, and cloth, one of your bulks will have.
Admit, your fool's face be the mother of laughter,
  Yet, for his brain, it must always come after;
And, though that do feed him, it's a pitiful case,
  His body is beholding to such a bad face.   20

                                                   One knocks

VOLPONE
Who's there? My couch, away, look, Nano, see:
Give me my caps, first – go, inquire.

             [*Exeunt* NANO, ANDROGYNO, *and* CASTRONE]

                          Now, Cupid
Send it be Mosca, and with fair return.

        [VOLPONE *lies on his bed;* NANO *enters*]

NANO
It is the beauteous madam –
VOLPONE   Would-Be – is it?
NANO
The same.
VOLPONE   Now, torment on me! Squire her in;   25
For she will enter, or dwell here forever.
Nay, quickly, that my fit were past.

                         [*Exit* NANO]

                  I fear
A second hell too, that my loathing this
Will quite expel my appetite to the other:
Would she were taking, now, her tedious leave.   30
Lord, how it threats me, what I am to suffer!

15 *feat* dainty
19 *that* his face
22 s.d. *Exeunt* NANO No re-entry is marked for Nano before his next line; perhaps he
    speaks through the doorway.
22–3 *Cupid ... return* may Cupid grant my wish that it is Mosca knocking, and
    bringing good news
27 *that my fit were past* so that I can get it over with
29 *the other* the other woman, Celia

Act III, Scene iv

[*Enter* NANO, *bringing*] LADY WOULD-BE

LADY WOULD-BE
[*To* NANO] I thank you, good sir. 'Pray you signify
Unto your patron, I am here. This band
Shows not my neck enough – I trouble you, sir,
Let me request you, bid one of my women
Come hither to me –

                                       [*Exit* NANO]

                    In good faith, I, am dressed   5
Most favourably, today, it is no matter,
'Tis well enough.

      [*Enter* NANO *with first* SERVING-WOMAN]

           Look, see, these petulant things,
How they have done this!
VOLPONE   [*Aside*] I do feel the fever
Ent'ring, in at mine ears: O, for a charm
To fright it hence.
LADY WOULD-BE   Come nearer: is this curl   10
In his right place? or this? Why is this higher
Than all the rest? You ha' not washed your eyes, yet?
Or do they not stand even in your head?
Where is your fellow? Call her.

            [*Exit first* SERVING-WOMAN]

NANO   [*Aside*] Now, St Mark
Deliver us: anon, she'll beat her women,   15
Because her nose is red.

    [*Enter first* SERVING-WOMAN *with another*]

---

2 *band* ruff or collar; this line may refer to what the English considered shockingly
low necklines on Italian dresses (Coryat I, 399–400, cited by Parker); it may also
refer to the band around the neck of a parrot, a bird the English commonly called
'Pol' or 'Polly', thus extending the avian metaphor to this fourth legacy-hunter.
5–6 *in good ... today* Lady Would-Be is speaking sarcastically.
9 *charm* magic spell
13 *do they ... head?* can't you see straight?
15 *anon* in a moment

LADY WOULD-BE   I pray you, view
  This tire, forsooth; are all things apt, or no?
1st WOMAN
  One hair a little, here, sticks out, forsooth.
LADY WOULD-BE
  Does't so, forsooth? And where was your dear sight
  When it did so, forsooth? What now? Bird-eyed?   20
  And you too? 'Pray you both approach, and mend it.
  Now, by that light, I muse you are not ashamed!
  I, that have preached these things so oft unto you,
  Read you the principles, argued all the grounds,
  Disputed every fitness, every grace,   25
  Called you to counsel of so frequent dressings –
NANO
  [Aside] More carefully, than of your fame, or honour.
LADY WOULD-BE
  Made you acquainted what an ample dowry
  The knowledge of these things would be unto you,
  Able, alone, to get you noble husbands   30
  At your return; and you, thus, to neglect it?
  Besides, you seeing what a curious nation
  Th' Italians are, what will they say of me?
  'The English lady cannot dress herself':
  Here's a fine imputation, to our country.   35
  Well, go your ways, and stay i' the next room.
  This fucus was too coarse too, it's no matter.
  Good sir, you'll give 'em entertainment?

                    [Exit NANO with serving-women]

VOLPONE
  [Aside] The storm comes toward me.
LADY WOULD-BE   How docs my Volp?
VOLPONE
  Troubled with noise, I cannot sleep: I dreamt   40
  That a strange fury entered, now, my house,
  And, with the dreadful tempest of her breath,
  Did cleave my roof asunder.

---

17 *tire* head-dress

22 *I muse* I am amazed

23–6 *preached ... counsel* Lady Would-Be invokes the high language of theological,
     logical, rhetorical, aesthetic, and legal education.

27 *fame* reputation

31 *return* return to England

32 *curious* attentive to details

37 *fucus* a paste or paint used as a cosmetic base

LADY WOULD-BE   Believe me, and I
Had the most fearful dream, could I remember't –
VOLPONE
[*Aside*] Out on my fate! I ha' giv'n her the occasion   45
How to torment me: she will tell me hers.
LADY WOULD-BE
Methought, the golden mediocrity,
Polite and delicate –
VOLPONE   O, if you do love me,
No more: I sweat, and suffer, at the mention
Of any dream; feel, how I tremble yet.   50
LADY WOULD-BE
Alas, good soul, the passion of the heart!
Seed-pearl were good now, boiled with syrup of apples,
Tincture of gold, and coral, citron-pills,
Your elecampane root, myrobalanes –
VOLPONE
[*Aside*] Ay me, I have ta'en a grasshopper by the wing.   55
LADY WOULD-BE
Burnt silk, and amber, you have muscadel
Good i' the house –
VOLPONE   You will not drink, and part?
LADY WOULD-BE
No, fear not that. I doubt, we shall not get
Some English saffron – half a dram would serve –
Your sixteen cloves, a little musk, dried mints,   60

45 *Out* Curses
    occasion opportunity
47 *golden mediocrity* Lady Would-Be's characteristically protracted and mannered
    term (out of Theophrastus) for the Horatian 'golden mean', and also a reminder
    that gold is what diverts all the play's characters from safe moderation. Unlike
    modern editors, neither Q nor F (both usually generous with commas) places a
    comma at the end of this line; so if Lady Would-Be's dream was indeed 'fearful',
    she may be preparing (after a 'but') to describe the shocking transformation of
    this supposedly decorous 'mediocrity' into something monstrous.
52–4 *Seed-pearl ... myrobalanes* A medley of popular remedies, mostly stimulants
    and cures for melancholy.
55 *ta'en a grasshopper by the wing* Volpone here complains about the constant
    whining noise of Lady Would-Be's voice, but may also have in mind a
    Renaissance locution: 'someone *seizes the grasshopper by the wing* when he
    incites and prompts someone else to do something, which the latter is prepared
    to do even more promptly and readily on his own initiative' (Parker, citing
    Stephanus's gloss to Erasmus's *Adagia*).
56 *Burnt silk* a treatment for smallpox
58 *doubt* fear

Bugloss, and barley-meal –
VOLPONE   [*Aside*] She's in again;
Before I feigned diseases, now I have one.
LADY WOULD-BE
And these applied with a right scarlet cloth –
VOLPONE
[*Aside*] Another flood of words! A very torrent!
LADY WOULD-BE
Shall I, sir, make you a poultice?
VOLPONE   No, no, no: 65
I'm very well; you need prescribe no more.
LADY WOULD-BE
I have, a little, studied physic; but, now,
I'm all for music – save, i' the forenoons,
An hour, or two, for painting. I would have
A lady, indeed, to have all, letters and arts,   70
Be able to discourse, to write, to paint,
But principal (as Plato holds) your music
(And, so does wise Pythagoras, I take it)
Is your true rapture: when there is concent
In face, in voice, and clothes; and is, indeed,   75
Our sex's chiefest ornament.
VOLPONE   The poet,
As old in time as Plato, and as knowing,
Says that your highest female grace is silence.
LADY WOULD-BE
Which o' your poets? Petrarch? or Tasso? or Dante?
Guarini? Ariosto? Aretine?   80
Cieco di Hadria? I have read them all.

61 *Bugloss* recommended (as are many of Lady Would-Be's remedies) in Burton's
   Anatomy of Melancholy, this one as a heart stimulant
63 *scarlet cloth* Smallpox patients were sometimes wrapped in scarlet cloth.
70, 75 *indeed* Apparently a familiar pretentious verbal tic in Jacobean society;
   overuse of 'indeed' is mocked in Marston's *What You Will*, III.iii.136 (Parker).
74 *concent* harmony
76 *The poet* Sophocles (*Ajax*, line 293, Loeb edition), or possibly Euripides
   (*Children of Hercules*, lines 476–7, Loeb edition).
79–81 *Petrarch ... Hadria* Yet another degrading downward succession, since
   Aretine was a notorious (if skilful) pornographer, and Cieco di Hadria far below
   the others in literary merit.

VOLPONE
  [*Aside*] Is every thing a cause, to my destruction?
LADY WOULD-BE
  I think I ha' two or three of 'em about me.
VOLPONE
  [*Aside*] The sun, the sea will sooner, both, stand still,
  Then her eternal tongue: nothing can scape it.   85
LADY WOULD-BE
  [*Holding up a book*] Here is *Pastor Fido* –
VOLPONE   [*Aside*] Profess obstinate silence,
  That's, now, my safest.
LADY WOULD-BE   All our English writers,
  I mean such as are happy in th' Italian,
  Will deign to steal out of this author, mainly –
  Almost as much, as from Montagni –   90
  He has so modern, and facile a vein,
  Fitting the time, and catching the court-ear.
  Your Petrarch is more passionate, yet he,
  In days of sonneting, trusted 'em with much;
  Dante is hard, and few can understand him.   95
  But, for a desperate wit, there's Aretine;
  Only, his pictures are a little obscene –
  You mark me not?
VOLPONE   Alas, my mind's perturbed.
LADY WOULD-BE
  Why, in such cases we must cure ourselves,
  Make use of our philosophy –

82 *cause* Again the comma allows a first meaning – *causa*, the classical term for a
    topic for debate – to emerge before being subsumed in the more conventional
    modern notion of cause and (destructive) effect, implying a sequence of thought
    and verbal association in the speaker.
86 Guarini's 1590 play appeared in English as *The Faithful Shepherd* in 1602, and
    though widely popular, was condemned by Jonson in the *Conversations with
    Drummond* (H&S I, 134).
94 *sonneting* Jonson also criticizes Petrarch's sonnets in the *Conversations* (H&S, I,
    133–34).
    trusted 'em with much entrusted his successors (Wyatt, Surrey, Sidney, and
    Spenser) with a legacy worth imitating
96 *desperate* outrageous
98 *You mark me not?* Are you listening to me? (though Jonson sometimes used the
    question mark in place of an exclamation mark, so this could be a more direct
    accusation)

VOLPONE   [*Aside*] O'ay me!   100
LADY WOULD-BE
    And, as we find our passions do rebel,
    Encounter them with reason; or divert them,
    By giving scope unto some other humour
    Of lesser danger; as, in politic bodies,
    There's nothing more doth overwhelm the judgement,   105
    And clouds the understanding, than too much
    Settling, and fixing, and (as 'twere) subsiding
    Upon one object. For the incorporating
    Of these same outward things, into that part
    Which we call mental, leaves some certain faeces,   110
    That stop the organs, and as Plato says,
    Assassinates our knowledge.
VOLPONE   [*Aside*] Now, the spirit
    Of patience help me.
LADY WOULD-BE   Come, in faith, I must
    Visit you more, a-days; and make you well:
    Laugh, and be lusty.
VOLPONE   [*Aside*] My good angel save me.   115
LADY WOULD-BE
    There was but one sole man, in all the world,
    With whom I e'er could sympathize; and he
    Would lie you often three, four hours together,
    To hear me speak: and be, sometime, so rapt,
    As he would answer me quite from the purpose,   120
    Like you, and you are like him, just. I'll discourse
    (And't be but only, sir, to bring you asleep)
    How we did spend our time, and loves, together,
    For some six years.

100 *O'ay me* A cry of anguish, like 'Alas'; perhaps a version of the Italian *Ohimé*,
     which Parker substitutes here; compare 'O me!' or 'Ay me!' several times later in
     this play (and in Milton's 'Lycidas', lines 56 and 154).
104 *politic bodies* Lady Would-Be seems to mean wise persons, though the term
     would normally refer to kingdoms.
107 *Settling ... subsiding* terms from alchemy – aptly, since all the characters here
     are diseased by their obsession with acquiring gold
115 *lusty* merry, but the modern sexual sense begins to impinge
118 *lie you* lie
119 *rapt* enraptured, or lost in thought
120 *quite from the purpose* entirely off the topic; her supposed paramour does not
     seem to have been listening.

VOLPONE   Oh, oh, oh, oh, oh, oh.

LADY WOULD-BE
  For we were *coaetanei*, and brought up –   125

VOLPONE
  [*Aside*] Some power, some fate, some fortune rescue me.

Act III, Scene v

[*Enter*] MOSCA

MOSCA
  God save you, madam.

LADY WOULD-BE   Good sir.

VOLPONE   Mosca? Welcome,
  Welcome to my redemption.

MOSCA   Why, sir?

VOLPONE   O,
  Rid me of this my torture, quickly, there:
  My madam, with the everlasting voice.
  The bells, in time of pestilence, ne'er made   5
  Like noise, or were in that perpetual motion;
  The cock-pit comes not near it. All my house,
  But now, steamed like a bath, with her thick breath.
  A lawyer could not have been heard; nor scarce
  Another woman, such a hail of words   10
  She has let fall. For hell's sake, rid her hence.

MOSCA
  Has she presented?

VOLPONE   O, I do not care,
  I'll take her absence, upon any price,
  With any loss.

MOSCA   Madam.

LADY WOULD-BE   I ha' brought your patron
  A toy, a cap here, of mine own work –

MOSCA   'Tis well;   15
  I had forgot to tell you, I saw your knight,

---

125 *coaetanei* of the same age

5–6 *The bells ... noise* The church-bells, even when the plague had them ringing
    death-knells constantly, never made so much noise

  7 *cock-pit* Cock fights were fashionable in this period – King James liked them –
    and were always raucous.

  8 *But now* Just a moment ago

12 *presented* given a present; Volpone's reply puns on 'presents' and 'presence'.

15 *toy* silly trifle

Where you'd little think it –
LADY WOULD-BE   Where?
MOSCA   Marry,
Where yet, if you make haste, you may apprehend him,
Rowing upon the water in a gondole,
With the most cunning courtesan of Venice.   20
LADY WOULD-BE
Is't true?
MOSCA   Pursue 'em, and believe your eyes;
Leave me to make your gift.

                    [*Exit* LADY WOULD-BE]

                    I knew't would take.
For lightly they, that use themselves most license,
Are still most jealous.
VOLPONE   Mosca, hearty thanks,
For thy quick fiction, and delivery of me.   25
Now, to my hopes, what sayst thou?

              [LADY WOULD-BE *enters*]

LADY WOULD-BE   But do you hear, sir?
VOLPONE
Again! I fear a paroxysm.
LADY WOULD-BE   Which way
Rowed they together?
MOSCA   Toward the Rialto.
LADY WOULD-BE
I pray you, lend me your dwarf.
MOSCA   I pray you, take him –

              [*Exit* LADY WOULD-BE]

Your hopes, sir, are like happy blossoms, fair,   30
And promise timely fruit, if you will stay
But the maturing: keep you at your couch,
Corbaccio will arrive straight, with the will;
When he is gone, I'll tell you more.   [*Exit*]
VOLPONE   My blood,
My spirits are returned: I am alive;   35

23 *lightly* usually
24 *still* always

And like your wanton gamester, at primero,
Whose thought had whispered to him not go less,
Methinks I lie, and draw – for an encounter.

Act III, Scene vi

[MOSCA *brings in* BONARIO *and hides him*]

MOSCA
    Sir, here concealed, you may hear all. But 'pray you

                              One knocks

    Have patience, sir; the same's your father, knocks:
    I am compelled to leave you.
BONARIO   Do so. Yet,
    Cannot my thought imagine this a truth.

Act III, Scene vii

[MOSCA *opens the door, enter*] CORVINO, CELIA

MOSCA
    Death on me! You are come too soon, what meant you?
    Did not I say, I would send?
CORVINO   Yes, but I feared
    You might forget it, and then they prevent us.
MOSCA
    [*Aside*] Prevent? Did e'er man haste so, for his horns?
    A courtier would not ply it so, for a place.   5
    [*To* CORVINO] Well, now there is no helping it, stay here;
    I'll presently return.   [MOSCA *goes to* BONARIO]
CORVINO   Where are you, Celia?
    You know not wherefore I have brought you hither?

---

36 *wanton gamester, at primero* reckless gambler playing a popular card-game;
    Volpone uses technical terms of the game – go less, lie, draw, encounter – as
    metaphors for his anticipated seduction of Celia.
 4 *Cannot ... truth* I cannot believe my father would really disinherit me as Mosca
    claims
 1 *Death on me!* Apparently an exclamatory curse, like 'Damn it!', but oddly par-
    allel to Corvino's 'Death of mine honour' at the beginning of II.v.
 4 *horns* marks of the cuckold
 5 *ply it so, for a place* strive so diligently for appointment to a higher office

CELIA
    Not well, except you told me.
CORVINO   Now, I will:
    Hark hither.
MOSCA (To BONARIO) Sir, your father hath sent word,   10
    It will be half an hour, ere he come;
    And therefore, if you please to walk, the while,
    Into that gallery – at the upper end,
    There are some books, to entertain the time;
    And I'll take care, no man shall come unto you, sir.   15
BONARIO
    Yes, I will stay there. [Aside] I do doubt this fellow. [Exit]
MOSCA
    There, he is far enough: he can hear nothing;
    And, for his father, I can keep him off. [Goes to VOLPONE]
CORVINO
    Nay, now, there is no starting back; and therefore,
    Resolve upon it: I have so decreed.   20
    It must be done. Nor would I move't afore,
    Because I would avoid all shifts and tricks
    That might deny me.
CELIA   Sir, let me beseech you,
    Affect not these strange trials. If you doubt
    My chastity, why, lock me up, for ever;   25
    Make me the heir of darkness. Let me live,
    Where I may please your fears, if not your trust.
CORVINO
    Believe it, I have no such humour, I.
    All that I speak, I mean; yet I am not mad –
    Not horn-mad, see you? Go to, show yourself   30

 9 *except you told me* unless you tell me, or possibly, except what little you have
   told me
10 *Hark hither* Listen here
19 *no starting back* no turning back, or possibly, no use drawing back startled
21 *Nor would I move't afore* Nor was I willing to suggest this plan earlier
22 *shifts* evasions
24 *Affect not* Do not attempt, or pretend to attempt
27 *please your fears, if not your trust* allay your jealous fears, if not earn your actual
   trust
30 *horn-mad* sexually jealous, or (almost the opposite), eager to be cuckolded

Obedient, and a wife.
CELIA   O heaven!
CORVINO   I say it,
Do so.
CELIA   Was this the train?
CORVINO   I've told you reasons:
What the physicians have set down; how much
It may concern me; what my engagements are;
My means; and the necessity of those means,   35
For my recovery. Wherefore, if you be
Loyal, and mine, be won, respect my venture.
CELIA
Before your honour?
CORVINO   Honour? tut, a breath;
There's no such thing, in nature: a mere term
Invented to awe fools. What is my gold   40
The worse, for touching? clothes, for being looked on?
Why, this 's no more. An old, decrepit wretch,
That has no sense, no sinew; takes his meat
With others' fingers; only knows to gape,
When you do scald his gums; a voice; a shadow;   45
And what can this man hurt you?
CELIA   Lord! what spirit
Is this hath entered him?
CORVINO   And for your fame,
That's such a jig; as if I would go tell it,
Cry it, on the Piazza! Who shall know it?
But he, that cannot speak it; and this fellow,   50
Whose lips are i' my pocket; save yourself –
If you'll proclaim't, you may – I know no other
Should come to know it.
CELIA   Are heaven and saints then nothing?
Will they be blind, or stupid?

32 *train* plan, trap
33 *set down* recorded as their prognosis (for Volpone's sexual impotence and immi-
      nent death)
34 *engagements* investments (in courting Volpone), perhaps also consequent debts
      to others
35 *means* method, means to the end, which is winning Volpone's inheritance
37 *venture* risky commercial undertaking
38 *tut, a breath* nonsense, an empty word
43 *no sense, no sinew* no sensory awareness, no physical strength
48 *jig* farcical diversion, silly excuse
51 *Whose lips are i' my pocket* Whose silence I have purchased
      save except

CORVINO   How?
CELIA   Good sir,
  Be jealous still, emulate them; and think   55
  What hate they burn with, toward every sin.
CORVINO
  I grant you; if I thought it were a sin,
  I would not urge you. Should I offer this
  To some young Frenchman, or hot Tuscan blood,
  That had read Aretine, conned all his prints,   60
  Knew every quirk within lust's labyrinth,
  And were professed critic in lechery,
  And I would look upon him, and applaud him,
  This were a sin; but here, 'tis contrary,
  A pious work, mere charity, for physic,   65
  And honest polity, to assure mine own.
CELIA
  O heaven! canst thou suffer such a change?
VOLPONE
  [Aside to MOSCA] Thou art mine honour, Mosca, and my pride,
  My joy, my tickling, my delight! Go, bring 'em.
MOSCA
  Please you draw near, sir.
CORVINO   Come on, what –   70

          [CELIA resists as he drags her toward the bed]

  You will not be rebellious? By that light –
MOSCA
  Sir, Signior Corvino, here, is come to see you.
VOLPONE
  Oh.
MOSCA And, hearing of the consultation had,
  So lately, for your health, is come to offer,
  Or rather, sir, to prostitute –
CORVINO   Thanks, sweet Mosca.   75
MOSCA
  Freely, unasked, or unentreated –
CORVINO   Well.
MOSCA
  As the true, fervent instance of his love,

---

60 *conned all his prints* studied all Aretine's pornographic illustrations
62 *professed critic* expert scholar
63 *And* If
66 *polity, to assure mine own* stratagem to secure the fortune that is rightfully mine
71 *You will not be rebellious?* Are you really going to disobey me? or, Didn't you
    promise to be an obedient wife?

His own most fair and proper wife: the beauty,
Only of price, in Venice –

CORVINO   'Tis well urged.

MOSCA

To be your comfortress, and to preserve you.   80

VOLPONE

Alas, I'm past already. 'Pray you, thank him,
For his good care, and promptness. But for that,
'Tis a vain labour, e'en to fight, 'gainst heaven:
Applying fire to a stone – uh, uh, uh, uh –
Making a dead leaf grow again. I take   85
His wishes gently, though; and, you may tell him,
What I've done for him. Marry, my state is hopeless.
Will him to pray for me; and t' use his fortune,
With reverence, when he comes to't.

MOSCA   Do you hear, sir?
Go to him, with your wife.

CORVINO   Heart of my father!   90
Wilt thou persist thus? Come, I pray thee, come.
Thou seest 'tis nothing, Celia. By this hand,
I shall grow violent. Come, do't, I say.

CELIA

Sir, kill me, rather: I will take down poison,
Eat burning coals, do anything –

CORVINO   Be damned!   95
Heart, I will drag thee hence, home, by the hair;
Cry thee a strumpet through the streets; rip up
Thy mouth, unto thine ears; and slit thy nose,
Like a raw rotchet – do not tempt me, come;
Yield, I am loath – Death, I will buy some slave,   100

78 *proper* Three meanings simultaneously: respectable, attractive, and privately owned
78–9 *the beauty, / Only of price* the most prized and precious beauty (but with a reminder that even she can be bought)
81–9 *Alas ... to't* The heavy punctuation in this speech (both in Q and in F) suggests Volpone struggling for breath as he speaks.
84 *Applying fire to a stone* A proverb for futility (Tilley S892), but Volpone is also playing slyly on 'stone' as Renaissance slang for 'testicle'.
92 *By this hand* A familiar oath, short for 'I swear by this hand', but also suggesting that Corvino raises his hand threateningly here.
95 *Eat burning coals* Portia, wife of Brutus and legendary for her virtue and loyalty, chose this method of suicide.
97 *Cry* Proclaim
99 *rotchet* a reddish fish; Jonson had been threatened with judicial nose-slitting for mocking Scots in *Eastward Ho!*

Whom I will kill, and bind thee to him, alive;
And, at my window, hang you forth; devising
Some monstrous crime, which I, in capital letters,
Will eat into thy flesh, with *aquafortis*,
And burning cor'sives, on this stubborn breast.   105
Now, by the blood thou hast incensed, I'll do't.

CELIA
Sir, what you please, you may: I am your martyr.

CORVINO
Be not thus obstinate, I ha' not deserved it.
Think who it is entreats you. 'Pray thee, sweet:
Good faith, thou shalt have jewels, gowns, attires,   110
What thou wilt think, and ask – do but go kiss him.
Or touch him, but. For my sake. At my suit.
This once. No? Not? I shall remember this.
Will you disgrace me, thus? Do you thirst my undoing?

MOSCA
Nay, gentle lady, be advised.

CORVINO   No, no.   115
She has watched her time. God's precious, this is scurvy;
'Tis very scurvy; and you are –

MOSCA   Nay, good, sir.

CORVINO
An errant locust, by heaven, a locust. Whore,
Crocodile, that hast thy tears prepared,
Expecting how thou'lt bid 'em flow.

MOSCA   Nay, 'pray you, sir,   120
She will consider.

---

104 *aquafortis* nitric acid, used for etching; Corvino threatens to engrave his false
     accusation against Celia in her flesh with corrosives.
111 *What thou wilt think, and ask* Anything you can imagine and ask for, or, Think
     of anything you wish for, and ask me for it
     but merely
112 *At my suit* Because I am begging you
115 *be advised* take your husband's advice, believe his warning
116 *watched her time* waited for the opportunity to do me the most damage
     God's precious I swear by God's precious blood
118 *errant* arrant, notorious; or possibly, erring, devious
     locust a Biblical plague, a pest that swallows up the harvest
119–20 *Crocodile ... flow* Crocodiles were believed to lure their victims with false
     tears.
120 *Expecting* Anticipating, Plotting

CELIA   Would my life would serve
  To satisfy –
CORVINO   'Sdeath, if she would but speak to him,
  And save my reputation, 'twere somewhat;
  But, spitefully to affect my utter ruin –
MOSCA
  Ay, now you've put your fortune in her hands.   125
  Why, i' faith, it is her modesty, I must 'quit her:
  If you were absent, she would be more coming;
  I know it, and dare undertake for her.
  What woman can, before her husband? 'Pray you,
  Let us depart, and leave her here.
CORVINO   Sweet Celia,   130
  Thou mayst redeem all, yet; I'll say no more:
  If not, esteem yourself as lost –

                 [CELIA *tries to exit*]

             Nay, stay there.

         [*Exeunt* CORVINO *and* MOSCA]

CELIA
  O God, and his good angels! Whither, whither.
  Is shame fled human breasts? that, with such ease,
  Men dare put off your honours, and their own?   135
  Is that, which ever was a cause of life,
  Now placed beneath the basest circumstance?
  And modesty an exile made, for money?

     He [VOLPONE] *leaps off from his couch*

VOLPONE
  Ay, in Corvino, and such earth-fed minds,
  That never tasted the true heav'n of love.   140
  Assure thee, Celia, he that would sell thee,

121–2 *Would my life … satisfy* I would be happy to be killed if only that would solve
     the problem
123 *'twere somewhat* that would count for something
124 *affect* attempt
126 *'quit* acquit, excuse; or possibly, leave her in privacy
127 *coming* forthcoming, agreeable, perhaps with sexual connotations
129 *can, before* can (commit adultery) in sight of
135 *put off your honours* ignore or betray the divine principles of honour, or, dis-
     honour the divine by doing so
136–7 *Is that … circumstance?* Is honour, which has always been considered a cause
     worth dying for, now valued less than the lowliest and most trivial advantage?

Only for hope of gain, and that uncertain,
He would have sold his part of Paradise
For ready money, had he met a cope-man.
Why art thou mazed, to see me thus revived?   145
Rather, applaud thy beauty's miracle:
'Tis thy great work, that hath, not now alone,
But sundry times, raised me, in several shapes,
And, but this morning, like a mountebank,
To see thee at thy window. Ay, before   150
I would have left my practice for thy love,
In varying figures, I would have contended
With the blue Proteus, or the hornèd flood.
Now, art thou welcome.

CELIA   Sir!
VOLPONE   Nay, fly me not;
Nor let thy false imagination   155
That I was bed-rid, make thee think, I am so:
Thou shalt not find it. I am, now, as fresh,
As hot, as high, and in as jovial plight,
As when (in that so celebrated scene,
At recitation of our comedy,   160
For entertainment of the great Valois)
I acted young Antinous; and attracted

142 *and that uncertain* when the gain is not even guaranteed
144 *cope-man* suitable merchant
145 *mazed* amazed, bewildered
151 *practice for* scheming to win
152 *figures* disguises, shapes
153 *blue Proteus, or the hornèd flood* Proteus was a sea-god who could change shape
    at will; the hornèd flood is the river-god Achelous who turned himself into vari-
    ous animals while battling Hercules for a woman's love.
158 *jovial plight* thriving condition, with some reference to Jove's persistent courting
    of beautiful mortal women
161 *Valois* Henry Valois, later King Henry III of France, was lavishly entertained in
    Venice in 1574.
162 *Antinous* either the manly chief suitor to Odysseus's chaste wife Penelope, or the
    boy beloved by the Emperor Hadrian; considering how often Jonson traps this
    play's characters into self-aggrandizing masculine poses that can be ironically re-
    interpreted as signs of sterility and perversion (which was evidently his view of
    homosexuality), the ambiguity may be deliberate.

The eyes and ears of all the ladies present,
To admire each graceful gesture, note, and footing.

Song

Come, my Celia, let us prove,   165
While we can, the sports of love:
Time will not be ours forever,
He, at length, our good will sever;
Spend not then his gifts, in vain.
Suns that set may rise again;   170
But if, once, we lose this light,
'Tis with us perpetual night.
Why should we defer our joys?
Fame and rumour are but toys.
Cannot we delude the eyes   175
Of a few poor household-spies?
Or his easier ears beguile,
Thus removèd by our wile?
'Tis no sin, love's fruits to steal,
But the sweet thefts to reveal;   180
To be taken, to be seen,
These have crimes accounted been.

CELIA
Some serene blast me, or dire lightning strike
This my offending face.
VOLPONE   Why droops my Celia?
Thou hast, in place of a base husband, found   185
A worthy lover: use thy fortune well,
With secrecy, and pleasure. See, behold, [*Shows the treasure*]
What thou art queen of; not in expectation,
As I feed others, but possessed, and crowned.

164 *footing* dance step
164 s.d. *Song* Jonson based this *carpe diem* song on Catullus's Ode V, had his friend
    Antonio Ferrabosco set it to music, and later reprinted it in his poetry collection
    The Forest.
165 *prove* experience, try out
168 *our good will sever* will cut off our good times
174 *toys* silly trifles
177 *his* Corvino's
178 *Thus removèd by our wile* Since we have cleverly got him out of the room
181 *taken* caught
183 *Some serene blast me* I wish some poisonous mist would destroy me
184 *offending* Her beauty has committed an offence, she feels, in provoking this
    sinful proposal.

See, here, a rope of pearl; and each more orient   190
Than that the brave Egyptian queen caroused:
Dissolve, and drink 'em. See, a carbuncle,
May put out both the eyes of our St Mark;
A diamond, would have bought Lollia Paulina,
When she came in, like starlight, hid with jewels,   195
That were the spoils of provinces. Take these,
And wear, and lose 'em; yet remains an earring
To purchase them again, and this whole state.
A gem but worth a private patrimony
Is nothing: we will eat such at a meal.   200
The heads of parrots, tongues of nightingales,
The brains of peacocks, and of ostriches
Shall be our food; and, could we get the phoenix,
Though nature lost her kind, she were our dish.

CELIA
Good sir, these things might move a mind affected   205
With such delights; but I, whose innocence
Is all I can think wealthy, or worth th' enjoying,
And which, once lost, I have nought to lose beyond it,
Cannot be taken with these sensual baits.
If you have conscience –

190 *orient* rare, fine, precious; see the note at I.v.9.
191 *the brave Egyptian queen caroused* The glamorous Cleopatra, according to
   Pliny, was challenged by her lover Antony to spend a fortune on a meal, which
   she did by dissolving a pearl in vinegar and drinking it.
192 *carbuncle* a round red gem
193 *put out both the eyes of our St Mark* Perhaps Venice, known to possess some
   precious rubies, had a statue of its patron saint with carbuncles for the eyes.
   Volpone (possibly echoing Pietro Aretino) offers a jewel that will either put to
   shame, or bribe into looking the other way, the grand patron saint of the city. In
   any case – as when Volpone's worship of gold 'darkens' the sun in the opening
   scene – Jonson suggests monetary values eclipsing religious ones (Kernan).
194 *Lollia Paulina* consort of the Emperor Caligula; Pliny describes her as covered
   with jewels. Volpone neglects to mention that her opulent story, like that of
   Cleopatra, ends in suicide.
196 *spoils of provinces* greatest treasures stolen from conquered territories
197–98 *yet remains ... whole state* there would still be left an earring that would
   purchase all the aforementioned jewellry, and all of Venice too
199 *but worth a private patrimony* worth only as much as a single person's estate
203 *phoenix* a mythical bird, supposedly reborn from its own ashes every five hundred years; Volpone is willing to render the species ('kind') extinct by eating it.

VOLPONE   'Tis the beggar's virtue;   210
If thou hast wisdom, hear me, Celia.
Thy baths shall be the juice of July-flowers,
Spirit of roses, and of violets,
The milk of unicorns, and panthers' breath
Gathered in bags, and mixed with Cretan wines.   215
Our drink shall be preparèd gold, and amber;
Which we will take, until my roof whirl round
With the vertigo; and my dwarf shall dance,
My eunuch sing, my fool make up the antic.
Whilst, we, in changèd shapes, act Ovid's tales,   220
Thou, like Europa now, and I like Jove,
Then I like Mars, and thou like Erycine,
So, of the rest, till we have quite run through
And wearied all the fables of the gods.
Then will I have thee, in more modern forms,   225
Attirèd like some sprightly dame of France,
Brave Tuscan lady, or proud Spanish beauty;
Sometimes, unto the Persian Sophy's wife;
Or the Grand Signior's Mistress; and, for change,
To one of our most artful courtesans,   230
Or some quick Negro, or cold Russian;
And I will meet thee, in as many shapes,
Where we may, so, transfuse our wand'ring souls,
Out at our lips, and score up sums of pleasures,

[*Sings*] That the curious shall not know,   235
         How to tell them, as they flow;

210 *'Tis the beggar's virtue* Conscience is good only for those so poor they can't
    afford great pleasures anyway
212 *July-flowers* gillyflowers, or clove-scented pinks, which Perdita in Shakespeare's
    Winter's Tale (IV.iv) mistrusts as an exotic graft
214 *panthers' breath* Panthers were supposed to lure their prey with sweet breath (as
    Volpone is luring Celia with sweet words).
219 *antic* strange dance
220 *Ovid's tales* Ovid's *Metamorphoses* recounts many transformations and seduc-
    tions, such as Zeus disguising himself as a bull to capture Europa; Jonson mocks
    the male appetite for such pornographic role-playing in several of his works.
222 *Erycine* Venus
228 *Persian Sophy* Shah of Iran
229 *Grand Signior* Sultan of Turkey
231 *quick* lively, hot-blooded
233 *transfuse* cause to flow from one to another (OED); this exotic but finally
    pathetic wandering through many identities recalls the degrading transmigration
    of Pythagoras's soul in I.ii.1–62.
236 *tell* count

And the envious, when they find
What their number is, be pined.

CELIA
If you have ears, that will be pierced – or eyes,
That can be opened – a heart, may be touched –   240
Or any part, that yet sounds man, about you –
If you have touch of holy saints – or Heaven –
Do me the grace, to let me 'scape – if not,
Be bountiful, and kill me – you do know,
I am a creature, hither ill betrayed,   245
By one whose shame I would forget it were –
If you will deign me neither of these graces,
Yet feed your wrath, sir, rather than your lust –
It is a vice, comes nearer manliness –
And punish that unhappy crime of nature,   250
Which you miscall my beauty – flay my face,
Or poison it, with ointments, for seducing
Your blood to this rebellion – rub these hands,
With what may cause an eating leprosy,
E'en to my bones and marrow – anything,   255
That may disfavour me, save in my honour –
And I will kneel to you, pray for you, pay down
A thousand hourly vows, sir, for your health –
Report, and think you virtuous –
VOLPONE   Think me cold,
Frozen, and impotent, and so report me?   260
That I had Nestor's hernia, thou wouldst think.
I do degenerate, and abuse my nation,

238 *pined* pained, caused to pine away with envy
239–59 Q's punctuation of Celia's speech with dashes suggests breathless panic, or
    struggles to escape Volpone's embraces or his bedchamber; F provides gram-
    matically and logically accurate punctuation instead. This edition, trusting the
    theatrical wisdom of Jonson in 1606 and recognizing that the 1616 version may
    reflect Jonson's effort to impose a consistent form on the page rather than a
    rethinking of Celia's demeanour on the stage here, preserves Q's dashes. Still, it
    is worth acknowledging a feminist argument for the F version, which would
    create a much stronger Celia – less a wide-eyed damsel in distress than a well-
    spoken, cool-headed defender of her chastity, appealing eloquently to what little
    is left of Volpone's reason and (though this immediately backfires) to his manly
    pride.
241 *yet sounds man* still retains some echo of manly honour or humane mercy
256 *disfavour* disfigure, destroy whatever makes me sexually appealing
261 *Nestor's hernia* impotence; Nestor was the aged Greek commander in Homer's
    Iliad (cf. Juvenal's *Satires* VI, 326).
262 *abuse my nation* dishonour the reputation of Italians for ferocious virility

To play with opportunity thus long:
I should have done the act, and then have parleyed.
Yield, or I'll force thee.
CELIA   O, just God!
VOLPONE   In vain –   265

He [BONARIO] *leaps out from where Mosca had*
placed him

BONARIO
Forbear, foul ravisher, libidinous swine!
Free the forced lady, or thou diest, impostor.
But that I am loath to snatch thy punishment
Out of the hand of justice, thou shouldst yet
Be made the timely sacrifice of vengeance,   270
Before this altar, and this dross [*Gesturing toward the*
gold], thy idol.
Lady, let's quit the place: it is the den
Of villainy. Fear nought, you have a guard;
And he, ere long, shall meet his just reward.

VOLPONE
Fall on me, roof, and bury me in ruin,   275
Become my grave, that wert my shelter. O!
I am unmasked, unspirited, undone,
Betrayed to beggary, to infamy –

Act III, Scene viii

[*Enter*] MOSCA, [*bleeding*]

MOSCA
Where shall I run, most wretched shame of men,
To beat out my unlucky brains?
VOLPONE   Here, here.
What! dost thou bleed?
MOSCA   O, that his well-driven sword
Had been so courteous to have cleft me down
Unto the navel, ere I lived to see   5
My life, my hopes, my spirits, my patron, all
Thus desperately engagèd, by my error.

---

271 *dross* a dismissive term for Volpone's gold
274 *he* presumably Volpone; but the situation conventionally suggests (though this
    play stubbornly refuses to fulfil the expectation) that Bonario should be
    rewarded with the hand of the young woman he has saved.
7 *engagèd* entrapped, entangled, or thrown into debt

VOLPONE
  Woe on thy fortune.
MOSCA   And my follies, sir.
VOLPONE
  Th' hast made me miserable.
MOSCA   And myself, sir.
  Who would have thought he would have hearkened so?   10
VOLPONE
  What shall we do?
MOSCA   I know not; if my heart
  Could expiate the mischance, I'd pluck it out.
  Will you be pleased to hang me? Or cut my throat?
  And I'll requite you, sir. Let's die like Romans,
  Since we have lived like Grecians.

                              They knock without

VOLPONE   Hark, who's there?   15
  I hear some footing: officers, the *Saffi*,
  Come to apprehend us! I do feel the brand
  Hissing, already, at my forehead; now,
  Mine ears are boring.
MOSCA   To your couch, sir; you
  Make that place good, however. [VOLPONE *gets into bed*]
                              Guilty men   20
  Suspect what they deserve still. [*Opens the door*] Signior
    Corbaccio!

---

10 *he would have hearkened* Bonario would have eavesdropped
14 *requite* repay you in kind
   Romans Ancient Rome had a Stoic tradition of answering adversity and pre-
     serving honour by suicide.
15 *like Grecians* craftily, and (above all) for high pleasures
16 *Saffi* bailiffs assigned to make arrests
17–19 *brand … boring* permanently disfiguring punishments with hot or sharp
     metal; Jonson himself had been branded on the thumb for killing a fellow-actor.
20 *Make that place good, however* Try to resume playing the dying man convinc-
     ingly, in whatever way you can, or whatever happens
21 *Suspect what they deserve still* Always expect, with dread, their due punishment

Act III, Scene ix

[Enter] CORBACCIO; VOLTORE *[enters unnoticed behind him]*

CORBACCIO
Why, how now, Mosca?
MOSCA   O, undone, amazed, sir.
Your son (I know not by what accident)
Acquainted with your purpose to my patron,
Touching your will, and making him your heir,
Entered our house with violence, his sword drawn,   5
Sought for you, called you wretch, unnatural,
Vowed he would kill you.
CORBACCIO   Me?
MOSCA   Yes, and my patron.
CORBACCIO
This act shall disinherit him indeed:
Here is the will.
MOSCA   'Tis well, sir.
CORBACCIO   Right, and well.
Be you as careful, now, for me.
MOSCA   My life, sir,   10
Is not more tendered; I am only yours.
CORBACCIO
How does he? Will he die shortly, think'st thou?
MOSCA   I fear
He'll outlast May.
CORBACCIO   Today?
MOSCA   No, last out May, sir.
CORBACCIO
Couldst thou not gi' him a dram?
MOSCA   O, by no means, sir.
CORBACCIO
Nay, I'll not bid you.
VOLTORE   This is a knave, I see.   15
MOSCA
[Aside] How, Signior Voltore! Did he hear me?

---

1 *undone, amazed* ruined, bewildered
3–4 *your purpose ... will* your intention toward Volpone, regarding your last will
   and testament
11 *tendered* tenderly cared for
14 *dram* drug, presumably a fatal overdose or poison
15 *This* Mosca

VOLTORE   Parasite!
MOSCA
  Who's that? O, sir, most timely welcome –
VOLTORE   Scarce,
  To the discovery of your tricks, I fear.
  You are his, only? and mine, also? are you not?
MOSCA
  Who? I, sir?
VOLTORE   You, sir. What device is this   20
  About a will?
MOSCA   A plot for you, sir.
VOLTORE   Come,
  Put not your foists upon me, I shall scent 'em.
MOSCA
  Did you not hear it?
VOLTORE   Yes, I hear, Corbaccio
  Hath made your patron, there, his heir.
MOSCA   'Tis true;
  By my device, drawn to it by my plot,   25
  With hope –
VOLTORE   Your patron should reciprocate?
  And you have promised?
MOSCA   For your good, I did, sir.
  Nay, more, I told his son, brought, hid him here,
  Where he might hear his father pass the deed;
  Being persuaded to it by this thought, sir: 30
  That the unnaturalness, first, of the act,
  And then, his father's oft disclaiming in him,
  Which I did mean t' help on, would sure enrage him
  To do some violence upon his parent,
  On which the law should take sufficient hold,   35
  And you be stated in a double hope.
  Truth be my comfort, and my conscience,
  My only aim was, to dig you a fortune
  Out of these two, old, rotten sepulchres –
VOLTORE
  I cry thee mercy, Mosca.

---

17 *Scarce* Hardly welcome, or, Just in time
22 *foists* tricks, but with a secondary meaning of 'odours of decay', which a vulture
   would be attuned to notice
32 *oft disclaiming in him* repeatedly disowning him
35 *sufficient hold* severe enough penalty to make Bonario ineligible for Corbaccio's
   inheritance
36 *stated in a double hope* instated with both inheritances
40 *cry thee mercy* beg your pardon

MOSCA   Worth your patience,   40
  And your great merit, sir. And, see the change!
VOLTORE
  Why? what success?
MOSCA   Most hapless! You must help, sir.
  Whilst we expected th' old raven, in comes
  Corvino's wife, sent hither by her husband –
VOLTORE
  What, with a present?
MOSCA   No, sir, on visitation   45
  (I'll tell you how, anon); and, staying long,
  The youth, he grows impatient, rushes forth,
  Seizeth the lady, wounds me, makes her swear –
  Or he would murder her, that was his vow –
  T' affirm my patron would have done her rape –   50
  Which how unlike it is, you see! – and, hence,
  With that pretext, he's gone t' accuse his father;
  Defame my patron; defeat you –
VOLTORE   Where's her husband?
  Let him be sent for, straight.
MOSCA   Sir, I'll go fetch him.
VOLTORE
  Bring him to the *Scrutineo*.
MOSCA   Sir, I will.   55
VOLTORE
  This must be stopped.
MOSCA   O, you do nobly, sir.
  Alas, 'twas laboured all, sir, for your good;
  Nor was there want of counsel in the plot;
  But fortune can, at any time, o'erthrow
  The projects of a hundred learned clerks, sir.   60
CORBACCIO
  What's that?
VOLTORE   Will't please you, sir, to go along?

                [*Exeunt* VOLTORE *and* CORBACCIO]

MOSCA
  Patron, go in, and pray for our success.

---

42 *what success?* how successful was this?
   hapless unlucky
55 *Scrutineo* The law court in the Venetian Senate House
58 *want of counsel* lack of deliberation
60 *clerks* learnèd men

VOLPONE
 Need makes devotion: heaven your labour bless.

[*Exeunt*]

Act IV, Scene i

[*Enter*] POLITIC, PEREGRINE

SIR POLITIC
 I told you, sir, it was a plot: you see
 What observation is. You mentioned me
 For some instructions: I will tell you, sir,
 Since we are met, here, in this height of Venice,
 Some few particulars I have set down   5
 Only for this meridian, fit to be known
 Of your crude traveller; and they are these.
 I will not touch, sir, at your phrase, or clothes,
 For they are old.
PEREGRINE   Sir, I have better.
SIR POLITIC   Pardon,
 I meant, as they are themes.
PEREGRINE   O, sir, proceed: 10
 I'll slander you no more of wit, good sir.
SIR POLITIC
 First, for your garb, it must be grave, and serious;
 Very reserved, and locked; not tell a secret,
 On any terms, not to your father; scarce
 A fable, but with caution; make sure choice   15
 Both of your company, and discourse; beware

1–2 *I told you ... what observation is* You see how observant I was to suspect (at
   II.iii.10–12) that the mountebank scene was all a plot to entrap me
2 *mentioned* asked
4 *height of Venice* Cf. II.i.12 and the explanatory note there.
7 *crude* raw (implying inexperience and also, perhaps, vulgarity)
8 *touch, sir, at your phrase* make mention, sir, of your style of speech; but
   Peregrine mischievously pretends to mistake the sense of 'touch' as well as the
   referent of 'old' here.
11 *slander you no more of wit* never again mistakenly think you capable of a witty
   insult
12 *garb* bearing, demeanour; like Polonius's advice to Laertes in *Hamlet*, Sir Pol's
   advice emphasizes shallow social tactics rather than deep moral sense.
14 *not* not even
14–15 *scarce ... caution* hardly even risk telling a fictional story without caution

You never speak a truth –
PEREGRINE   How!
SIR POLITIC   Not to strangers,
  For those be they you must converse with most;
  Others I would not know, sir, but, at distance,
  So as I still might be a saver in 'em: 20
  You shall have tricks, else, passed upon you, hourly.
  And then, for your religion, profess none;
  But wonder, at the diversity of all;
  And, for your part, protest, were there no other
  But simply the laws o' th' land, you could content you: 25
  Nick Machiavel and Monsieur Bodin, both,
  Were of this mind. Then, must you learn the use,
  And handling of your silver fork, at meals;
  The metal of your glass – these are main matters,
  With your Italian – and to know the hour,   30
  When you must eat your melons, and your figs.
PEREGRINE
  Is that a point of state, too?
SIR POLITIC   Here it is.
  For your Venetian, if he see a man
  Preposterous in the least, he has him straight;
  He has: he strips him. I'll acquaint you, sir,   35
  I now have lived here, 'tis some fourteen months;
  Within the first week of my landing here,
  All took me for a citizen of Venice;
  I knew the forms so well –
PEREGRINE   [Aside] And nothing else.
SIR POLITIC
  I had read Contarine, took me a house,   40

19 *Others* presumably, other travellers from your own country
20 *be a saver in 'em* be safer around them (by being an acquaintance) or save time
    and money (by not becoming close enough to be asked for favours or loans)
26 *Nick Machiavel and Monsieur Bodin* Sir Pol has a characteristically fashionable
    misunderstanding of Niccolo Machiavelli (whose book arguably advocated
    putting political considerations ahead of religious ones) and Jean Bodin (who
    argued for religious toleration, a cause that might have appealed to Jonson, him-
    self a convert to the banned Catholicism).
28 *fork* Forks were still uncommon silverware in Jacobean England.
29 *metal* material
34 *Preposterous* Disordered, Incorrect
    has him straight instantly sees through his pretences and takes advantage of him
35 *strips him* exposes him to ridicule
40 *Contarine* Cardinal Gasparo Contarini's book on Venice was translated into
    English in 1599.

Dealt with my Jews, to furnish it with movables –
Well, if I could but find one man – one man,
To mine own heart, whom I durst trust – I would –
PEREGRINE
What? What, sir?
SIR POLITIC   Make him rich; make him a fortune:
He should not think again. I would command it.   45
PEREGRINE
As how?
SIR POLITIC With certain projects, that I have;
Which, I may not discover.
PEREGRINE   [Aside] If I had
But one to wager with, I would lay odds, now,
He tells me, instantly.
SIR POLITIC   One is – and that
I care not greatly who knows – to serve the state   50
Of Venice with red herrings, for three years,
And at a certain rate, from Rotterdam,
Where I have correspondence. There's a letter,
Sent me from one o' th' States, and to that purpose;
                        [Shows a letter]
He cannot write his name, but that's his mark.   55
PEREGRINE
He is a chandler?
SIR POLITIC   No, a cheesemonger.
There are some other too, with whom I treat
About the same negotiation;

41 *Jews* Venice supported a Jewish community to handle the money-lending business which was forbidden to Christians but necessary for their capitalist economy; cf. Shakespeare's misrepresentation of this relationship in *The Merchant of
Venice*.
   movables furniture other than fixtures
46 *projects* In this period, the word connotes highly speculative schemes; Jonson
mocks such ingenious 'projectors' again in *The Devil is an Ass*.
47 *may not discover* must not reveal
51 *red herrings* a basic cheap food in England, but considered a dainty in Venice;
the modern meaning of strategic diversion or delusion was not yet common, but
seems relevant, especially in parallel with the same three-year period Volpone
has been misleading the legacy-hunters (Parker).
54 *th' States* Holland
56 *chandler* candle-maker or retailer of provisions; Peregrine may be joking about
the messiness of the paper or the size of the seal.
   cheesemonger Sir Pol has settled on an illiterate cheese-seller as his source for
correspondence and herrings; a further joke lies in the standard English mockery
of the Dutch fondness for butter and cheese.

And I will undertake it. For, 'tis thus,
I'll do't with ease, I've cast it all: your hoy   60
Carries but three men in her, and a boy;
And she shall make me three returns, a year;
So, if there come but one of three, I save,
If two, I can defalk. But this is now
If my main project fail.

PEREGRINE   Then, you have others?   65

SIR POLITIC
I should be loath to draw the subtle air
Of such a place without my thousand aims.
I'll not dissemble, sir: where'er I come,
I love to be considerative; and, 'tis true,
I have, at my free hours, thought upon   70
Some certain goods unto the state of Venice,
Which I do call my cautions; and, sir, which
I mean (in hope of pension) to propound
To the Great Council, then unto the Forty,
So to the Ten. My means are made already –   75

PEREGRINE
By whom?

SIR POLITIC Sir, one, that though his place be obscure,
Yet, he can sway, and they will hear him. He's
A *commandatore*.

PEREGRINE   What, a common sergeant?

SIR POLITIC
Sir, such as they are, put it in their mouths,
What they should say, sometimes, as well as greater.   80
I think I have my notes, to show you –

60 *cast* calculated
     hoy small boat for coastal transportation; probably not adequate for safe voy-
     aging between Venice and Rotterdam
63–4 *if there come ... defalk* The sense of this seems to be that Sir Pol can afford to
     have only one of his three shiploads arrive safely, and that if two arrive he can
     reduce his debt, or maybe his price; but Jonson may not intend Sir Pol's plans to
     make perfect sense.
64 *now* only
66 *draw the subtle air* breathe the atmosphere of intrigue
71 *goods* benefits; Sir Pol intends to offer such valuable precautionary schemes to
     the three highest levels of the Venetian government that they will pay him a pen-
     sion.
78 *commandatore* officer charged with bringing offenders to court – the disguise
     Volpone will later assume
79–80 *such as ... greater* lowly officials such as sergeants, as well as more exalted
     ones, sometimes advise these authorities what to say

PEREGRINE   Good, sir.
SIR POLITIC
   But, you shall swear unto me, on your gentry,
   Not to anticipate –
PEREGRINE   I, sir?
SIR POLITIC   Nor reveal
   A circumstance – My paper is not with me.
PEREGRINE
   O, but, you can remember, sir.
SIR POLITIC   My first is   85
   Concerning tinderboxes. You must know,
   No family is, here, without its box.
   Now sir, it being so portable a thing,
   Put case, that you or I were ill affected
   Unto the state: sir, with it in our pockets,   90
   Might not I go into the Arsenale?
   Or you? Come out again? And none the wiser?
PEREGRINE
   Except yourself, sir.
SIR POLITIC   Go to, then. I, therefore,
   Advertise to the state how fit it were
   That none, but such as were known patriots,   95
   Sound lovers of their country, should be suffered
   T' enjoy them in their houses; and even those,
   Sealed, at some office, and at such a bigness,
   As might not lurk in pockets.
PEREGRINE   Admirable!
SIR POLITIC
   My next is, how t' enquire, and be resolved   100
   By present demonstration, whether a ship,
   Newly arrived from *Soria*, or from
   Any suspected part of all the Levant,
   Be guilty of the plague: and, where they use

82–3 *swear unto ... anticipate* swear, on your good name, not to use my ideas before
   I do
89 *Put case, that* What if, suppose hypothetically
91 *Arsenale* the place Venice kept its ships and weapons, where a spark from a tin-
   derbox could have devastating effects; it had exploded and burnt in 1568–9, and
   a Jacobean audience might again have been reminded of the 1605 Gunpowder
   Plot.
96 *suffered* allowed; Sir Pol's scheme would make it impossible for most Venetians
   to maintain the fires they need for cooking and heating.
98 *Sealed* Licensed, perhaps sealed shut
101 *present* immediate
102 *Sorìa* Sir Pol suavely employs the Italian name for Syria.

To lie out forty, fifty days, sometimes,   105
About the Lazaretto, for their trial,
I'll save that charge and loss unto the merchant,
And, in an hour, clear the doubt.
PEREGRINE   Indeed, sir?
SIR POLITIC
Or – I will lose my labour.
PEREGRINE   My faith, that's much.
SIR POLITIC
Nay, sir, conceive me. 'Twill cost me, in onions,   110
Some thirty *livres* –
PEREGRINE   Which is one pound sterling.
SIR POLITIC
Beside my waterworks. For this I do, sir:
First, I bring in your ship, 'twixt two brick walls
(But those the state shall venture); on the one
I strain me a fair tarpaulin; and, in that,   115
I stick my onions, cut in halves; the other
Is full of loopholes, out at which, I thrust
The noses of my bellows; and those bellows
I keep, with waterworks, in perpetual motion
(Which is the easiest matter of a hundred).   120
Now, sir, your onion, which doth naturally
Attract th' infection, and your bellows, blowing
The air upon him, will show, instantly,
By his changed colour, if there be contagion;
Or else, remain as fair as at the first.   125
Now 'tis known, 'tis nothing.
PEREGRINE   You are right, sir.
SIR POLITIC
I would I had my note.

---

106 *About the Lazaretto* Near Venice's quarantine areas for those suspected of
     bubonic plague or leprosy; as a world port, Venice had various schemes to pre-
     vent importation of disease, including lengthy quarantines and purifying incom-
     ing goods with vinegar.
109 *that's much* Peregrine is unimpressed, to the point of sarcasm, with the 'labour'
     that much have gone into Pol's scheme.
111 *livres* French coins
114 *venture* invest in
115 *strain* stretch
126 *Now 'tis known ... right, sir* With false humility, Pol acknowledges that the idea
     may seem obvious once it has been explained; but Peregrine exploits Pol's word-
     ing to suggest (with characteristic suave irony) that the idea is worthless rather
     than obvious.

PEREGRINE   Faith, so would I;
But, you ha' done well, for once, sir.
SIR POLITIC   Were I false,
Or would be made so, I could show you reasons,
How I could sell this state, now, to the Turk;   130
Spite of their galleys, or their –
PEREGRINE   'Pray you, Sir Pol.
SIR POLITIC
I have 'em not, about me.
PEREGRINE   That I feared.
They're there, sir?
SIR POLITIC   No. This is my diary,
Wherein I note my actions of the day.
PEREGRINE
'Pray you, let's see, sir. What is here? '*Notandum*,   135
A rat had gnawn my spur leathers; notwithstanding,
I put on new, and did go forth; but, first,
I threw three beans over the threshold. *Item*,
I went and bought two toothpicks, whereof one
I burst, immediately, in a discourse   140
With a Dutch merchant, 'bout *ragion' del stato*.
From him, I went and paid a *moccenigo*,
For piecing my silk stockings; by the way,
I cheapened sprats; and at St Mark's, I urined'.
Faith, these are politic notes!
SIR POLITIC   Sir, I do slip   145
No action of my life, thus, but I quote it.
PEREGRINE
Believe me, it is wise!

128 *false* treacherous
131 *'Pray you* Probably, a version of 'Please', either asking Pol to finish his sentence,
     or asking him to show his papers, or asking him to forget about his papers:
     throughout the scene Jonson suggests stage-business in which Pol fumbles with
     miscellaneous documents.
133 *diary* Travellers in this period were notorious for keeping diaries filled with self-
     serious trivia.
138 *threw three beans* a superstition (drawn from Theophrastus)
141 *ragion' del stato* reasons of state, politics
142 *moccenigo* small coin
143 *piecing* mending, piecing together
144 *cheapened sprats* bargained for herring
145 *slip* allow to pass

SIR POLITIC   Nay, sir, read forth.

Act IV, Scene ii

[*Enter*] LADY WOULD-BE, NANO, SERVING-WOMEN

LADY WOULD-BE
Where should this loose knight be, trow? Sure he's housed.
NANO
Why, then he's fast.
LADY WOULD-BE   Ay, he plays both with me.
I pray you, stay. This heat will do more harm
To my complexion than his heart is worth.
I do not care to hinder, but to take him.   5
[*Rubbing her cheeks*] How it comes off!
1st WOMAN   My master's yonder.
LADY WOULD-BE   Where?
1st WOMAN
With a young gentleman.
LADY WOULD-BE   That same's the party,
In man's apparel! 'Pray you, sir, jog my knight.
I will be tender to his reputation,
However he demerit.
SIR POLITIC   My lady!
PEREGRINE   Where?   10
SIR POLITIC
'Tis she indeed, sir, you shall know her. She is,
Were she not mine, a lady of that merit,
For fashion, and behaviour; and, for beauty
I durst compare –
PEREGRINE   It seems you are not jealous,
That dare commend her.

---

1 *loose* promiscuous, wandering
  housed hidden away, presumably in a house of prostitution, maybe in the prostitute herself
2 *fast* caught, with a pun on the game of fast-and-loose, referred to at I.ii.8
5 *take him* catch him in the act
6 *How it comes off* Perspiration is making Lady Would-Be's heavy make-up run.
8 *man's apparel* Lady Would-Be's error here is partly explained by a tradition of Venetian courtesans dressing as men.
  jog nudge (to get his attention)
10 *However he demerit* Even though, or even if, he doesn't deserve it

SIR POLITIC   Nay, and for discourse –   15
PEREGRINE
  Being your wife, she cannot miss that.
SIR POLITIC [*Approaching* LADY WOULD-BE *to introduce*
    PEREGRINE] Madam,
  Here is a gentleman, 'pray you, use him fairly,
  He seems a youth, but he is –
LADY WOULD-BE   None?
SIR POLITIC   Yes, one
  Has put his face, as soon, into the world –
LADY WOULD-BE
  You mean, as early? But today?
SIR POLITIC   How's this?   20
LADY WOULD-BE
  Why, in this habit, sir: you apprehend me.
  Well, Master Would-Be, this doth not become you.
  I had thought, the odour, sir, of your good name
  Had been more precious to you; that you would not
  Have done this dire massàcre on your honour –   25
  One of your gravity, and rank, besides –
  But, knights, I see, care little for the oath
  They make to ladies; chiefly their own ladies.
SIR POLITIC
  Now, by my spurs, the symbol of my knighthood –
PEREGRINE
  [*Aside*] Lord, how his brain is humbled for an oath!   30
SIR POLITIC
  I reach you not.
LADY WOULD-BE Right, sir, your polity
  May bear it through thus. [*To* PEREGRINE] Sir, a word with
    you.
  I would be loath, to contest, publicly,
  With any gentlewoman or to seem
  Froward, or violent: as *The Courtier* says,   35

21 *habit* clothing; Lady Would-Be is sardonically suggesting that Peregrine is new in
   the world because the supposed courtesan had only newly assumed this male
   'disguise'.
26 *gravity* seriousness
30 *humbled* brought low – down to the level of his spurs, which seem to be an
   important item to Sir Pol, and probably notable in his costume
31 *reach* understand
31–2 *your polity / May bear it through* sustaining your clever bluff may spare you
   having to confess your adultery
35 *Froward* Ill-humoured, unreasonable
   The Courtier Castiglione's famous sixteenth-century courtesy manual

It comes too near rusticity, in a lady,
Which I would shun, by all means; and, however
I may deserve from Master Would-Be, yet,
To have one fair gentlewoman, thus, be made
The unkind instrument to wrong another,   40
And one she knows not; ay, and to persèver;
In my poor judgement, is not warranted
From being a solecism in our sex,
If not in manners.
PEREGRINE   How is this?
SIR POLITIC   Sweet madam,
Come nearer to your aim.
LADY WOULD-BE   Marry, and will, sir.   45
Since you provoke me, with your impudence,
And laughter of your light land-siren, here,
Your Sporus, your hermaphrodite –
PEREGRINE   What's here?
Poetic fury, and historic storms?
SIR POLITIC
The gentleman, believe it, is of worth,   50
And of our nation.
LADY WOULD-BE   Ay, your Whitefriars nation!
Come, I blush for you, Master Would-Be, I;
And am ashamed you should ha' no more forehead
Than thus to be the patron or St George
To a lewd harlot, a base fricatrice,   55

36 *rusticity* crude country-bumpkin conduct
41 *persèver* persist (in denying involvement?); accented on second syllable
42 *warranted* exempted
43 *solecism* breach of propriety (usually in grammar)
47 *light land-siren* immoral temptress
48 *Sporus* a young man whom the emperor Nero, finding him attractive, had castrated, and dressed as a woman; this recalls Volpone's attachment to Androgyno
and Castrone.
49 *Poetic fury* Peregrine plays off Plato's term for poetic inspiration (in the *Ion* dialogue).
historic Now Peregrine balances 'poetic' with the historical Sporus reference, and
perhaps plays off 'hysterical' and 'histrionic'.
51 *Whitefriars* a section of London (called a 'liberty') which was exempt from the
City's jurisdiction, and therefore became a haven for criminals and prostitutes;
Q ends this line with a question mark.
53 *forehead* sense of shame, ability to blush
54 *St George* England's patron saint was also a patron saint of Venice, and was
famous for rescuing a princess from a dragon.
55 *fricatrice* masseuse, prostitute

A female devil, in a male outside.
SIR POLITIC　　　　　　　　　　　　Nay,
And you be such a one, I must bid adieu
To your delights! The case appears too liquid.　　　[*Exit*]
LADY WOULD-BE
Ay, you may carry't clear, with your state-face!
But, for your carnival concupiscence,　　　　　　　　60
Who here is fled for liberty of conscience,
From furious persecution of the marshal,
Her will I disc'ple.
PEREGRINE　　　　　　This is fine, i' faith!
And do you use this, often? Is this part
Of your wit's exercise, 'gainst you have occasion?　　65
Madam –
LADY WOULD-BE　Go to, sir.
PEREGRINE　　　　　　　　Do you hear me, lady?
Why, if your knight have set you to beg shirts,
Or to invite me home, you might have done it
A nearer way, by far.
LADY WOULD-BE　　　　This cannot work you
Out of my snare.
PEREGRINE　　　　Why, am I in it, then?　　　　　70
Indeed, your husband told me you were fair,
And so you are; only, your nose inclines
(That side, that's next the sun) to the queen-apple.

57　*you* either Peregrine, whom Sir Pol (always looking for obscure plots) now sus-
　　pects may actually be the courtesan his wife claims, or perhaps Lady Would-Be
　　herself
58　*liquid* transparent, or perhaps hard to grasp; Sir Pol may also be punning on his
　　wife's sweat and tears ('case' often meant 'mask').
59　*state-face* calculated, dignified public demeanour
61　*liberty of conscience* religious freedom, for which Venice was famous, here
　　turned into an ironic euphemism for sexual licentiousness (playing on the pre-
　　vious reference to the Whitefriars liberty)
63　*disc'ple* discipline; in many productions, Lady Would-Be here attacks Peregrine
　　physically.
64　*use this* behave this way
65　*'gainst you have occasion* to keep your wit in practice, so it will be ready when
　　really needed; or possibly, whenever you have an opportunity
67　*beg shirts* Lady Would-Be may be tugging at Peregrine's shirt here (trying to
　　expose a courtesan's breasts?), or Peregrine may be referring to a common cover-
　　story for sexual solicitation.
69　*nearer* more direct
73　*queen-apple* large red fruit; Peregrine plays off the common idealization of 'fair'
　　(pale) complexion, which Lady Would-Be's heavy make-up has failed to sustain.

LADY WOULD-BE
  This cannot be endured, by any patience.

Act IV, Scene iii

[Enter] MOSCA

MOSCA
  What's the matter, madam?
LADY WOULD-BE   If the Senate
  Right not my quest in this, I will protest 'em,
  To all the world, no aristocracy.
MOSCA
  What is the injury, lady?
LADY WOULD-BE   Why, the callet
  You told me of, here I have ta'en disguised.   5
MOSCA
  Who? This? What means your ladyship? The creature
  I mentioned to you is apprehended, now,
  Before the Senate, you shall see her –
LADY WOULD-BE   Where?
MOSCA
  I'll bring you to her. This young gentleman,
  I saw him land, this morning, at the port.   10
LADY WOULD-BE
  Is't possible? How has my judgement wandered!
  Sir, I must, blushing, say to you, I have erred;
  And plead your pardon.
PEREGRINE   What, more changes, yet?
LADY WOULD-BE
  I hope y' ha' not the malice to remember
  A gentlewoman's passion. If you stay   15
  In Venice here, please you to use me, sir –
MOSCA
  Will you go, madam?
LADY WOULD-BE   'Pray you, sir, use me. In faith,
  The more you use me the more I shall conceive
  You have forgot our quarrel.

---

  2 *Right not ... protest 'em* Does not enforce my complaint against this courtesan,
    I will proclaim that they are; Machiavelli argued that the leading Venetians were
    not truly aristocrats, since they were merchants.
  4 *callet* prostitute
  16 *use me* let me be helpful, find me useful; but the common sense of sexual use
    comes through strongly, especially in conjunction with 'conceive' in the next line.

[*Exeunt* LADY WOULD-BE, SERVING-WOMEN,
MOSCA, NANO]

PEREGRINE   This is rare!
Sir Politic Would-Be? No, Sir Politic Bawd!   20
To bring me, thus, acquainted with his wife!
Well, wise Sir Pol: since you have practised, thus,
Upon my freshmanship, I will try your salt-head,
What proof it is against a counter-plot.   [*Exit*]

Act IV, Scene iv

[*Enter*] VOLTORE, CORBACCIO, CORVINO, MOSCA

VOLTORE
Well, now you know the carriage of the business,
Your constancy is all that is required
Unto the safety of it.
MOSCA   Is the lie
Safely conveyed amongst us? Is that sure?
Knows every man his burden?
CORVINO   Yes.
MOSCA   Then, shrink not.   5
CORVINO
[*Taking* MOSCA *aside*] But, knows the advocate the truth?
MOSCA   O, sir,
By no means. I devised a formal tale,
That salved your reputation. But, be valiant, sir.
CORVINO
I fear no one but him: that this his pleading
Should make him stand for a co-heir –

21 *acquainted* Since Peregrine suspects Sir Pol of being a wittol who abets his wife's
    adulteries, there may be a pun here on 'quaint', Jacobean slang for a woman's
    genitalia.
22–4 *practised ... proof it is* plotted thus to take advantage of my inexperience here,
    I'll test how well your more seasoned mind can defend you
1 *the carriage* the management, how to carry it off
5 *burden* the refrain of a song; hence, his part in the group performance
7 *formal tale* elaborate fiction (to conceal Corvino's attempt to prostitute his wife
    – a thematic connection to the Would-Be scene that just ended)

MOSCA   Co-halter.   10
  Hang him: we will but use his tongue, his noise,
  As we do Croaker's here.
CORVINO   Ay, what shall he do?
MOSCA
  When we have done, you mean?
CORVINO   Yes.
MOSCA   Why, we'll think:
  Sell him for mummia, he's half dust already.
  (*To* VOLTORE) Do not you smile, to see this buffalo,   15
  How he does sport it with his head? [*To himself*] I should
  If all were well, and past. (*To* CORBACCIO) Sir, only you
  Are he that shall enjoy the crop of all,
  And these not know for whom they toil.
CORBACCIO   Ay, peace.
MOSCA
  (*To* CORVINO) But you shall eat it. [*To himself*] Much! (*To*
     VOLTORE) Worshipful sir,   20
  Mercury sit upon your thund'ring tongue,
  Or the French Hercules, and make your language
  As conquering as his club, to beat along,
  As with a tempest, flat, our adversaries;
  But, much more, yours, sir.
VOLTORE   Here they come, ha' done.   25
MOSCA
  I have another witness, if you need, sir,
  I can produce.

---

12 *Croaker* Corbaccio, whose voice may have been crow-like
14 *mummia* a supposedly medicinal substance derived from preserved corpses
15 *buffalo* Mosca is now confiding in Voltore instead, joking about the cuckold's
    horns Corvino has earned.
20 *Much!* Probably an ironic exclamation, like the sarcastic, 'that's likely' or 'fat
    chance'; Mosca may be speaking to Voltore to assure him that the previous
    assurances to Corvino and Corbaccio were merely ploys. Mosca's handling of
    these three rival suitors in the same room at the same time is a bravura juggling
    act.
21 *Mercury* the god of eloquence, but also associated with thievery
22 *French Hercules* Late in life Hercules was believed to have fathered the Celts in
    Gaul, and to have compensated for his lost physical strength with oratorical
    powers.
25 *yours* your adversaries
    ha' done stop, be quiet

VOLTORE   Who is it?
MOSCA   Sir, I have her.

Act IV, Scene v

[*Enter*] *four* AVOCATORI, BONARIO, CELIA, NOTARIO,
                    COMMANDATORI

1st AVOCATORE
  The like of this the Senate never heard of.
2nd AVOCATORE
  'Twill come most strange to them, when we report it.
4th AVOCATORE
  The gentlewoman has been ever held
  Of unreprovèd name.
3rd AVOCATORE   So has the youth.
4th AVOCATORE
  The more unnatural part that of his father.   5
2nd AVOCATORE
  More of the husband.
1st AVOCATORE   I not know to give
  His act a name, it is so monstrous!
4th AVOCATORE
  But the impostor, he is a thing created
  T' exceed example!
1st AVOCATORE   And all after-times!
2nd AVOCATORE
  I never heard a true voluptuary   10
  Described but him.
3rd AVOCATORE   Appear yet those were cited?
NOTARIO
  All but the old *magnifico*, Volpone.
1st AVOCATORE
  Why is not he here?
MOSCA   Please your fatherhoods,
  Here is his advocate. Himself's so weak,
  So feeble –

---

27 *her* Lady Would-Be
 9 *example* precedent
11 *cited* subpoenaed, summoned
12 *magnifico* nobleman
13 *fatherhoods* As Kernan points out, this is not only a technically correct form of
    address, but also a rhetorically advantageous one, since it inclines the judges to
    side with the father Corbaccio.

4th AVOCATORE What are you?
BONARIO   His parasite,   15
  His knave, his pander! I beseech the court
  He may be forced to come, that your grave eyes
  May bear strong witness of his strange impostures.
VOLTORE
  Upon my faith, and credit with your virtues,
  He is not able to endure the air.   20
2nd AVOCATORE
  Bring him, however.
3rd AVOCATORE   We will see him.
4th AVOCATORE   Fetch him.

                         [*Exit* COMMANDATORE]

VOLTORE
  Your fatherhoods' fit pleasures be obeyed,
  But sure, the sight will rather move your pities,
  Than indignation. May it please the court,
  In the meantime, he may be heard in me;   25
  I know this place most void of prejudice,
  And therefore crave it, since we have no reason
  To fear our truth should hurt our cause.
3rd AVOCATORE   Speak free.
VOLTORE
  Then know, most honoured fathers, I must now
  Discover, to your strangely abused ears,   30
  The most prodigious, and most frontless piece
  Of solid impudence, and treachery,
  That ever vicious nature yet brought forth
  To shame the state of Venice. This lewd woman, [*Pointing
    to* CELIA]
  That wants no artificial looks, or tears,   35
  To help the visor, she has now put on,
  Hath long been known a close adulteress,
  To that lascivious youth there [*Pointing to* BONARIO]; not
    suspected,
  I say, but known; and taken, in the act;
  With him; and by this man [*Pointing to* CORVINO], the easy   40
    husband,

31 *frontless* shameless
35 *wants* lacks
36 *visor* mask; either Celia has now modestly masked herself, or Voltore is imply-
    ing that her appearance of anguished innocence is merely a disguise.
37 *close* secret
40 *easy* lenient

Pardoned; whose timeless bounty makes him, now,
Stand here, the most unhappy, innocent person
That ever man's own virtue made accused.
For these, not knowing how to owe a gift
Of that dear grace but with their shame, being placed   45
So above all powers of their gratitude,
Began to hate the benefit; and, in place
Of thanks, devise t' extirp the memory
Of such an act. Wherein, I pray your fatherhoods,
To observe the malice, yea, the rage of creatures   50
Discovered in their evils; and what heart
Such take, even from their crimes. But that, anon,
Will more appear. This gentleman [*Pointing to* CORBACCIO],
    the father,
Hearing of this foul fact, with many others,
Which daily struck at his too tender ears,   55
And, grieved in nothing more than that he could not
Preserve himself a parent (his son's ills
Growing to that strange flood), at last decreed
To disinherit him.

1st AVOCATORE   These be strange turns!

2nd AVOCATORE
The young man's fame was ever fair and honest.   60

VOLTORE
So much more full of danger is his vice,
That can beguile so, under shade of virtue.
But as I said, my honoured sires, his father
Having this settled purpose – by what means
To him betrayed, we know not – and this day   65
Appointed for the deed, that parricide
(I cannot style him better), by confederacy
Preparing this his paramour to be there,
Entered Volpone's house – who was the man
Your fatherhoods must understand, designed   70
For the inheritance – there, sought his father.
But, with what purpose sought he him, my sires?
I tremble to pronounce it, that a son
Unto a father, and to such a father,

44–7 *For these ... benefit* Celia and Bonario do not know how to respond to such
    generosity except by feeling shamed, since it goes beyond their sadly limited
    capacity for gratitude, and so they began to resent the gift
48 *extirp* eradicate
51 *heart* audacity, encouragement
65 *To him betrayed* Revealed to Bonario
70 *designed* designated, intended

Should have so foul, felonious intent: 75
It was, to murder him. When, being prevented
By his more happy absence, what then did he?
Not check his wicked thoughts; no, now new deeds –
Mischief doth ever end, where it begins –
An act of horror, fathers! He dragged forth   80
The agèd gentleman, that had there lain, bed-rid,
Three years and more, out off his innocent couch,
Naked upon the floor, there left him; wounded
His servant in the face; and, with this strumpet,
The stale to his forged practice, who was glad   85
To be so active (I shall here desire
Your fatherhoods to note but my collections,
As most remarkable), thought at once to stop
His father's ends; discredit his free choice
In the old gentleman; redeem themselves,   90
By laying infamy upon this man
To whom, with blushing, they should owe their lives.

1st AVOCATORE
  What proofs have you of this?
BONARIO   Most honoured fathers,
  I humbly crave there be no credit given
  To this man's mercenary tongue.
2nd AVOCATORE   Forbear.   95
BONARIO
  His soul moves in his fee.
3rd AVOCATORE   O, sir.
BONARIO   This fellow,
  For six sols more, would plead against his Maker.
1st AVOCATORE
  You do forget yourself.
VOLTORE   Nay, nay, grave fathers,
  Let him have scope: can any man imagine
  That he will spare 's accuser, that would not   100
  Have spared his parent?

---

77 *his more happy* Corbaccio's fortunate
85 *The stale ... practice* The prostitute used as a lure for his deceptive plot
87 *collections* conclusions, inferences
89 *ends* intentions
90 *the old gentleman* Volpone, whom Corbaccio had chosen as his heir
91 *this man* Corvino
97 *sols* low-value French coins

1st AVOCATORE	Well, produce your proofs.

CELIA
I would I could forget I were a creature.
VOLTORE
Signior Corbaccio.
4th AVOCATORE   What is he?
VOLTORE   The father.
2nd AVOCATORE
Has he had an oath?
NOTARIO   Yes.
CORBACCIO   What must I do now?
NOTARIO
Your testimony's craved.
CORBACCIO   Speak to the knave?   105
I'll ha' my mouth, first, stopped with earth! My heart
Abhors his knowledge; I disclaim in him.
1st AVOCATORE
But, for what cause?
CORBACCIO   The mere portent of nature.
He is an utter stranger to my loins.
BONARIO
Have they made you to this?
CORBACCIO   I will not hear thee,   110
Monster of men, swine, goat, wolf, parricide;
Speak not, thou viper.
BONARIO   Sir, I will sit down,
And rather wish my innocence should suffer,
Than I resist the authority of a father.
VOLTORE
Signior Corvino.
2nd AVOCATORE   This is strange!
1st AVOCATORE   Who's this?   115
NOTARIO
The husband.

---

102 *I would ... creature* I wish I could forget that I am created by God (so I could
    choose suicide), or, I wish I could separate myself totally from these beasts
105 *Speak to the knave?* The half-deaf Corbaccio has misheard the Notario's
    response.
107 *Abhors his knowledge* Hates to acknowledge him, or, Hates even to think about
    him
108 *The mere portent* An absolute freak; unnatural births were considered porten-
    tous, and Corbaccio is distancing himself from his natural fatherhood of
    Bonario.
110 *made you* forced you, or, put you up

4th AVOCATORE Is he sworn?

NOTARIO   He is.

3rd AVOCATORE   Speak, then.

CORVINO

    This woman, please your fatherhoods, is a whore,

    Of most hot exercise, more than a partridge,

    Upon recòrd –

1st AVOCATORE No more.

CORVINO   Neighs like a jennet.

NOTARIO

    Preserve the honour of the court.

CORVINO   I shall,   120

    And modesty of your most reverend ears.

    And yet I hope that I may say, these eyes

    Have seen her glued unto that piece of cedar,

    That fine well-timbered gallant; and that, here, [*Pointing to

      his forehead*]

    The letters may be read, thorough the horn,   125

    That make the story perfect.

MOSCA   [*Aside to* CORVINO] Excellent, sir!

CORVINO

    [*Aside to* MOSCA] There is no shame in this, now, is there?

MOSCA   [*Aside to* CORVINO] None.

CORVINO

    Or if I said, I hoped that she were onward

    To her damnation, if there be a hell

    Greater than whore, and woman: a good Catholic   130

    May make the doubt.

---

118 *partridge* nature's most lecherous creature, according to Pliny's *Natural History*

119 *Upon recòrd* A recorded fact

    jennet small, lively Spanish horse

124 *well-timbered gallant* well-built young man (Bonario)

124–6 *here ... perfect* here on my forehead is legible the letter V that makes the shape of cuckold's horns – or maybe the word 'cuckold' that can be read through the transparent horn that covered the printed sheets on which Elizabethan schoolchildren were taught their letters – that completes the story of my betrayal

127 *There is ... None* Corvino wants reassurance that he has not humiliated himself by claiming to have been cuckolded; Mosca's gives the desired answer, but (by changing Q's 'harm' to F's 'shame' here) Jonson allows him a sly implication that Corvino's performance was shameless.

128 *onward* well on her way

131 *make the doubt* suspect that women and whores are themselves hell; Jonson was apparently no longer a Catholic at the time of F, allowing him to replace Q's 'a good Christian' with a more pointed implication about Catholicism's powerful ambivalence toward women.

3rd AVOCATORE   His grief hath made him frantic.
1st AVOCATORE
  Remove him, hence.

[CELIA] swoons

2nd AVOCATORE   Look to the woman.
CORVINO   Rare!
  Prettily feigned! Again!
4th AVOCATORE   Stand from about her.
1st AVOCATORE
  Give her the air.
3rd AVOCATORE [To MOSCA] What can you say?
MOSCA   My wound,
  May it please your wisdoms, speaks for me, received   135
  In aid of my good patron, when he missed
  His sought-for father, when that well-taught dame
  Had her cue given her, to cry out a rape.
BONARIO
  O, most laid impudence! Fathers –
3rd AVOCATORE   Sir, be silent,
  You had your hearing free, so must they theirs.   140
2nd AVOCATORE
  I do begin to doubt th' imposture, here.
4th AVOCATORE
  This woman has too many moods.
VOLTORE   Grave fathers,
  She is a creature of a most professed
  And prostituted lewdness.
CORVINO   Most impetuous!
  Unsatisfied, grave fathers!
VOLTORE   May her feignings   145
  Not take your wisdoms; but this day, she baited
  A stranger, a grave knight, with her loose eyes,
  And more lascivious kisses. This man saw them
  Together, on the water, in a gondola.
MOSCA
  Here is the lady herself, that saw 'em too,   150
  Without; who then had in the open streets
  Pursued them, but for saving her knight's honour.

<hr>

136 *he* Bonario
139 *most laid* deeply plotted
141 *doubt th' imposture* suspect fraud by Celia and Bonario
146 *take* take in, deceive, charm
    but this day this very day
151 *Without* Outside

1st AVOCATORE
  Produce that lady.
2nd AVOCATORE   Let her come.

                              [*Exit* MOSCA]

4th AVOCATORE   These things,
  They strike with wonder!
3rd AVOCATORE   I am turned a stone!

Act IV, Scene vi

[*Enter*] MOSCA [*with*] LADY WOULD-BE

MOSCA
  Be resolute, Madam.
LADY WOULD-BE [*Pointing at* CELIA] Ay, this same is she.
  Out, thou chameleon harlot; now thine eyes
  Vie tears with the hyena. Dar'st thou look
  Upon my wrongèd face? [*To the* AVOCATORI] I cry your
    pardons.
  I fear I have, forgettingly, transgressed   5
  Against the dignity of the court –
2nd AVOCATORE   No, madam.
LADY WOULD-BE
  And been exorbitant –
2nd AVOCATORE   You have not, lady.
4th AVOCATORE
  These proofs are strong.

2 *chameleon* creature famous for its changing camouflage; Lady Would-Be now
   assumes that Celia was the woman disguised as a man she heard was accompanying her husband.
3 *hyena* Lady Would-Be confuses the hyena, which was thought to capture people
   by imitating a human voice, with the crocodile, which was thought to use unfelt
   tears for the same purpose; in fact, in her make-up and shifting stories, her
   destructive voice and eagerness to feed on Volpone's moribund flesh, she herself
   becomes both chameleon and hyena, extending Jonson's fable of human beings
   who degrade themselves into beasts.
7 *exorbitant* excessive or disorderly
   s.p. *2nd* AVOCATORE Both parts of the reply are given to the 4th Avocatore by Q
   and F, but with separate speech headings, so this edition (like others) follows F3
   (Jonson's 1692 *Works*) in giving the first part to the 2nd Avocatore; in any case,
   the judges (like Volpone earlier) seem desperate throughout the scene to forestall,
   by futile interruptions, any long explanations from Lady Would-Be.

LADY WOULD-BE   Surely, I had no purpose,
  To scandalise your honours, or my sex's.
3rd AVOCATORE
  We do believe it.
LADY WOULD-BE   Surely, you may believe it.   10
2nd AVOCATORE
  Madam, we do.
LADY WOULD-BE   Indeed, you may: my breeding
  Is not so coarse –
4th AVOCATORE   We know it.
LADY WOULD-BE   To offend
  With pertinacy –
3rd AVOCATORE   Lady.
LADY WOULD-BE   Such a presence;
  No, surely.
1st AVOCATORE   We well think it.
LADY WOULD-BE   You may think it.
1st AVOCATORE
  Let her o'ercome. [To CELIA and BONARIO] What witnesses
    have you,   15
  To make good your report?
BONARIO   Our consciences.
CELIA
  And heaven, that never fails the innocent.
4th AVOCATORE
  These are no testimonies.
BONARIO   Not in your courts,
  Where multitude and clamour overcomes.
1st AVOCATORE
  Nay, then you do wax insolent.

             VOLPONE *is brought in, as impotent*

VOLTORE   Here, here,   20
  The testimony comes, that will convince,
  And put to utter dumbness, their bold tongues.
  See here, grave fathers, here is the ravisher,
  The rider on men's wives, the great impostor,

---

13 *pertinacy* pertinacity, stubborness; or possibly Lady Would-Be's mistake for
   'impertinence'
15 *o'ercome* conquer – either by believing her testimony against Celia, or by letting
   her characteristic verbal persistence grant her the last word in the exchange of
   courteous remarks
19 *multitude and clamour* the larger number of witnesses, and louder ones
20 s.d. *as impotent* seemingly devoid of bodily strength; Volpone is presumably
   carried in draped on a litter or stretcher

The grand voluptuary! Do you not think,   25
These limbs should affect venery? or these eyes
Covet a concubine? 'Pray you, mark these hands:
Are they not fit to stroke a lady's breasts?
Perhaps, he doth dissemble.

BONARIO   So he does.

VOLTORE
Would you have him tortured?

BONARIO   I would have him proved.   30

VOLTORE
Best try him, then, with goads, or burning irons;
Put him to the *strappado*! I have heard,
The rack hath cured the gout: 'faith, give it him,
And help him of a malady, be courteous.
I will undertake, before these honoured fathers,   35
He shall have, yet, as many left diseases,
As she has known adulterers, or thou strumpets.
O, my most equal hearers, if these deeds –
Acts of this bold and most exorbitant strain –
May pass with sufferance, what one citizen   40
But owes the forfeit of his life, yea, fame,
To him that dares traduce him? Which of you
Are safe, my honoured fathers? I would ask,
With leave of your grave fatherhoods, if their plot
Have any face, or colour like to truth?   45
Or if, unto the dullest nostril here,
It smell not rank, and most abhorrèd slander?
I crave your care of this good gentleman,
Whose life is much endangered by their fable;
And, as for them, I will conclude with this: 50
That vicious persons when they are hot, and fleshed

26 *affect venery* pursue sexual pleasure
30 *proved* tested
32 *strappado* hoisting prisoners by a rope tied to their wrists behind their back and then dropping them; all these forms of torture were practised by the Venetian republic.
34 *help* relieve
38 *equal* fair-minded
39 *strain* type
40–42 *May pass ... traduce him?* May occur and be tolerated, can any citizen defend his life or even his reputation against anyone who has the nerve to slander him?
44 *leave* permission
45 *face, or colour* resemblance; but the irony is that Voltore's own case consists entirely of face (surface and shamelessness) and colour (rhetorical devices)
51 *fleshed* initiated (as in the passion of a hunt)

In impious acts, their constancy abounds:
Damned deeds are done with greatest confidence.
1st AVOCATORE
Take 'em to custody, and sever them.

    [CELIA *and* BONARIO *are led out separately*]

2nd AVOCATORE
'Tis pity two such prodigies should live.   55
1st AVOCATORE
Let the old gentleman be returned, with care;
I'm sorry, our credulity wronged him.

    [VOLPONE *is carried out*]

4th AVOCATORE
These are two creatures!
3rd AVOCATORE   I have an earthquake in me!
2nd AVOCATORE
Their shame, even in their cradles, fled their faces.
4th AVOCATORE
[*To* VOLTORE] You've done a worthy service to the state, sir,   60
In their discovery.
1st AVOCATORE   You shall hear, ere night,
What punishment the court decrees upon 'em.
VOLTORE
We thank your fatherhoods.

    [*Exeunt* AVOCATORI, NOTARIO, *and all other* OFFICIALS]

                How like you it?
MOSCA   Rare.
I'd ha' your tongue, sir, tipped with gold, for this;
I'd ha' you be the heir to the whole city;   65
The earth I'd have want men, ere you want living!
They're bound to erect your statue, in St Mark's.
Signior Corvino, I would have you go
And show yourself, that you have conquered.
CORVINO   Yes.
MOSCA
It was much better that you should profess   70

---

52 *constancy* resolution
54 *sever them* keep them separate
55 *prodigies* ominous monsters
63 *Rare* Unusually good; Jonson's tombstone reads simply, 'O Rare Ben Jonson'
66 *The earth ... living* I would rather have the earth lack human beings than have
    you lack a lawyer's livelihood

Yourself a cuckold, thus, than that the other
Should have been proved.
CORVINO   Nay, I considered that:
 Now, it is her fault:
MOSCA   Then, it had been yours.
CORVINO
 True. I do doubt this advocate, still.
MOSCA   I' faith,
 You need not, I dare ease you of that care.   75
CORVINO
 I trust thee, Mosca.
MOSCA   As your own soul, sir.

                                    [*Exit* CORVINO]

CORBACCIO   Mosca.
MOSCA
 Now for your business, sir.
CORBACCIO   How? Ha' you business?
MOSCA
 Yes, yours, sir.
CORBACCIO   O, none else?
MOSCA   None else, not I.
CORBACCIO
 Be careful, then.
MOSCA   Rest you, with both your eyes, sir.
CORBACCIO
 Dispatch it.
MOSCA   Instantly.
CORBACCIO   And look that all,   80
 Whatever, be put in: jewels, plate, moneys,
 Household stuff, bedding, curtains.
MOSCA   Curtain-rings, sir.
 Only, the advocate's fee must be deducted.
CORBACCIO
 I'll pay him now: you'll be too prodigal.
MOSCA
 Sir, I must tender it.
CORBACCIO   Two chequins is well?   85
MOSCA
 No, six, sir.

71 *the other* that Corvino had deliberately prostituted his own wife
74 *I do ... still* I still don't trust this lawyer Voltore
79 *Rest ... eyes* Relax completely
80 *Dispatch it* Quickly begin an inventory of Volpone's property
85 *tender* give

CORBACCIO   'Tis too much.
MOSCA   He talked a great while;
  You must consider that, sir.
CORBACCIO [*Giving* MOSCA *coins*] Well, there's three –
MOSCA
  I'll give it him.
CORBACCIO   Do so, and there's for thee.
                   [*Gives* MOSCA *a small tip and exits*]

MOSCA
  Bountiful bones! What horrid strange offence
  Did he commit 'gainst nature, in his youth,   90
  Worthy this age? [*To* VOLTORE] You see, sir, how I work
  Unto your ends; take you no notice.
VOLTORE   No,
  I'll leave you.
MOSCA   All is yours –

                       [*Exit* VOLTORE]

           the devil and all,
  Good advocate. [*To* LADY WOULD-BE] Madam, I'll bring
    you home.
LADY WOULD-BE
  No, I'll go see your patron.
MOSCA   That you shall not.   95
  I'll tell you why. My purpose is, to urge
  My patron to reform his will; and, for
  The zeal you've shown today, whereas before
  You were but third or fourth, you shall be now
  Put in the first; which would appear as begged,   100
  If you be present. Therefore –
LADY WOULD-BE   You shall sway me.

                    [*Exeunt*]

---

89 *Bountiful bones* A sarcastic exclamation associating Corbaccio's stinginess with
    his shrunken, skeletal physique; the connection between moral and physical con-
    dition is important throughout the play.
91 *Worthy this age* To have earned such an ugly old age
92 *take you no notice* don't worry that I seem to be conspiring with your rivals, or,
    don't acknowledge what I am doing for or saying to you (because Lady Would-
    Be is still present)
101 *sway* persuade, perhaps (as often with Lady Would-Be) with a secondary sexual
    meaning

Act V, Scene i

[*Enter*] VOLPONE

VOLPONE
Well, I am here; and all this brunt is past!
I ne'er was in dislike with my disguise,
Till this fled moment: here, 'twas good, in private,
But in your public – *cavè*, whilst I breathe.
'Fore God, my left leg 'gan to have the cramp;   5
And I appre'nded, straight, some power had struck me
With a dead palsy! Well, I must be merry,
And shake it off. A many of these fears
Would put me into some villainous disease,
Should they come thick upon me: I'll prevent 'em.   10
Give me a bowl of lusty wine, to fright
This humour from my heart – hum, hum, hum; (*He drinks*)
'Tis almost gone already: I shall conquer.
Any device, now, of rare, ingenious knavery,
That would possess me with a violent laughter,   15
Would make me up, again! So, so, so, so. (*Drinks again*)
This heat is life; 'tis blood, by this time! Mosca!

Act V, Scene ii

[*Enter*] MOSCA

MOSCA
How now, sir? Does the day look clear again?
Are we recovered? And wrought out of error,
Into our way? To see our path before us?
Is our trade free once more?
VOLPONE   Exquisite Mosca!
MOSCA
Was it not carried learnèdly?

---

  1 *brunt* stress, attack, crisis
  3 *fled* past
  4 *cavè* beware; Volpone is warning the audience, himself, or an attendant to make
    sure he isn't seen standing up.
  6 *appre'nded, straight* thought immediately
  7 *dead palsy* total paralysis; Jonson suffered some kind of palsy later in life.
 16 s.d. *Drinks again* Some productions emphasize Volpone's over-indulgence here to
    explain his rash decision to play dead; Tilley, F651, records 'foxed' as a
    euphemism for 'drunk' (Parker).

VOLPONE   And stoutly.   5
  Good wits are greatest in extremities.
MOSCA
  It were a folly, beyond thought, to trust
  Any grand act unto a cowardly spirit.
  You are not taken with it enough, methinks?
VOLPONE
  O, more than if I had enjoyed the wench!   10
  The pleasure of all womankind's not like it.
MOSCA
  Why, now you speak, sir. We must here be fixed;
  Here, we must rest; this is our masterpiece;
  We cannot think to go beyond this.
VOLPONE   True,
  Thou hast played thy prize, my precious Mosca.
MOSCA   Nay sir,   15
  To gull the court –
VOLPONE   And quite divert the torrent
  Upon the innocent.
MOSCA   Yes, and to make
  So rare a music out of discords –
VOLPONE   Right.
  That, yet, to me's the strangest! How thou'st borne it!
  That these, being so divided 'mongst themselves,   20
  Should not scent somewhat, or in me, or thee,
  Or doubt their own side.
MOSCA   True. They will not see it:
  Too much light blinds them, I think; each of 'em
  Is so possessed, and stuffed with his own hopes,
  That anything unto the contrary,   25
  Never so true, or never so apparent,
  Never so palpable, they will resist it –
VOLPONE
  Like a temptation of the devil.

  7 *beyond thought* unthinkable
  9 *taken* pleased
 15 *prize* masterpiece; but Mosca may have another prize in view.
 16 *gull* trick, make fools of (as in 'gullible')
 18 *discords* the conflicting testimonies, and/or the feuding rival heirs
 19 *borne* managed
 23 *light* hope, perhaps with a gesture toward the gleaming treasure, as in the play's
    opening line
 24 *possessed* The word (like much about Mosca) hovers between material and
    demonic possessions.

MOSCA   Right, sir.
Merchants may talk of trade, and your great signiors
Of land that yields well; but if Italy   30
Have any glebe more fruitful than these fellows,
I am deceived. Did not your advocate rare?

VOLPONE
[*Mimicking* VOLTORE] 'O, my most honoured fathers, my
    grave fathers,
Under correction of your fatherhoods,
What face of truth is, here? If these strange deeds   35
May pass, most honoured fathers' – I had much ado
To forbear laughing.

MOSCA   'T seemed to me, you sweat, sir.

VOLPONE
In troth, I did a little.

MOSCA   But confess, sir,
Were you not daunted?

VOLPONE   In good faith, I was
A little in a mist; but not dejected;   40
Never, but still myself.

MOSCA   I think it, sir.
Now (so truth help me) I must needs say this, sir,
And, out of conscience, for your advocate:
He's taken pains, in faith, sir, and deserved,
In my poor judgement (I speak it, under favour,   45
Not to contrary you, sir), very richly –
Well – to be cozened.

VOLPONE   Troth, and I think so too,
By that I heard him in the latter end.

MOSCA
O, but before, sir; had you heard him, first,
Draw it to certain heads, then aggravate,   50
Then use his vehement figures – I looked still,
When he would shift a shirt; and, doing this
Out of pure love, no hope of gain –

31 *glebe* agricultural field
32 *rare* extremely well
45 *under favour* with your permission; Mosca may be parodying the lawyer
    Voltore's obsequious grandiloquence here.
47 *cozened* cheated
48 *By that I heard him* Judging by what I heard him say
50 *Draw ... aggravate* Gather his arguments into specific topics, then emphasize
51 *figures* rhetorical tropes (figures of speech), or gestures
51-2 *I looked ... shirt* I kept expecting him to change his clothing (because his
    extreme efforts must have made him sweat)

VOLPONE   'Tis right.
  I cannot answer him, Mosca, as I would,
  Not yet; but, for thy sake, at thy entreaty,   55
  I will begin, even now, to vex 'em all;
  This very instant.
MOSCA   Good, sir.
VOLPONE   Call the dwarf
  And eunuch forth.
MOSCA   Castrone, Nano.

          [*Enter* CASTRONE, NANO]

NANO   Here.
VOLPONE
  Shall we have a jig now?
MOSCA   What you please, sir.
VOLPONE   Go,
  Straight, give out, about the streets, you two,   60
  That I am dead; do it, with constancy,
  Sadly, do you hear? Impute it to the grief
  Of this late slander.

          [*Exeunt* CASTRONE, NANO]

MOSCA   What do you mean, sir?
VOLPONE   O,
  I shall have, instantly, my vulture, crow,
  Raven, come flying hither, on the news,   65
  To peck for carrion; my she-wolf, and all,
  Greedy, and full of expectation –
MOSCA
  And then, to have it ravished from their mouths?
VOLPONE
  'Tis true, I will ha' thee put on a gown,
  And take upon thee as thou wert mine heir;   70
  Show 'em a will. Open that chest, and reach
  Forth one of those, that has the blanks. I'll straight
  Put in thy name.

---

54 *answer* repay
59 *jig* a lively dance, often performed at the end of an Elizabethan play; but Volpone
   seems to be using it as a metaphor for the final satiric dance of death he intends
   to choreograph for the legacy-hunters.
60 *Straight ... about* Immediately report throughout
61 *with constancy* with conviction and straight faces
63 *mean* intend
70 *take upon thee as* act as if

MOSCA   It will be rare, sir.
VOLPONE   Aye,
  When they e'en gape, and find themselves deluded –
MOSCA
  Yes.
VOLPONE And thou use them scurvily. Dispatch,   75
  Get on thy gown.
MOSCA   But, what, sir, if they ask
  After the body?
VOLPONE   Say, it was corrupted.
MOSCA
  I'll say it stunk, sir; and was fain t' have it
  Coffined up instantly, and sent away.
VOLPONE
  Anything, what thou wilt. Hold, here's my will.   80
  Get thee a cap, a count-book, pen and ink,
  Papers afore thee; sit, as thou wert taking
  An inventory of parcels. I'll get up,
  Behind the curtain, on a stool, and hearken;
  Sometime, peep over; see, how they do look;   85
  With what degrees, their blood doth leave their faces!
  O, 'twill afford me a rare meal of laughter.
MOSCA
  Your advocate will turn stark dull upon it.
VOLPONE
  It will take off his oratory's edge.
MOSCA
  But your *clarissimo*, old round-back, he   90
  Will crump you, like a hog-louse, with the touch.
VOLPONE
  And what Corvino?
MOSCA   O, sir, look for him,
  Tomorrow morning, with a rope, and a dagger,
  To visit all the streets: he must run mad.
  My lady too, that came into the court,   95

---

78 *fain* eager, compelled
81 *count-book* account-book, financial ledger
88 *turn stark dull* be struck dumb; Volpone's reply puns on another meaning of
    'dull'.
90 *clarissimo* high-ranking Venetian
90–1 *old round-back ... touch* Corbaccio, who evidently stoops with age, will curl
    (or crumple) up like a wood-louse (pill-bug) from the impact of this development
93 *rope, dagger* These were standard symbols of suicidal madness, ones Jonson
    would have used as props when he played the grieving Hieronimo in Kyd's
    Spanish Tragedy.

To bear false witness for your worship.
VOLPONE   Yes,
And kissed me 'fore the fathers; when my face
Flowed all with oils.
MOSCA   And sweat – sir. Why, your gold
Is such another med'cine, it dries up
All those offensive savours! It transforms   100
The most deformèd, and restores 'em lovely,
As 'twere the strange poetical girdle. Jove
Could not invent, t' himself, a shroud more subtle,
To pass Acrisius' guards. It is the thing
Makes all the world her grace, her youth, her beauty.   105
VOLPONE
I think she loves me.
MOSCA   Who? The lady, sir?
She is jealous of you.
VOLPONE   Dost thou say so?

                              [*A knock at the door*]

MOSCA   Hark,
There's some already.
VOLPONE   Look.
MOSCA   It is the vulture:
He has the quickest scent.
VOLPONE   I'll to my place,
Thou, to thy posture.
MOSCA   I'm set.
VOLPONE   But, Mosca,   110
Play the artificer now, torture 'em, rarely.

---

98 *And sweat – sir* Mosca needles Volpone with a reminder that he was panicked,
   not just performing, at the trial; the dash may suggest a pause before reverting
   to deference with 'sir'.

99 *such another* so great a

102 *girdle* F inserts '*Cestus*' in the margin at the end of this line, probably to clarify
    the reference to Venus's girdle of that name, which is capable (according to
    Homer's *Iliad*, XIV) of transforming ugliness to beauty and reviving passion in
    the aged.

104 *Acrisius* the father of Danae, who locked her in a brazen tower to forestall a
    prophecy that her son would kill him; but Jove descended on her in a shower of
    gold and impregnated her with Perseus

106 *The lady* Perhaps Lady Would-Be, and some commentators suggest Celia, but
    the previous lines feminize the gold itself, which is the thing Volpone seeks love
    from, and which proves to be his jealous god.

110 *posture* pose, imposture

111 *Play the artificer* Perform craftily and elaborately

Act V, Scene iii

[*Enter* VOLTORE]

VOLTORE
  How now, my Mosca?
MOSCA   Turkey carpets, nine –
VOLTORE
  Taking an inventory? That is well.
MOSCA
  Two suits of bedding, tissue –
VOLTORE   Where's the will?
  Let me read that, the while.

[CORBACCIO *is carried in*]

CORBACCIO   So, set me down;
  And get you home.

                    [*Exeunt* Chair-Bearers]

VOLTORE   Is he come, now, to trouble us?   5
MOSCA
  Of cloth of gold, two more –
CORBACCIO   Is it done, Mosca?
MOSCA
  Of several vellets, eight –
VOLTORE   I like his care.
CORBACCIO
  Dost thou not hear?

[*Enter* CORVINO]

CORVINO   Ha? Is the hour come, Mosca?

VOLPONE *peeps from behind a traverse*

VOLPONE
  Ay, now they muster.
CORVINO   What does the advocate here?
  Or this Corbaccio?

---

1 *Turkey carpets* imported through Italy, and used as table covers or wall hangings
3 *suits of bedding* sets of bed covers in expensive fabrics
  tissue cloth with silver or gold
4 *the while* while you are completing the inventory
7 *several vellets* separate velvet hangings

CORBACCIO   What do these here?

[*Enter* LADY WOULD-BE]

LADY WOULD-BE   Mosca?   10
  Is his thread spun?
MOSCA   Eight chests of linen –
VOLPONE   O,
  My fine Dame Would-Be, too!
CORVINO   Mosca, the will,
  That I may show it these, and rid 'em hence.
MOSCA
  Six chests of diaper, four of damask – There. [*Points to
    papers on a table*]
CORBACCIO
  Is that the will?
MOSCA   Down-beds, and bolsters –
VOLPONE   Rare!   15
  Be busy still. Now they begin to flutter;
  They never think of me. Look, see, see, see!
  How their swift eyes run over the long deed,
  Unto the name, and to the legacies,
  What is bequeathed them there –
MOSCA   Ten suits of hangings –   20
VOLPONE
  Ay, i' their garters, Mosca. Now their hopes
  Are at the gasp.
VOLTORE   Mosca the heir!
CORBACCIO   What's that?
VOLPONE
  My advocate is dumb. Look to my merchant,
  He has heard of some strange storm, a ship is lost:
  He faints. My lady will swoon. Old glazen-eyes,   25
  He hath not reached his despair, yet.
CORBACCIO   All these
  Are out of hope, I'm sure the man.

11 *Is his thread spun* Lady Would-Be alludes to the myth of the Three Fates to ask,
   in characteristically pompous fashion, whether Volpone is dead; she may also
   subconsciously be responding to the sight of all these expensive fabrics.
14 *diaper* linen woven into a diamond pattern
   damask intricately woven table-linen
20 *suits of hangings* sets of draperies for poster-beds
21 *i' their garters* Volpone puns on a jeering Elizabethan invitation to suicide, 'Hang
   yourself in your own garters' (Tilley G42).
22 *gasp* last gasp

CORVINO   But, Mosca –
MOSCA
  Two cabinets.
CORVINO   Is this in earnest?
MOSCA   One
  Of ebony –
CORVINO   Or, do you but delude me?
MOSCA
  The other, mother of pearl – I am very busy.   30
  Good faith, it is a fortune thrown upon me –
  Item, one salt of agate – not my seeking.
LADY WOULD-BE
  Do you hear, sir?
MOSCA   A perfumed box – 'pray you forbear,
  You see I'm troubled – made of an onyx –
LADY WOULD-BE   How!
MOSCA
  Tomorrow, or next day, I shall be at leisure   35
  To talk with you all.
CORVINO   Is this my large hope's issue?
LADY WOULD-BE
  Sir, I must have a fairer answer.
MOSCA   Madam!
  Marry, and shall: 'pray you, fairly quit my house.
  Nay, raise no tempest with your looks; but, hark you:
  Remember what your ladyship offered me,   40
  To put you in, an heir; go to, think on't.
  And what you said e'en your best madams did
  For maintenance, and why not you? Enough.
  Go home, and use the poor Sir Pol, your knight, well,
  For fear I tell some riddles: go, be melancholic.   45

                          [*Exit* LADY WOULD-BE]

VOLPONE
  O, my fine devil!
CORVINO   Mosca, 'pray you a word.
MOSCA
  Lord! Will not you take your dispatch hence, yet?

---

32 *salt* salt-cellar
38 *fairly* simply, completely; but with a sense of poetic justice, a play off her pre-
    ceding line, and another dig at her compromised cosmetic 'fairness' (cf. IV.ii.73).
40 *what . . . me* Lady Would-Be has offered herself sexually to Mosca, either by her
    salacious double-entendres, as at IV.vi.101, or by a more explicit offer we are
    now invited to imagine.
47 *dispatch* sending off

Methinks, of all, you should have been th' example.
Why should you stay here? With what thought? What
    promise?
Hear you: do not you know, I know you an ass?   50
And that you would, most fain, have been a wittol,
If fortune would have let you? That you are
A declared cuckold, on good terms? This pearl,
You'll say, was yours? Right. This diamond?
I will not deny't, but thank you. Much here else?   55
It may be so. Why, think that these good works
May help to hide your bad; I'll not betray you;
Although you be but extraordinary,
And have it only in title, it sufficeth.
Go home; be melancholic too, or mad.   60

                             [Exit CORVINO]

VOLPONE
Rare, Mosca! How his villainy becomes him!
VOLTORE
Certain, he doth delude all these for me.
CORBACCIO
Mosca the heir?
VOLPONE   O, his four eyes have found it.
CORBACCIO
I'm cozened, cheated, by a parasite slave;
Harlot, th'ast gulled me.
MOSCA   Yes, sir. Stop your mouth,   65
Or I shall draw the only tooth is left.
Are not you he – that filthy covetous wretch,
With the three legs – that, here, in hope of prey,
Have, any time this three year, snuffed about,
With your most grov'ling nose; and would have hired   70
Me to the pois'ning of my patron? Sir?
Are not you he, that have, today, in court,
Professed the disinheriting of your son?

51 *fain ... wittol* eagerly have been a pimp to your own wife
56–7 *think that ... bad* think of these unrewarded gifts of yours as charity to expi-
    ate your evil deeds
58–9 *Although ... sufficeth* Although you are unusual in being a cuckold in public
    name rather than physical fact, that is bad enough
63 *four eyes* Corbaccio evidently wears spectacles.
65 *Harlot* Rogue, low-born man; not yet exclusively a synonym for female prosti-
    tute
68 *three legs* Corbaccio walks with a cane.
69 *any time this three year* constantly during the past three years

Perjured yourself? Go home, and die, and stink;
If you but croak a syllable, all comes out: 75
Away, and call your porters, go, go stink.

                                        [*Exit* CORBACCIO]

VOLPONE
Excellent varlet!
VOLTORE   Now, my faithful Mosca,
I find thy constancy.   .
MOSCA   Sir?
VOLTORE   Sincere.
MOSCA   A table
Of porphyry – I mar'l you'll be thus troublesome.
VOLTORE
Nay, leave off now, they are gone.
MOSCA   Why, who are you?   80
What? Who did send for you? O, cry you mercy,
Reverend sir! Good faith, I am grieved for you,
That any chance of mine should thus defeat
Your (I must needs say) most deserving travails;
But, I protest, sir, it was cast upon me,   85
And I could, almost, wish to be without it,
But that the will o' th' dead must be observed.
Marry, my joy is, that you need it not,
You have a gift, sir, (thank your education)
Will never let you want, while there are men,   90
And malice to breed causes. Would I had
But half the like, for all my fortune, sir.
If I have any suits – as I do hope,
Things being so easy and direct, I shall not –
I will make bold with your obstreperous aid –   95
Conceive me, for your fee, sir. In meantime,
You, that have so much law, I know ha' the conscience
Not to be covetous of what is mine.
Good sir, I thank you, for my plate: 'twill help
To set up a young man. Good faith, you look   100
As you were costive: best go home, and purge, sir.

79 *mar'l* marvel, am astonished
81 *cry you mercy* I beg your pardon
83 *chance* luck
91 *causes* lawsuits
95–6 *I will ... fee* I will not hesitate to enlist your strong voice (in any litigation over
    Volpone's will) – and, please understand, I will pay your usual fee
99 *my plate* the valuable piece Voltore gave Volpone at I.iii.10
101 *costive* constipated

[*Exit* VOLTORE]

VOLPONE
　　Bid him eat lettuce well! My witty mischief,
　　Let me embrace thee. O, that I could now
　　Transform thee to a Venus – Mosca, go,
　　Straight, take my habit of *clarissimo*,　　　　　　　105
　　And walk the streets; be seen, torment 'em more:
　　We must pursue, as well as plot. Who would
　　Have lost this feast?
MOSCA　　　　　　　　I doubt it will lose them.
VOLPONE
　　O, my recovery shall recover all.
　　That I could now but think on some disguise,　　　110
　　To meet 'em in; and ask 'em questions.
　　How I would vex 'em still, at every turn!
MOSCA
　　Sir, I can fit you.
VOLPONE　　　　　　Canst thou?
MOSCA　　　　　　　　　　　　Yes. I know
　　One o' th' *commandatori*, sir, so like you;
　　Him will I straight make drunk, and bring you his habit.　　115
VOLPONE
　　A rare disguise, and answering thy brain!
　　O, I will be a sharp disease unto 'em.
MOSCA
　　Sir, you must look for curses –

102 *lettuce* considered a good laxative
104 *Venus* Flies were believed to be bisexual (Parker). This wish renews the Venus
　　allegory and the hermaphroditic theme that have surfaced several times in the
　　play.
105 *habit of clarissimo* The strict Venetian dress code dictated that such gentlemen
　　should wear black gowns edged with black taffeta, and a brimless black felt cap
　　(Parker).
107–8 *Who would ... feast?* Would anyone willingly miss out on this delicious
　　opportunity to gloat and taunt?
108 *I doubt it will lose them* either (as Volpone understands it), I'm afraid it will
　　make it impossible to exploit these gulls any further; or possibly, I'm afraid it
　　won't get rid of them
110 *That* I wish that
113 *fit you* fit you out for that, provide what you asked for
114 *commandatori* officers charged with bringing offenders to court (cf. IV.i.78)
116 *answering* worthy of
118 *look for* expect

VOLPONE   Till they burst;
The fox fares ever best when he is cursed.

                                   [*Exeunt*]

Act V, Scene iv

[*Enter*] PEREGRINE [*in disguise, and three* MERCHANTS]

PEREGRINE
  Am I enough disguised?
1st MERCHANT   I warrant you.
PEREGRINE
  All my ambition is to fright him, only.
2nd MERCHANT
  If you could ship him away, 'twere excellent.
3rd MERCHANT
  To Zant, or to Aleppo?
PEREGRINE   Yes, and ha' his
  Adventures put i' th' *Book of Voyages*,   5
  And his gulled story registered for truth?
  Well, gentlemen, when I am in a while,
  And that you think us warm in our discourse,
  Know your approaches.
1st MERCHANT   Trust it to our care.

                          [*Exeunt* MERCHANTS]

                    [*Enter* WOMAN]

PEREGRINE
  'Save you, fair lady. Is Sir Pol within?   10
WOMAN
  I do not know, sir.

---

119 *The fox ... cursed* This proverb (Tilley F632) probably meant that hunters curse
   the fox when they cannot catch him.
  1 *warrant* assure
  4 *Zant* an Ionian island, controlled at that time by Venice
  5 *Book of Voyages* probably one of the travel books (such as Hakluyt's) popular
   in this period
  6 *gulled story* Previous editors have assumed this means, the story of Pol's humil-
   iating gulling; but Peregrine may be warning that Sir Pol's grandiose version of
   his downfall might end up recorded as heroic historical truth. Jonson may thus
   be scoffing at the other grandiose tales so recorded.
  9 *Know your approaches* Remember exactly how and when to enter

PEREGRINE   'Pray you, say unto him,
  Here is a merchant, upon earnest business,
  Desires to speak with him.
WOMAN   I will see, sir.   [*Exit* WOMAN]
PEREGRINE   'Pray you.
  I see, the family is all female, here.

                [*Enter* WOMAN]

WOMAN
  He says, sir, he has weighty affairs of state,   15
  That now require him whole; some other time,
  You may possess him.
PEREGRINE   'Pray you say again,
  If those require him whole, these will exact him,
  Whereof I bring him tidings.

                            [*Exit* WOMAN]

                    What might be
  His grave affair of state, now? How to make   20
  Bolognian sausages, here, in Venice, sparing
  One o' th' ingredients?

                [*Enter* WOMAN]

WOMAN   Sir, he says he knows
  By your word 'tidings' that you are no statesman,
  And therefore, wills you stay.
PEREGRINE   Sweet, 'pray you return him,
  I have not read so many proclamations,   25
  And studied them, for words, as he has done,
  But – here he deigns to come.

                [*Enter* SIR POLITIC]

                            [*Exit* WOMAN]

SIR POLITIC   Sir, I must crave
  Your courteous pardon. There hath chanced, today,

---

  16 *require him whole* demand his complete attention
  18–19 *these ... tidings* the state affairs of which I bring him news will draw him out;
      Peregrine here mocks Pol's pretentious phrasing.
  24 *wills you stay* says – because you said 'tidings' instead of the sophisticated spy-
      jargon, 'intelligences' – you are not dangerous and may stay, or (almost the
      opposite), are not important and must wait
      return him say to him in response

Unkind disaster 'twixt my Lady and me;
And I was penning my apology   30
To give her satisfaction, as you came, now.
PEREGRINE
Sir, I am grieved, I bring you worse disaster:
The gentleman you met at th' port, today,
That told you he was newly arrived –
SIR POLITIC   Ay, was
A fugitive punk?
PEREGRINE   No, sir, a spy, set on you,   35
And he has made relation to the Senate,
That you professed to him to have a plot
To sell the state of Venice to the Turk.
SIR POLITIC
O me!
PEREGRINE For which, warrants are signed by this time,
To apprehend you, and to search your study,   40
For papers –
SIR POLITIC   Alas, sir. I have none, but notes,
Drawn out of play-books –
PEREGRINE   All the better, sir.
SIR POLITIC
And some essays. What shall I do?
PEREGRINE   Sir, best
Convey yourself into a sugar-chest,
Or, if you could lie round, a frail were rare;   45
And I could send you aboard.
SIR POLITIC   Sir, I but talked so,
For discourse sake, merely.
PEREGRINE   Hark, they are there.

                              They knock without

SIR POLITIC
I am a wretch, a wretch.
PEREGRINE   What will you do, sir?
Ha' you ne'er a currant-butt to leap into?

---

35 *punk* prostitute
36 *made relation to* told (Peregrine again adopts Pol's overblown lingo, cf. II.i.96)
42 *Drawn ... better, sir* As in the Epistle accompanying this play (lines 64–74),
     Jonson often complained that he was persecuted by the government because
     people insisted on reading sinister political implications into his plays.
45 *lie round ... rare* curl up, a basket of rushes (such as figs were packed in) would
     be ideal
49 *currant-butt* cask or small barrel used to hold currants or currant-wine

They'll put you to the rack, you must be sudden.   50
SIR POLITIC
    Sir, I have an engine –
3rd MERCHANT [*From off-stage*] Sir Politic Would-Be?
2nd MERCHANT
    [*From off-stage*] Where is he?
SIR POLITIC   – that I have thought upon beforetime.
PEREGRINE
    What is it?
SIR POLITIC [*Aside*] I shall ne'er endure the torture.
    [*To* PEREGRINE] Marry, it is, sir, of a tortoise-shell,
    Fitted for these extremities; 'pray you sir, help me. [*Climbs*   55
        into the tortoise shell]
    Here, I've a place, sir, to put back my legs;
    Please you to lay it on, sir. With this cap,
    And my black gloves, I'll lie, sir, like a tortoise,
    Till they are gone.
PEREGRINE   And call you this an engine?
SIR POLITIC
    Mine own device – Good sir, bid my wife's women   60
    To burn my papers.

                                        [*Exit* PEREGRINE]

                    [*The* MERCHANTS] *rush in*

1st MERCHANT   Where's he hid?
3rd MERCHANT   We must,
    And will, sure, find him.
2nd MERCHANT   Which is his study?

                    [*Enter* PEREGRINE]

1st MERCHANT   What
    Are you, sir?
PEREGRINE   I'm a merchant, that came here
    To look upon this tortoise.
3rd MERCHANT   How?
1st MERCHANT   St Mark!
    What beast is this?

50 *sudden* quick
55 *Fitted for these extremities* Prepared (Q 'apted') for emergencies like this, but
    perhaps also, Made to fit my limbs; tortoises were sold in the Venetian markets,
    and (as Peregrine's remark at line 80 suggests) were a symbol of wise policy.
59 *engine* piece of engineering

PEREGRINE   It is a fish.

2nd MERCHANT   Come out here.   65

PEREGRINE
Nay, you may strike him, sir, and tread upon him:
He'll bear a cart.

1st MERCHANT   What, to run over him?

PEREGRINE   Yes.

3rd MERCHANT
Let's jump upon him.

2nd MERCHANT   Can he not go?

PEREGRINE   He creeps, sir.

1st MERCHANT
[*Prodding* SIR POLITIC *through the openings in the shell*]
Let's see him creep.

PEREGRINE   No, good sir, you will hurt him.

2nd MERCHANT
'Heart, I'll see him creep; or prick his guts.   70

3rd MERCHANT
Come out here.

PEREGRINE   'Pray you, sir. [*Aside to* SIR POLITIC] Creep a
little.

1st MERCHANT Forth.

2nd MERCHANT
Yet further.

PEREGRINE   Good sir. [*Aside to* SIR POLITIC] Creep.

2nd MERCHANT   We'll see his legs.

3rd MERCHANT
Godso, he has garters!

They pull off the shell and discover him.

1st MERCHANT   Ay, and gloves!

2nd MERCHANT   Is this
Your fearful tortoise?

PEREGRINE [*Taking off his own disguise*] Now, Sir Pol, we are
even;
For your next project, I shall be prepared!   75
I am sorry for the funeral of your notes, sir.

1st MERCHANT
'Twere a rare motion, to be seen in Fleet Street!

---

68 *go* move
74 *even* Peregrine still seems to believe that Pol's pretensions were partly some kind
   of plot against him, deserving vengeance.
76 *funeral* burning, as on a pyre; smoke was sometimes released from trap doors on
   the Jacobean stage.
77 *motion* puppet-show

2nd MERCHANT
  Ay, i' the term.
1st MERCHANT   Or Smithfield, in the fair.
3rd MERCHANT
  Methinks, 'tis but a melancholic sight!
PEREGRINE
  Farewell, most politic tortoise.

                    [*Exeunt* PEREGRINE *and* MERCHANTS]

              [*Enter* WOMAN]

SIR POLITIC   Where's my lady?   80
  Knows she of this?
WOMAN   I know not, sir.
SIR POLITIC   Inquire.

                              [*Exit* WOMAN]

  O, I shall be the fable of all feasts;
  The freight of the *gazetti*; ship-boys' tale;
  And, which is worst, even talk for ordinaries.

              [*Enter* WOMAN]

WOMAN
  My lady's come most melancholic home,   85
  And says, sir, she will straight to sea, for physic.
SIR POLITIC
  And I, to shun this place and clime forever;
  Creeping, with house on back; and think it well
  To shrink my poor head, in my politic shell.

                              [*Exeunt*]

78 *i' the term* when law courts were in session, which drew crowds to Fleet Street,
    where puppet-shows were often performed
    Smithfield Jonson's play *Bartholomew Fair*, set in Smithfield, culminates with a
    puppet-show.
80 s.d. *Enter* WOMAN Alternatively, the waiting woman could have remained on
    stage instead of exiting at line 27 above; her ongoing reactions to Sir Pol's
    humiliation would present interesting theatrical opportunities.
83 *freight of the gazetti* material for the newspapers
84 *ordinaries* taverns
86 *physic* health, medical purposes

Act V, Scene v

[*Enter*] VOLPONE, MOSCA; *the first, in the habit of a*
commandatore; the other, of a clarissimo

VOLPONE
  Am I then like him?
MOSCA   O, sir, you are he:
  No man can sever you.
VOLPONE   Good.
MOSCA   But, what am I?
VOLPONE
  'Fore heav'n, a brave *clarissimo*; thou becom'st it!
  Pity, thou wert not born one.
MOSCA   If I hold
  My made one, 'twill be well.
VOLPONE   I will go, and see   5
  What news, first, at the court.
MOSCA   Do so.

                              [*Exit* VOLPONE]

                              My fox
  Is out on his hole, and, ere he shall re-enter,
  I will make him languish, in his borrowed case,
  Except he come to composition with me.
  Androgyno, Castrone, Nano!

          [*Enter* ANDROGYNO, CASTRONE, NANO]

ALL   Here.   10
MOSCA
  Go, recreate yourselves, abroad; go, sport!

          [*Exeunt* ANDROGYNO, CASTRONE, NANO]

---

  1 *him* the *commandatore*
  2 *sever* distinguish
  3 *becom'st it* fill the role handsomely
4–5 *If ... one* If I can maintain my assumed role; what sounds like Mosca's modesty
      actually reveals his intentions.
6–7 *My fox ... hole* Volpone has made himself vulnerable (by playing dead and then
      leaving his house); 'Fox in the Hole' was a game in which the players hop and
      strike each other with gloves and a piece of leather.
  8 *case* disguise
  9 *Except he come to composition* Unless he negotiates a wealth-sharing agreement

So, now I have the keys, and am possessed.
Since he will needs be dead, afore his time,
I'll bury him, or gain by him. I'm his heir;
And so will keep me, till he share at least.   15
To cozen him of all, were but a cheat
Well placed; no man would construe it a sin.
Let his sport pay for't; this is called the fox-trap.   [*Exit*]

Act V, Scene vi

[*Enter*] CORBACCIO, CORVINO

CORBACCIO
They say the court is set.
CORVINO   We must maintain
Our first tale good, for both our reputations.
CORBACCIO
Why, mine's no tale: my son would, there, have killed me.
CORVINO
That's true, I had forgot; mine is, I am sure.
But, for your will, sir.
CORBACCIO   Ay, I'll come upon him   5
For that, hereafter, now his patron's dead.

[*Enter* VOLPONE, *disguised as a commandatore*]

VOLPONE
Signor Corvino! And Corbaccio! Sir,
Much joy unto you.
CORVINO   Of what?
VOLPONE   The sudden good,
Dropped down upon you –

12 *possessed* in possession of the riches; but Jonson again (as at V.ii.24 and many
    other places in the play) uses the word to remind us that gold is a demonic pos-
    sessor, a notion which will become explicit in V.xii.
13 *will needs be* insists on being
15 *keep me* remain
16–17 *were but ... placed* would only be poetic justice
18 *Let his sport pay for't* Let his amusement at this latest trick compensate him for
    what it will cost him
1–2 *maintain ... good* stick to the story we told the court the first time
 5 *come upon him* make a demand to Mosca

CORBACCIO   Where?
VOLPONE   – and none knows how –
  From old Volpone, sir.
CORBACCIO   Out, errant knave.   10
VOLPONE
  Let not your too much wealth, sir, make you furious.
CORBACCIO
  Away, thou varlet.
VOLPONE   Why, sir?
CORBACCIO   Dost thou mock me?
VOLPONE
  You mock the world, sir: did you not change wills?
CORBACCIO
  Out, harlot.
VOLPONE   O! Belike you are the man,
  Signor Corvino? 'Faith, you carry it well: 15
  You grow not mad withal; I love your spirit.
  You are not over-leavened with your fortune.
  You should ha' some would swell, now, like a wine-vat,
  With such an autumn – Did he gi' you all, sir?
CORVINO
  Avoid, you rascal.
VOLPONE   Troth, your wife has shown   20
  Herself a very woman; but, you are well,
  You need not care, you have a good estate,
  To bear it out sir, better by this chance.
  Except Corbaccio have a share?
CORVINO   Hence, varlet.
VOLPONE
  You will not be a'known, sir. Why, 'tis wise,   25
  Thus do all gamesters, at all games, dissemble:

---

10 *errant* As at III.vii.118, possibly Jonson's version of 'arrant', meaning 'notorious', but more likely 'erring', combining the accusation that he is mistaken with
  a dismissive view of the *commandatore*'s itinerant occupation.
13 *You mock the world* You are trying to conceal the truth from everyone, or perhaps, You can laugh at everyone
  change exchange (by naming each other as heirs)
14 *Belike* Perhaps
17 *over-leavened* puffed up
18 *You should ha' some* There would be some people who
19 *autumn* large harvest
21 *very* true
24 *Except* Unless
25 *a'known* acknowledged (as heir)
26 *gamesters* gamblers

No man will seem to win.

      [*Exeunt* CORVINO *and* CORBACCIO]
      Here comes my vulture,
Heaving his beak up i' the air, and snuffing.

Act V, Scene vii

     [*Enter*] VOLTORE

VOLTORE
 Out-stripped thus, by a parasite? a slave?
 Would run on errands? and make legs, for crumbs?
 Well, what I'll do –
VOLPONE   The court stays for your worship.
 I e'en rejoice, sir, at your worship's happiness,
 And that it fell into so learnèd hands,   5
 That understand the fingering.
VOLTORE   What do you mean?
VOLPONE
 I mean to be a suitor to your worship,
 For the small tenement, out of reparations:
 That, at the end of your long row of houses,
 By the *Piscaria*. It was, in Volpone's time,   10
 Your predecessor, ere he grew diseased,
 A handsome, pretty, customed bawdy-house
 As any was in Venice – none dispraised –
 But fell with him; his body and that house
 Decayed together.
VOLTORE   Come, sir, leave your prating. 15

27 *seem to win* acknowledge he is winning
 2 *make legs* bow
 3 *stays* waits
 5 *it* the inheritance
 6 *fingering* manipulation, how to handle it (playing off the reference to 'learned hands')
 8 *out of reparations* needing repairs
10 *Piscaria* Fish-market
12 *customed* well supplied with customers (or, possibly, permitted, either because bribes have been paid as 'customs', or because it has been established by custom)
  bawdy-house house of prostitution
13 *none dispraised* not to say anything bad of the others (Kernan)

VOLPONE
Why, if your worship give me but your hand,
That I may ha' the refusal, I have done.
'Tis a mere toy, to you, sir: candle-rents;
As your learned worship knows –
VOLTORE   What do I know?
VOLPONE
Marry, no end of your wealth, sir, God decrease it.   20
VOLTORE
Mistaking knave! What, mock'st thou my misfortune?
VOLPONE
His blessing on your heart, sir, would 'twere more.

                                   [*Exit* VOLTORE]

Now to my first again, at the next corner.

Act V, Scene viii

[*Enter*] CORBACCIO, CORVINO; MOSCA [*walking across
the stage dressed as a clarissimo*]

CORBACCIO
See, in our habit! See the impudent varlet!
CORVINO
That I could shoot mine eyes at him, like gunstones.

                                     [*Exit* MOSCA]

VOLPONE
But, is this true, sir, of the parasite?
CORBACCIO
Again, to afflict us? Monster!

16–17 *Why ... done* Well, if your honoured self will just give me your handshake (or
     handwriting) promising me first refusal on the property, I won't ask any more
     favours
  18 *toy* trifle
     candle-rents rents from deteriorating property
  20 *decrease* A deliberate slip for 'increase'; Volpone plays the sergeant like a
     Shakespearean comic constable, such as the malapropist Dogberry.
  22 *would 'twere more* Under the guise of politely wishing Voltore's fortune were
     even greater, Volpone can tauntingly wish that Voltore's *mis*fortune were even
     greater.
   1 *in our habit* dressed like us (despite his lower birth)

VOLPONE   In good faith, sir,
I'm heartily grieved a beard of your grave length   5
Should be so over-reached. I never brooked
That parasite's hair, methought his nose should cozen:
There still was somewhat, in his look, did promise
The bane of a *clarissimo*.
CORBACCIO   Knave –
VOLPONE   Methinks
Yet you, that are so traded i' the world,   10
A witty merchant, the fine bird, Corvino,
That have such moral emblems on your name,
Should not have sung your shame, and dropped your cheese,
To let the fox laugh at your emptiness.

CORVINO
Sirrah, you think the privilege of the place,   15
And your red saucy cap, that seems, to me,
Nailed to your jolt-head with those two chequins,
Can warrant your abuses. Come you, hither:
You shall perceive, sir, I dare beat you. Approach.

VOLPONE
No haste, sir, I do know your valour, well,   20
Since you durst publish what you are, sir.
CORVINO   Tarry,
I'd speak with you.

5–6 *a beard ... over-reached* that someone of your advanced age has been so out-
      smarted
  6 *brooked* could tolerate
  8 *still* always
  9 *bane* poison
 10 *traded* experienced (playing on Corvino's occupation)
12–14 *That have ... emptiness* Volpone here refers explicitly to one of the Aesop's
      fables that have informed the entire play: the fox who flatters the crow into drop-
      ping his cheese. Horace (*Satires*, II.v.55–7) alludes to this tale when describing a
      legacy-hunter much like Corvino: one who married his daughter to an old man,
      but was left out of the old man's will anyway.
 14 *emptiness* the now-empty beak, but also the empty head that made it so
 15 *place* either his role as a court official or the physical proximity to the high court
 17 *jolt-head* block-head
    chequins probably coin-like gold buttons on the cap
20–1 *I do know ... sir* I don't doubt your courage, since you were brave enough to
      announce publicly that you are a cuckold

VOLPONE   Sir, sir, another time –
CORVINO
Nay, now.
VOLPONE   O God, sir! I were a wise man,
Would stand the fury of a distracted cuckold.
CORBACCIO
What! Come again?

MOSCA *walks by 'em*

VOLPONE   [*Aside*] Upon 'em, Mosca: save me.   25
CORBACCIO
The air's infected where he breathes.
CORVINO   Let's fly him.

[*Exeunt* CORVINO *and* CORBACCIO]

VOLPONE
Excellent basilisk! Turn upon the vulture.

Act V, Scene ix

[*Enter*] VOLTORE

VOLTORE
Well, flesh-fly, it is summer with you now;
Your winter will come on.
MOSCA   Good advocate,
'Pray thee, not rail, nor threaten out of place, thus:
Thou'lt make a solecism (as Madam says).
Get you a biggin more: your brain breaks loose.   5
VOLTORE
Well, sir.
VOLPONE   Would you have me beat the insolent slave?
Throw dirt upon his first good clothes?
VOLTORE   This same
Is, doubtless, some familiar!
VOLPONE   Sir, the court,

23–4 *I were ... cuckold* I'd have to be very wise to stand still and endure the fury of
    an insane cuckold (spoken sarcastically)
27 *basilisk* a mythical serpent that could kill with just its glance
 1 *flesh-fly* the meaning of 'Mosca' – a fly that plants its eggs in dead flesh (OED)
 4 *Madam* Lady Would-Be (cf. IV.ii.43)
 5 *biggin* lawyer's cap
 8 *familiar* evil spirit (renewing the theme of demonic possession)

In troth, stays for you. I am mad a mule,
That never read Justinian, should get up,   10
And ride an advocate. Had you no quirk
To avoid gullage, sir, by such a creature?
I hope you do but jest; he has not done't.
This's but confederacy, to blind the rest.
You are the heir?
VOLTORE   A strange, officious,   15
Troublesome knave! Thou dost torment me.
VOLPONE   I know –
It cannot be, sir, that you should be cozened:
'Tis not within the wit of man, to do it;
You are so wise, so prudent – and 'tis fit
That wealth and wisdom still should go together –   20

                                        [*Exeunt*]

Act V, Scene x

[*Enter four*] AVOCATORI, NOTARIO, COMMANDATORI
[*including the disguised* VOLPONE], BONARIO, CELIA,
                CORBACCIO, CORVINO

1st AVOCATORE
Are all the parties here?
NOTARIO   All but the advocate.
2nd AVOCATORE
And here he comes.

                [*Enter* VOLTORE]

 9 *I am mad* It drives me crazy
9–11 *a mule ... advocate* Lawyers traditionally rode mules; Justinian was the great
     Roman code of law.
11 *quirk* trick
12 *gullage* being made a fool of
14 *confederacy* a conspiratorial subterfuge (with Mosca – but Volpone himself is
     dangerously blind to the possibility that he no longer has such a conspiracy with
     Mosca)
 2 *And here he comes* Here and at line 20, F gives the speech to 'AVO', Q to
     'AVOC', which might indicate the lines are spoken by several of the judges
     together; but editorial tradition has reasonably assigned these lines to individual
     judges.

1st AVOCATORE   Then bring 'em forth to sentence.
VOLTORE
  O, my most honoured fathers, let your mercy
  Once win upon your justice, to forgive –
  I am distracted –
VOLPONE   [Aside] What will he do now?
VOLTORE   O,   5
  I know not which t' address myself to first,
  Whether your fatherhoods, or these innocents –
CORVINO
  [Aside] Will he betray himself?
VOLTORE   Whom, equally,
  I have abused, out of most covetous ends –
CORVINO
  [Aside] The man is mad!
CORBACCIO   [Aside] What's that?
CORVINO   [Aside] He is possessed.   10
VOLTORE
  For which, now struck in conscience, here I prostrate
  Myself, at your offended feet, for pardon. [Throws himself
    down]
1st, 2nd AVOCATORI
  Arise.
CELIA   O heaven, how just thou art!
VOLPONE   [Aside] I'm caught
  I' mine own noose –
CORVINO [Aside to CORBACCIO] Be constant, sir: nought now
  Can help but impudence.
1st AVOCATORE   Speak forward.
COMMANDATORE   Silence.   15
VOLTORE
  It is not passion in me, reverend fathers,
  But only conscience – conscience, my good sires –
  That makes me, now, tell truth. That parasite,
  That knave hath been the instrument of all.
1st AVOCATORE
  Where is that knave? Fetch him.
VOLPONE   I go.   [Exit]

---

2 'em Celia and Bonario
4 win upon take precedence over
5 distracted mad, out of his wits
9 out of most covetous ends because of extremely greedy motives
15 impudence shamelessness (in sticking to their earlier lie)
16 passion frenzy

CORVINO   Grave fathers,   20
This man is distracted, he confessed it now;
For, hoping to be old Volpone's heir,
Who now is dead –
3rd AVOCATORE   How?
2nd AVOCATORE   Is Volpone dead?
CORVINO
Dead since, grave fathers –
BONARIO   O, sure vengeance!
1st AVOCATORE   Stay –
Then he was no deceiver?
VOLTORE   O, no, none;   25
The parasite, grave fathers –
CORVINO   He does speak
Out of mere envy, 'cause the servant's made
The thing he gaped for. Please your fatherhoods,
This is the truth; though, I'll not justify
The other, but he may be somewhere faulty.   30
VOLTORE
Ay, to your hopes, as well as mine, Corvino;
But I'll use modesty. Pleaseth your wisdoms
To view these certain notes, and but confer them:

[*Gives papers to the* AVOCATORI]

As I hope favour, they shall speak clear truth.
CORVINO
The devil has entered him!
BONARIO   Or bides in you.   35
4th AVOCATORE
We have done ill, by a public officer
To send for him, if he be heir.
2nd AVOCATORE   For whom?
4th AVOCATORE
Him that they call the parasite.
3rd AVOCATORE   'Tis true:
He is a man of great estate now left.
4th AVOCATORE
[*To* NOTARIO] Go you, and learn his name; and say, the court   40

---

32   *modesty* restraint, moderation
33   *certain* particular, or, offering reliable proof
     but confer simply compare them, or confer about them
35   *bides* abides, remains
40   *you* the Notario, a more decorous emissary

Entreats his presence here, but to the clearing
Of some few doubts.

                                    [*Exit* NOTARIO]

2nd AVOCATORE   This same's a labyrinth!
1st AVOCATORE
Stand you unto your first report?
CORVINO   My state,
My life, my fame –
BONARIO   Where is't?
CORVINO   Are at the stake
1st AVOCATORE
[*To* CORBACCIO] Is yours so too?
CORBACCIO   The advocate is a knave: 45
And has a forkèd tongue –
2nd AVOCATORE   Speak to the point.
CORBACCIO
So is the parasite, too.
1st AVOCATORE   This is confusion.
VOLTORE
I do beseech your fatherhoods, read but those –
CORVINO
And credit nothing the false spirit hath writ:
It cannot be, my sires, but he is possessed.   50

                                      [*Exeunt*]

Act V, Scene xi

[*Enter*] VOLPONE

VOLPONE
To make a snare for mine own neck! and run
My head into it, wilfully! with laughter!
When I had newly 'scaped, was free, and clear!
Out of mere wantonness! O, the dull devil

---

41 *but to* only for
43 *Stand you unto* Do you hold to
     state estate
44 *fame* reputation
49 *credit* believe
50 *It cannot be ... but* There is no possible explanation except that
 1 *snare* noose; but the same term would have been used for a fox-trap.
 4 *wantonness* playful enthusiasm, careless self-indulgence

Was in this brain of mine, when I devised it;   5
And Mosca gave it second: he must now
Help to sear up this vein, or we bleed dead.

[*Enter* NANO, ANDROGYNO, *and* CASTRONE]

How now! Who let you loose? Whither go you, now?
What? To buy gingerbread? Or to drown kitlings?
NANO
Sir, Master Mosca called us out of doors,   10
And bid us all go play, and took the keys.
ANDROGYNO   Yes.
VOLPONE
Did Master Mosca take the keys? Why, so!
I am farther in. These are my fine conceits!
I must be merry, with a mischief to me!
What a vile wretch was I, that could not bear   15
My fortune soberly? I must ha' my crotchets!
And my conundrums! Well, go you, and seek him;
His meaning may be truer than my fear.
Bid him, he straight come to me, to the court;
Thither will I, and, if't be possible,   20
Unscrew my advocate, upon new hopes:
When I provoked him, then I lost myself.

                                        [*Exeunt*]

6 *gave it second* seconded the idea
7 *sear* cauterize
9 *kitlings* kittens; Volpone suggests the pastimes of naughty or cruel children.
13 *farther in* in even more trouble than I realized; Volpone now suspects Mosca's
    true intentions, so the remainder of the line is spoken sarcastically.
    conceits schemes
14 *I must ... to me* I had to enjoy myself with something that would do me harm
16 *My fortune soberly* My wealth, or my good luck in court, wisely
16–17 *my crochets ... my conundrums* my perverse and clever whims
18 *truer* more honest and loyal
19 *Bid* Instruct, or Ask
21 *Unscrew* Reverse the course of, or perhaps, Calm the fierce resolution of
    upon by offering him

Act V, Scene xii

[*Enter*] AVOCATORI, [NOTARIO, COMMANDATORI,
BONARIO, CELIA, VOLTORE, CORBACCIO, CORVINO]

1st AVOCATORE
    [*Studying* VOLTORE'*s notes*] These things can ne'er be
      reconciled. He here
    Professeth, that the gentleman was wronged;
    And that the gentlewoman was brought thither,
    Forced by her husband; and there left.
VOLTORE   Most true.
CELIA
    How ready is heaven to those that pray!
1st AVOCATORE   But, that   5
    Volpone would have ravished her, he holds
    Utterly false, knowing his impotence.
CORVINO
    Grave fathers, he is possessed; again I say,
    Possessed; nay, if there be possession
    And obsession, he has both.
3rd AVOCATORE   Here comes our officer.   10

[*Enter* VOLPONE, *still disguised*]

VOLPONE
    The parasite will straight be here, grave fathers.
4th AVOCATORE
    You might invent some other name, sir varlet.
3rd AVOCATORE
    Did not the notary meet him?
VOLPONE   Not that I know.
4th AVOCATORE
    His coming will clear all.
2nd AVOCATORE   Yet it is misty.
VOLTORE
    May't please your fatherhoods –

VOLPONE *whispers* [*to*] *the advocate* [VOLTORE]

---

  1 *He* Voltore
  5 *ready* promptly responsive
10 *obsession* a devil's assault on a person from the outside (as opposed to pos-
     session, which is from the inside)
12 *invent* find, choose (because Mosca's wealth makes him suddenly worthy of a
     nobler term)
14 *Yet it is misty* Still, up to this moment, it remains unclear

VOLPONE   Sir, the parasite   15
Willed me to tell you that his master lives;
That you are still the man; your hopes the same;
And this was only a jest –
VOLTORE   How?
VOLPONE   Sir, to try
If you were firm, and how you stood affected.
VOLTORE
Art sure he lives?
VOLPONE   Do I live, sir?
VOLTORE   O me!   20
I was too violent.
VOLPONE   Sir, you may redeem it.
They said you were possessed; fall down, and seem so:

        VOLTORE *falls*

I'll help to make it good. [*Aloud*] God bless the man!
[*Aside to* VOLTORE] Stop your wind hard, and swell.
    [*Aloud*] See, see, see, see!
He vomits crooked pins! His eyes are set,   25
Like a dead hare's, hung in a poulter's shop!
His mouth's running away! Do you see, Signor?
Now 'tis in his belly!
CORVINO   Ay, the devil!
VOLPONE
Now, in his throat.
CORVINO   Ay, I perceive it plain.
VOLPONE
'Twill out, 'twill out: stand clear. See, where it flies!   30
In shape of a blue toad, with a bat's wings!
Do not you see it, sir?

---

19 *stood affected* truly felt (about Volpone)
20 *Do I live* This normally means something like, 'as surely as I am here talking to
    you', with an added irony in this situation; but Volpone may also lift off his dis-
    guise momentarily for Voltore here, which would explain Voltore's instant
    change of tactics, though it does not explain how he would hope to inherit any-
    time soon from such a radically revived man.
23 *good* convincing
24 *Stop your wind* Hold your breath
25–31 *He vomits ... bat's wings* Similar phenomena were reported during Jacobean
    exorcisms (of which King James became a prominent debunker).
26 *poulter* seller of poultry and small game such as hares
27 *running away* moving wildly – perhaps twitching side to side, perhaps silently
    imitating rapid speech

CORBACCIO   What? I think I do.
CORVINO
    'Tis too manifest.
VOLPONE   Look! He comes t' himself!
VOLTORE
    Where am I?
VOLPONE   Take good heart, the worst is past, sir.
    You are dispossessed.
1st AVOCATORE   What accident is this?   35
2nd AVOCATORE
    Sudden, and full of wonder!
3rd AVOCATORE   If he were
    Possessed, as it appears, all this is nothing.
CORVINO
    He has been, often, subject to these fits.
1st AVOCATORE
    Show him that writing. [*To* VOLTORE] Do you know it, sir?
VOLPONE
    [*Aside to* VOLTORE] Deny it, sir, forswear it, know it not.   40
VOLTORE
    Yes, I do know it well, it is my hand;
    But all that it contains is false.
BONARIO   O practice!
2nd AVOCATORE
    What maze is this!
1st AVOCATORE   Is he not guilty, then,
    Whom you there name the parasite?
VOLTORE   Grave fathers,
    No more than his good patron, old Volpone.   45
4th AVOCATORE
    Why, he is dead!
VOLTORE   O no, my honoured fathers,
    He lives –
1st AVOCATORE How! Lives?
VOLTORE   Lives.
2nd AVOCATORE   This is subtler yet!
3rd AVOCATORE
    You said he was dead!

34 *Take good heart* Cheer up, be encouraged
35 *accident* unforeseen event
37 *this* Probably indicating Voltore's notes to the court.
41 *hand* handwriting
42 *O practice!* This is a treachery!
47 *subtler* trickier

VOLTORE   Never.
3rd AVOCATORE [*To* CORVINO] You said so!
CORVINO   I heard so.
4th AVOCATORE
  Here comes the gentleman, make him way.

                    [*Enter* MOSCA]

3rd AVOCATORE   A stool.
4th AVOCATORE
  A proper man! And, were Volpone dead,   50
  A fit match for my daughter.
3rd AVOCATORE   Give him way.
VOLPONE
  [*Aside to* MOSCA] Mosca, I was almost lost, the advocate
  Had betrayed all; but now it is recovered:
  All's on the hinge again – say I am living.
MOSCA
  What busy knave is this! Most reverend fathers,   55
  I sooner had attended your grave pleasures,
  But that my order for the funeral
  Of my dear patron did require me –
VOLPONE   [*Aside*] Mosca!
MOSCA
  Whom I intend to bury like a gentleman –
VOLPONE
  [*Aside*] Ay, quick, and cozen me of all.
2nd AVOCATORE   Still stranger!   60
  More intricate!
1st AVOCATORE And come about again!
4th AVOCATORE
  It is a match, my daughter is bestowed.
MOSCA
  [*Aside to* VOLPONE] Will you gi' me half?
VOLPONE   First I'll be hanged.
MOSCA   [*Aside to* VOLPONE] I know,
  Your voice is good, cry not so loud.

50 *proper* handsome
53 *recovered* revived, repaired, or covered up again
54 *on the hinge* working properly
55 *busy* meddling, officious
56 *sooner ... pleasures* would have responded sooner to the summons from you
      important men
60 *quick* alive
61 *come about* reversed (because Volpone is reported dead after all)
64 *cry* shout; Mosca is apparently warning Volpone that his exasperated reply in
      the previous line was dangerously audible.

1st AVOCATORE   Demand
  The advocate. Sir, did not you affirm   65
  Volpone was alive?
VOLPONE   Yes, and he is;
  This gent'man told me so. [*Aside to* MOSCA] Thou shalt
  have half.
MOSCA
  Whose drunkard is this same? Speak, some that know him:
  I never saw his face. [*Aside to* VOLPONE] I cannot now
  Afford it you so cheap.
VOLPONE [*Aside to* MOSCA] No?
1st AVOCATORE   [*To* VOLTORE] What say you?   70
VOLTORE
  The officer told me.
VOLPONE   I did, grave fathers,
  And will maintain he lives with mine own life,
  And that this creature told me. [*Aside*] I was born
  With all good stars my enemies.
MOSCA   Most grave fathers,
  If such an insolence as this must pass   75
  Upon me, I am silent; 'twas not this
  For which you sent, I hope.
2nd AVOCATORE [*Indicating* VOLPONE] Take him away.
VOLPONE
  [*Aside to* MOSCA] Mosca.
3rd AVOCATORE   Let him be whipped.
VOLPONE   [*Aside to* MOSCA] Wilt thou betray me?
  Cozen me?
3rd AVOCATORE And taught to bear himself
  Toward a person of his rank.
4th AVOCATORE   Away.   80

    [*Officers begin to drag* VOLPONE *away*]

MOSCA
  I humbly thank your fatherhoods.
VOLPONE   Soft, soft. [*Aside*] Whipped?
  And lose all that I have? If I confess,
  It cannot be much more.

    —

72 *And will ... lives* I would bet my life he is alive (repeating the joke from line 20)
74 *With all good stars my enemies* Under a bad astrological sign; hence, unlucky
75–6 *pass / Upon me* will be tolerated against me
80 *his* Mosca's
81 *Soft* Take it easy, wait a minute

4th AVOCATORE [*To* MOSCA] Sir, are you married?
VOLPONE
  They'll be allied, anon: I must be resolute;
  The fox shall, here, uncase.

              He puts off his disguise

MOSCA   [*Aside to* VOLPONE] Patron.
VOLPONE   Nay, now,   85
  My ruins shall not come alone. Your match
  I'll hinder sure; my substance shall not glue you,
  Nor screw you, into a family.
MOSCA   [*Aside to* VOLPONE] Why, patron!
VOLPONE
  I am Volpone, and this [*Indicating* MOSCA] is my knave;
  This, his own knave; this, avarice's fool;   90
  This [*Indicating* CORVINO], a chimera of wittol, fool, and
    knave;
  And, reverend fathers, since we all can hope
  Nought but a sentence, let's not now despair it.
  You hear me brief.
CORVINO   May it please your fatherhoods –
COMMANDATORI   Silence.
1st AVOCATORE
  The knot is now undone, by miracle!   95
2nd AVOCATORE
  Nothing can be more clear.
3rd AVOCATORE   Or can more prove
  These innocent.
1st AVOCATORE   Give 'em their liberty.
BONARIO
  Heaven could not, long, let such gross crimes be hid.
2nd AVOCATORE
  If this be held the high way, to get riches,
  May I be poor.

---

84 *allied, anon* made allies (by marriage) soon
85 *uncase* drop his disguise, and perhaps also (like a hunted fox) break from his
    cover, or, possibly, (like a captured fox) have his coat flayed off
86-7 *Your match ... sure* I'll definitely ruin your plans to marry into the aristocracy
89 *knave* low-ranking servant, with a connotation of low ethics
90 *avarice's fool* a person duped by greed; the 'knave' is probably Voltore and the
    'fool' Corbaccio, as some editors stipulate, but it could be the other way around.
91 *chimera* a mythical beast combining lion, goat, and serpent
93 *let's ... despair it* don't disappoint us (spoken with bitter irony)
94 *brief* keeping my remarks brief (to get this over with)

3rd AVOCATORE   This's not the gain, but torment.   100
1st AVOCATORE
  These possess wealth, as sick men possess fevers,
  Which, trulier, may be said to possess them.
2nd AVOCATORE
  Disrobe that parasite.
CORVINO, MOSCA   Most honoured fathers –
1st AVOCATORE
  Can you plead aught to stay the course of justice?
  If you can, speak.
CORVINO, VOLTORE   We beg favour.
CELIA   And mercy.   105
1st AVOCATORE
  You hurt your innocence, suing for the guilty.
  Stand forth; and, first, the parasite. You appear
  To have been the chiefest minister, if not plotter,
  In all these lewd impostures; and now, lastly,
  Have, with your impudence, abused the court,   110
  And habit of a gentleman of Venice,
  Being a fellow of no birth or blood;
  For which, our sentence is, first thou be whipped;
  Then live perpetual prisoner in our galleys.
VOLPONE
  I thank you, for him.
MOSCA   Bane to thy wolfish nature.   115
1st AVOCATORE
  Deliver him to the *Saffi*. Thou, Volpone,
  By blood and rank a gentleman, canst not fall
  Under like censure; but our judgement on thee
  Is, that thy substance all be straight confiscate
  To the hospital of the *Incurabili*;   120
  And, since the most was gotten by imposture,
  By feigning lame, gout, palsy and such diseases,
  Thou art to lie in prison, cramped with irons,

---

100 *This's … torment* This one gained nothing but torment, or, This is not profit but
    torment
109 *lewd impostures* wicked falsehoods
115 VOLPONE F and Q give this line to Voltore, but – considering Mosca's immedi-
    ate response, and the vengeful parallel with line 81 – it fits better spoken by
    Volpone. This is particularly true if the scene is staged with each miscreant led
    offstage immediately after his sentencing.
    Bane Mosca is cursing Volpone; wolf's-bane was a powerful poison
116 *Saffi* bailiffs
119 *substance* wealth, material goods
120 *Incurabili* incurables – mostly victims of venereal disease

Till thou be'st sick and lame indeed. Remove him.
VOLPONE
  This is called mortifying of a fox.   125
1st AVOCATORE
  Thou, Voltore, to take away the scandal
  Thou hast giv'n all worthy men of thy profession,
  Art banished from their fellowship, and our state.
  Corbaccio, bring him near. We here possess
  Thy son of all thy estate; and confine thee   130
  To the monastery of *San' Spirito*;
  Where since thou knew'st not how to live well here,
  Thou shalt be learned to die well.
CORBACCIO   Ha! What said he?
COMMANDATORE
  You shall know anon, sir.
1st AVOCATORE   Thou Corvino, shalt
  Be straight embarked from thine own house, and rowed   135
  Round about Venice, through the Grand Canal,
  Wearing a cap, with fair, long ass's ears,
  Instead of horns; and so to mount, a paper
  Pinned on thy breast, to the *Berlino* –
CORVINO   Yes,
  And have mine eyes beat out with stinking fish,   140
  Bruised fruit and rotten eggs – 'Tis well. I'm glad
  I shall not see my shame, yet.
1st AVOCATORE   And to expiate
  Thy wrongs done to thy wife, thou art to send her
  Home, to her father, with her dowry trebled;

125 *mortifying* a quintuple pun – the word means not only 'humiliation' and 'bring-
    ing toward death', but also 'tenderizing animal meat', 'teaching sinners, by pun-
    ishment, to overcome their worldly appetites', and even 'disposing of property
    for charitable purposes' (Parker).
126–7 *the scandal ... profession* the disgrace you have brought on all honourable
    lawyers; the Dedication and Epistle suggest that Jonson was aiming his play at
    an audience which included many legal scholars.
133 *die well* The arts of dying well – the *ars moriendi* – were a central religious prac-
    tice throughout the Renaissance.
135 *embarked* sent out on a boat
137–8 *ass's ears ... horns* Because Corvino behaved like an ass but was never actu-
    ally a cuckold.
138 *so to mount* to climb in that costume
139 *Berlino* the pillory, where malefactors were exposed to public humiliation
142 *I shall not see my shame, yet* I still won't be forced to witness my own humili-
    ation, not even such a prominent humiliation (since my eyes will be smashed by
    the garbage that people throw at those in the pillory)

And these are all your judgements –
ALL   Honoured fathers.   145
1st AVOCATORE
Which may not be revoked. Now you begin,
When crimes are done, and past, and to be punished,
To think what your crimes are; away with them.
Let all that see these vices thus rewarded
Take heart, and love to study 'em. Mischiefs feed   150
Like beasts, till they be fat, and then they bleed.

                                  [*Exeunt*]

        [*Enter*] VOLPONE [*as* EPILOGUE]

The seasoning of a play is the applause.
Now, though the fox be punished by the laws,
He yet doth hope there is no suff'ring due
For any fact which he hath done 'gainst you.
If there be, censure him; here he doubtful stands.   5
If not, fare jovially, and clap your hands.

THE END

---

150 *Take heart ... study 'em* Be encouraged, and love to practice those vices (spoken
    ironically)
  4 *fact* crime
  6 *fare jovially* be cheerful; Jonson here translates a standard closing plea for
    applause from classical comedies, and alters the familiar phrase 'farewell' to
    invoke the supposedly happy planetary influence of Jupiter.

TO

THE MOST
NOBLE AND
MOST EQVALL
SISTERS

THE TWO FAMOVS

VNIVERSITIES
FOR THEIR LOVE

AND

ACCEPTANCE

SHEW'N TO HIS POEME IN THE

PRESENTATION

BEN. IONSON

THE GRATEFVLL ACKNOWLEDGER

DEDICATES

BOTH IT AND HIMSELFE.

EQUAL equal to each other in quality, and fair (equitable) in their judgements; Jonson was granted honorary degrees from both Oxford and Cambridge, partly perhaps in appreciation of this play.
UNIVERSITIES Oxford and Cambridge
POEM *Volpone*, which was performed at Oxford and Cambridge between its early 1606 London premiere and its early 1607 Quarto printing.

Jonson's dedicatory letter to Oxford and Cambridge Universities defends literature (Jonson uses the term 'poetry' broadly) against its accusers (including, implicitly, Puritans), though it concedes that sloppy and slanderous writers have recently injured literature's ancient prestige. The Epistle draws its didactic justification of literary art from Jonson's own 'Apologetical Dialogue' in *Poetaster* five years earlier, as well as from Erasmus, Minturno, and Jonson's perennial favourite, Horace.

Jonson strives for an erudite elegance of style in addressing his university audience, which makes for interesting but difficult reading for more modern audiences. His rich and varied sentences provide some sense of how the best literary minds of Jacobean England chose ceremoniously to communicate their beliefs. The Epistle is so convoluted in syntax and so mannered in diction, however, that a single modern paraphrase – here presented on left-hand pages facing the relevant original text – seems preferable to dozens of piecemeal glosses, and I have added footnotes only where they add substance, not where they merely provide translation.

The sense of the Epistle is:

Since no writer is great enough to succeed without favourable circumstances, including admirers, writers should especially defend themselves when that entails defending their admirers also. So, while the endorsement of you great universities should be enough in itself, further justification is called for in an era when writers are so widely condemned.

Undisciplined writers have certainly damaged the reputation of literature; otherwise these accusations would be completely outrageous. Good writers have to be good men, and anyone who can provide the benefits true literature provides should be spared snobbish, ill-informed accusations. But the accusers will object that modern writers hardly correspond to the high dignity traditionally associated with literature; many people claim the title of author, while (especially in drama) producing only stupid and offensive works. I cannot deny that, but it is unfair to judge all writers by

9 *the bounty of your act* your generous patronage (which Jonson is trying to repay by explaining to the world why support of literature is justified)

16 *their mistress* poetry; 'poetasters' are weak, pretentious, dilettante poets, whose failings oblige true poets to defend their profession.

38–41 *especially ... practised* Jonson here echoes some of the Puritans' principal objections to the English theatre.

42 *features* plays, though it also suggests a condemnation of the authors' faces

THE EPISTLE

Never, most equal Sisters, had any man a wit so presently
excellent, as that it could raise itself; but there must come
both matter, occasion, commenders, and favourers to it. If
this be true, and that the fortune of all writers doth daily
prove it, it behooves the careful to provide well towards   5
these accidents; and, having acquired them, to preserve that
part of reputation most tenderly, wherein the benefit of a
friend is also defended. Hence is it that I now render myself
grateful, and am studious to justify the bounty of your act;
to which, though your mere authority were satisfying, yet,   10
it being an age wherein poetry and the professors of it hear
so ill on all sides, there will a reason be looked for in the
subject.

It is certain, nor can it with any forehead be opposed,
that the too much licence of poetasters in this time hath   15
much deformed their mistress; that, every day, their manifold and manifest ignorance doth stick unnatural
reproaches upon her. But for their petulancy, it were an act
of the greatest injustice, either to let the learned suffer, or
so divine a skill – which indeed should not be attempted   20
with unclean hands – to fall under the least contempt. For,
if men will impartially, and not asquint, look toward the
offices and function of a poet, they will easily conclude to
themselves the impossibility of any man's being the good
poet, without first being a good man. He that is said to be   25
able to inform young men to all good disciplines, inflame
grown men to all great virtues, keep old men in their best
and supreme state, or, as they decline to childhood, recover
them to their first strength; that comes forth the interpreter
and arbiter of nature, a teacher of things divine no less than 30
human, a master in manners; and can alone, or with a few,
effect the business of mankind: this, I take him, is no subject for pride and ignorance to exercise their railing rhetoric
upon. But it will here be hastily answered, that the writers
of these days are other things; that not only their manners,   35
but their natures, are inverted; and nothing remaining with
them of the dignity of poet, but the abused name, which
every scribe usurps; that now, especially in dramatic, or (as
they term it) stage-poetry, nothing but ribaldry, profana-
tion, blasphemy, all licence of offence to God and man is   40
practised. I dare not deny a great part of this, and am sorry
I dare not, because in some men's abortive features – and

these bad pretenders. I have always tried to avoid blasphemy or bawdiness; and though my satires are considered biting, what society have I offended, what public person have I insulted? My works are licensed, because I avoid excessive or personal criticisms, attacking only bad kinds of people, who richly deserve it. Any text can be wilfully misinterpreted, and it is unfair to blame me if malicious commentators try to interpret my works as attacks on individuals (whom the commentators themselves want to attack indirectly).

Those writers who seek popularity by recklessly slandering people will get no competition from me: I would rather go unread than become famous that way. Nor can I blame the government who, recognizing the damage slander can do, would rather see stupid, old-fashioned slapstick comedies and morality plays than satires on individuals, leaders, or nations. As Horace writes,

'Everyone is afraid and angry, even if personally uninjured'.

46-50 Jonson's rowdy conduct throughout his life – including persistent drunkenness, nasty insults, censored plays, brawling, killing a fellow-actor, and fathering illegitimate children – makes this claim that he 'can – and from a most clear conscience – affirm that I have ever trembled to think toward the least profaneness' seem like a wildly self-serving falsehood. If it were not for the context of a serious defence of poetic morality, it would be tempting to read it as a self-deprecating in-joke designed to elicit mocking whoops of laughter from an audience.

58 *entirely mine* Jonson must make an exception for collaborations such as *The Isle of Dogs, Eastward Ho!* and perhaps the first version of *Sejanus*, which landed Jonson in serious trouble with the authorities.

60 *particular* aiming at a specific person; satirists traditionally defended themselves by claiming they were attacking the faults, not any actual individual person; and that for anyone to complain of slander was foolishly to confess to the vices the satires depicted.

68 *Application* Interpretation designed to apply the satire to specific persons or events, the seeking out of personal allusions and political allegories; Volpone himself was apparently taken as a caricature of the wealthy Thomas Sutton.

78-9 *whose living faces ... petulant styles* what actual persons' public image they mutilate with their writing (punning on 'stiles', meaning pens); writers convicted of slandering royalty sometimes had their faces scarred in punishment, and Jonson himself had been in danger of that disfigurement, though he here insists he would never compete with such gossip-columnists.

82 *providing* foreseeing; Jonson here provisionally sides with those who, for the good of the society, prefer old-fashioned entertainments to the current trends in satire.

88 *Sibi ... odit* Horace, *Satires*, II.1.23, which Jonson translates (in *Poetaster*, III.v.41) as 'In satires, each man, though untouched, Complains / As he were hurt; and hates such biting strains'.

would they had never boasted the light – it is over-true. But,
that all are embarked in this bold adventure for hell, is a
most uncharitable thought, and, uttered, a more malicious   45
slander. For my particular, I can (and from a most clear
conscience) affirm, that I have ever trembled to think
toward the least profaneness; have loathed the use of such
foul and unwashed bawdry, as is now made the food of the
scene. And, howsoever I cannot escape, from some, the   50
imputation of sharpness, but that they will say, I have taken
a pride, or lust, to be bitter, and not my youngest infant but
hath come into the world with all his teeth; I would ask of
these supercilious politics, what nation, society, or general
order or state I have provoked? What public person?   55
Whether I have not in all these preserved their dignity, as
mine own person, safe? My works are read, allowed, (I
speak of those that are entirely mine). Look into them:
what broad reproofs have I used? where have I been
particular? where personal? except to a mimic, cheater,   60
bawd, or buffoon – creatures, for their insolencies, worthy
to be taxed? Or to which of these so pointingly, as he might
not either ingenuously have confessed, or wisely dissembled
his disease? But it is not rumour can make men guilty,
much less entitle me to other men's crimes. I know that   65
nothing can be so innocently writ or carried, but may be
made obnoxious to construction; marry, whilst I bear mine
innocence about me, I fear it not. Application is now grown
a trade with many; and there are that profess to have a key
for the deciphering of every thing: but let wise and noble   70
persons take heed how they be too credulous, or give leave
to these invading interpreters to be over-familiar with their
fames, who cunningly, and often, utter their own virulent
malice, under other men's simplest meanings.
     As for those that will – by faults which charity hath   75
raked up, or common honesty concealed – make themselves
a name with the multitude, or, to draw their rude and
beastly claps, care not whose living faces they entrench with
their petulant styles, may they do it without a rival, for me:
I choose rather to live graved in obscurity, than share with   80
them in so preposterous a fame. Nor can I blame the wishes
of those grave and wiser patriots, who providing the hurts
these licentious spirits may do in a state, desire rather to see
fools and devils, and those antique relics of barbarism
retrieved, with all other ridiculous and exploded follies,   85
than behold the wounds of private men, of princes and
nations: for, as Horace makes Trebatius speak, in these,

     – *Sibi quisque timet, quanquam est intactus, & odit.*

Some writers seem to enjoy that; but all worthy observers already abhor it, as they abhor the chaotic practices of the popular theatre, and the ugly, incorrect, nonsensical writing that offends anyone who cares about language, morality, or Christianity.

I am naturally concerned when my own reputation, and that of many virtuous scholars, is at risk; when the traditionally noble title of author is made scornful by these bad imitators; when those traditionally honoured by monarchs must endure the insults of every loud-mouthed, self-appointed preacher. That is what compels me to write this defence, and what always made me careful to distinguish myself from those bad writers. Therefore, in this new play *Volpone*, which you have honoured me by approving, I have tried to teach them all a lesson by copying the virtues of ancient literature: the structure, the style, the decorum, and finally the moral instruction, which is the principal purpose of literature – to teach people how to live, and why.

And though the ending of the play may be criticized as diverging from the traditions of comedy, strictly defined, I ask the knowledgeable and generous reader to recognize that it was done deliberately (except that I do not want to seem boastful, I could show here how easily I could have followed those traditional rules). But, because I was especially concerned to stifle those who claim that plays never punish sin, I took some liberty (though even my variations have precedents in the classics, where comedies often end with some characters appropriately punished, about which I will write more adequately soon).

104 *vernaculous* ill-bred, probably also implicating those who accuse in the vernacular language because they (and their low-class audience) lack the ability to use Latin

110 *to my crown* to my credit and glory (playing on the laureate crown granted to great poets)

111 *reduce* restore; Jonson often claims to be reviving the forms and mores of the classics.

116 *catastrophe* denouement, final act; Jonson concedes that *Volpone* lacks the happy ending traditional to the genre.

120 *his scale* the traditional measurements used by a learned critic (with a pun on the variations that can be played on a musical scale)

128 *mulcted* punished; the classical precedents Jonson broadly claims here for his harsh ending have been hard for modern scholars to find.

And men may justly impute such rages, if continued, to the
writer, as his sports. The increase of which lust in liberty,   90
together with the present trade of the stage, in all their mis-
cellane interludes, what learned or liberal soul doth not
already abhor, where nothing but the garbage of the time is
uttered, and that with such impropriety of phrase, such
plenty of solecisms, such dearth of sense, so bold prolepses,   95
so racked metaphors, with brothelry able to violate the ear
of a pagan, and blasphemy to turn the blood of a Christian
to water?

I cannot but be serious in a cause of this nature, wherein
my fame, and the reputation of diverse honest and learned   100
are the question; when a name so full of authority, anti-
quity, and all great mark, is, through their insolence,
become the lowest scorn of the age; and those men subject
to the petulancy of every vernaculous orator, that were
wont to be the care of kings and happiest monarchs. This it   105
is that hath not only rapt me to present indignation, but
made me studious heretofore, and by all my actions, to
stand off from them; which may most appear in this my
latest work, which you, most learned arbitresses, have seen,
judged, and to my crown, approved; wherein I have   110
laboured for their instruction and amendment, to reduce
not only the ancient forms, but manners of the scene, the
easiness, the propriety, the innocence, and last, the doctrine, which is the principal end of poesy, to inform men in
the best reason of living.   115

And though my catastrophe may, in the strict rigour of
comic law, meet with censure, as turning back to my
promise, I desire the learned and charitable critic to have so
much faith in me to think it was done of industry: for, with
what case I could have varied it nearer his scale (but that I   120
fear to boast my own faculty) I could here insert. But my
special aim being to put the snaffle in their mouths, that cry
out, We never punish vice in our interludes, etc., I took the
more liberty; though not without some lines of example,
drawn even in the ancients themselves, the goings-out of   125
whose comedies are not always joyful, but oft-times the
bawds, the servants, the rivals, yea, and the masters are
mulcted; and fitly, it being the office of a comic poet to imitate justice, and instruct to life, as well as purity of language, or stir up gentle affections; to which, upon my next   130
opportunity toward the examining and digesting of my
notes, I shall speak more wealthily, and pay the world a
debt.

Meanwhile, since I have been careful to show my gratitude for your support, and to show the world, in this epistle, why your support was justified, I hope I can count on that patronage continuing, which will give me time to complete even better works, which will restore the great ancient reputation of literature which has lately been besmirched.

As for those nasty and lazy commentators who have never tried to do anything positive, or who know themselves so sinful that they fear literature's ability to reveal truth, and therefore, as a precaution, defend themselves by long-winded attacks on it: they will find that literature's servants (whose feelings are easily aroused) will throw some ink at them that will disfigure their reputations more deeply than acid would disfigure their bodies; and not even a skilful plastic surgeon will be able to remove the scars, which will remain until death, announcing their unworthiness.

152 *Cinnamus* cf. Martial, *Epigrams* VI, 24–6; barbers were surgeons in the Renaissance, and Jonson, whose thumb had been branded for killing a fellow-actor, would have had reason to ponder the permanence of such marks of disgrace.

In the meantime, most reverenced Sisters, as I have cared
to be thankful for your affections past, and here made the   135
understanding acquainted with some ground of your
favours, let me not despair their continuance, to the maturing of some worthier fruits; wherein, if my muses be true to
me, I shall raise the despised head of poetry again, and
stripping her out of those rotten and base rags wherewith   140
the times have adulterated her form, restore her to her
primitive habit, feature, and majesty, and render her
worthy to be embraced and kissed of all the great and
master-spirits of our world.

As for the vile and slothful, who never affected an act   145
worthy of celebration, or are so inward with their own
vicious natures as they worthily fear her, and think it a high
point of policy to keep her in contempt, with their declam-
atory and windy invectives: she shall out of just rage incite
her servants (who are *genus irritabile*) to spout ink in their   150
faces, that shall eat farther than their marrow into their
fames; and not Cinnamus the barber, with his art, shall be
able to take out the brands; but they shall live, and be read,
till the wretches die, as things worst deserving of themselves
in chief, and then of all mankind.

From my House in the Black-Friars,
this 11th of February, 1607.